Gold & Silver: The Greatest Bull Market has Begun

A ONCE-IN-A-LIFETIME INVESTMENT OPPORTUNITY

JORDAN ROY-BYRNE, CMT, MFTA

PYRAMID
Publishers

Minneapolis, MN

Printed in the United States of America
ISBN 979-8-9908128-2-6

Cover Design by Aristotle Ordonez
Interior Design by Patrick Day

Dedication

I dedicate this book to my paying subscribers for their support of my work, allowing me to do what I love.

I also dedicate this book to my everything, my wonderful wife and best friend for her brilliance, wisdom and constant love, support, and encouragement.

Table of Contents

Introduction

Chapter 1: What Really Drives Gold....1

Chapter 2: Gold's Relationship with Stock Market....15

Chapter 3: Gold's Relationship with Bonds & Currencies....28

Chapter 4: What Really Drives Silver....34

Chapter 5: Technical Analysis of Gold & Silver....41

Chapter 6: Fundamental Drivers for Gold in 2020s & 2030s...54

Chapter 6 Part 2: Dedollarization....65

Chapter 7: Current Valuations....75

Chapter 8: About Gold Mining Stocks....86

Chapter 9: About Junior Gold Stocks....92

Chapter 10: Trading & Investing Rules....104

Chapter 11: My Predictions....107

Bonus Chapter....118

References....128

Acknowledgments....133

Introduction

My expectations and framework for the future changed after the first edition of this book in 2015 but have crystalized over the past few years.

Initially, some ten years ago, I argued that the stock market was in a cyclical bull market within a secular bear that could not end until Gold made a final run, similar to 1976 to 1980. While I was correct that the precious metals sector was at a major low, my larger framework was wrong.

In writing the second edition of this book in 2019, I correctly argued that the stock market was in a secular bull market and the best historical comparison for precious metals was the early 1960s.

As 2025 beckons, the reality is clear. Gold's breakout out of its 13-year cup-and-handle pattern, coupled with the new secular bear market in Bonds, undoubtedly signals the beginning of a new secular bull market in precious metals and hard assets. However, it will only be confirmed and begin in earnest once the secular bull market in stocks and conventional assets ends.

The continued secular bull markets in US stocks and the US Dollar (which are aligned) are the root answer to many questions concerning precious metals. This is why gold mining stocks are extremely under-owned and trade at historically low valuations despite a record Gold price, strong operating results, and improved financial health. It's partially why the leveraged plays on Gold (gold stocks, Silver, junior resource companies, and exploration companies) have underperformed despite a spectacular breakout in Gold and a 70% gain over the past 24 months.

We can use two key indicators to track when Gold and the entire precious metals sector are ripe for a huge move. First, I analyze Gold against the total return of a 60/40 investment portfolio. The conventional investment portfolio places 60% of capital in stocks and 40% in bonds. This ratio confirmed new secular bull markets in Gold and precious metals at the end of 1971 and 2001 but has yet to do so since our publishing. The second indicator is the stock market falling below its 40-month moving average, which occurred roughly one year after secular peaks in 1930, 1968, and 2000.

Beyond the secular turning point, which could occur within a few years, we explore everything we think is most important to you as an investor, be it a generalist or precious metals investor. We explore the history of markets and market cycles to assess what will come in the next 15 years.

Concerning precious metals, we provide a background on Gold, Silver, and the mining companies. We discuss the root fundamental drivers and historical tendencies and provide a lengthy discussion on the fundamental drivers over the next 15 years. We detail how current valuations set the stage for a new secular bull market to come. Finally, we cover the gold mining and junior resource sectors, which have amazing potential that will begin to come to fruition once the secular turn is in place.

Chapter 1

What Really Drives Gold

Gold as an investment is simple to understand yet is muddled by the endless misinformation and disinformation from detractors and proponents alike. We often hear phrases such as "end of the world trade," "just a rock," "flight to quality," "you cannot eat it," "hedge for uncertainty," "inflation hedge," and "deflation hedge."

Such phrases mischaracterize Gold and miss the simple fact that Gold is the ultimate money. Over 100 years ago, JP Morgan said, "Gold is money; everything else is credit."

Gold (and, secondarily, Silver) has been used as money for thousands of years because it better fits the characteristics of money than anything else: It's durable, divisible, convenient (portable), and has intrinsic value.

In today's fiat world, Gold is money but, more so, an alternative currency that performs well when the value of fiat currencies or perceived value is declining. One way to track any currency's current trend and perceived value is to compare it to the direction of real interest rates or real yields on government bonds.

Over the past 100 years, the best indicator of the trend in the Gold price has been the trend in real interest rates, which is essentially interest rates minus the inflation rate. Gold will rise when real rates are negative or decline towards negative territory. Gold declines when real interest rates rise and faces long-term headwinds when real rates are sharply positive, as they were for the majority of the 1980s and 1990s.

Suppose we can earn a real (inflation-adjusted) return on our capital in a savings account, certificate of deposit, or government bond. In that case, there is no reason to seek alternative currencies like Gold. Conversely, capital moves towards alternative currencies when the inflation rate exceeds the interest rate on the securities mentioned above. First and foremost, that means Gold, and secondly, Silver.

There are various ways to measure real interest rates. We will focus on two.

1. Calculate real rates by subtracting the inflation rate (using the Consumer Price Index) from the Federal Funds Rate or various bond yields. This works best in a historical and educational sense. The downside is that the Consumer Price Index is backward-looking.

2. The second method, established in the late 1990s with the advent of TIPS, or Treasury Inflation-Protected Securities, is a fluid, market-based calculation of real interest rates. The real yield is the difference between the yield on a government bond and the yield on the corresponding TIPS security.

According to research from PIMCO, the real yield on the 10-year Treasury Note (as calculated from the 10-year TIPS security) has been the best indicator for Gold. In other words, Gold is inversely correlated to the real 10-year yield.

Figure 1.1 in the graph below plots Gold along with the real Fed Funds Rate, dating back to 1914. The vertical lines show the secular peaks in commodity prices and/or Gold. The dates include 1920, 1951, 1980, and 2011. Historical secular bull markets in Gold and Commodities concluded when real rates, after being in negative territory for many years, surged into positive territory.

Figure 1.1: Gold & Real Fed Funds Rate

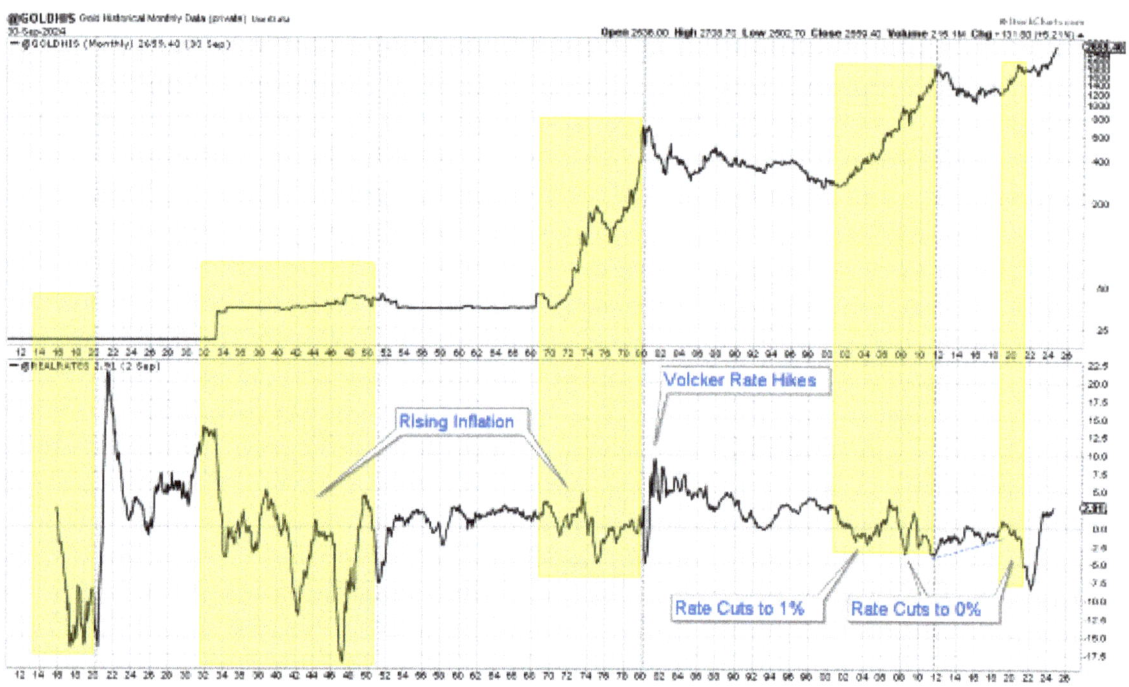

Commodity prices made secular peaks in 1920 and 1951, while Gold, which was fixed at $35/oz under the Bretton Woods Agreement until 1971, peaked in 1980. Commodity prices peaked in 1920 as the real Fed Funds Rate exploded from -19% to nearly 20%. Then, in 1951, commodity prices peaked as the real Fed Funds Rate increased from -7% to almost 2%. From 1979 to 1980, when the Gold price went parabolic and collapsed, the real Fed Funds Rate increased by nearly 15%. It advanced from a low of -5% to 10%.

Although the real Fed Funds Rate trended lower after the early 1980s, it was strongly positive for most of the 1980s and 1990s. A reduction from a sharply positive real interest rate to a modestly positive real interest rate did not move the needle regarding Gold's fundamentals.

The negative correlation between the trend in the Gold price and real interest rates over the past 25 years should be particularly illuminating.

The real Fed Funds Rate declined from 3.2% in 2001 to a low of -3.7% in 2011. That decline was interrupted by a sharp but temporary rise of around 6% during the financial crisis in 2008. Then, the Gold price declined by over 30%.

While 2011 was a significant peak in Gold and precious metals, it was not a multi-decade peak because real interest rates only increased slightly over the next few years. However, from 2011 to 2015, the real Fed Funds Rate rose by over 4%. That was the fundamental explanation for the 2011-2015 bear market.

Gold surged higher in 2016 as the real Fed Funds Rate declined by more than 2% over 18 months. However, Gold failed to build on its 2016 gains or break out in 2017 and 2018 due to the nearly 3% rebound in real interest rates (as the Federal Reserve raised interest rates).

Before and during the Covid crash, the real Fed Funds Rate crashed as a historic amount of fiscal stimulus and transfer payments, along with interest rate cuts to 0%, caused the highest inflation rate in 40 years. That spurred Gold to break the $1375/oz resistance level (which had held for six years) and reach nearly $2100/oz in August 2020.

Then, Gold peaked and consolidated for the following three and a half years as the Federal Reserve embarked on the second most aggressive tightening cycle in its history. In 2023, it hiked short-term rates from 0% to 5.5%. Not surprisingly, this coincided with a sharp increase in the real Fed Funds Rate from deeply negative to nearly 3%.

There have been some slight discrepancies over the past few years, and to explain them, we employ the better indicator, the real 10-year yield, as calculated from the TIPS market.

Figure 1.2 on the next page shows Gold and the real 10-year yield.

Figure 1.2: Gold & Real 10-Year Yield

The real Fed Funds Rate and real 10-year yield continued to decline after Gold peaked in August 2020. How do we explain this and some other discrepancies?

In Figure 1.2, we see that Gold leads the real 10-year yield at important turning points. In other words, the Gold price will bottom and rebound before real yields peak and start falling, and it will peak and decline before real yields bottom and turn higher.

For example, Gold peaked in the summer of 2011, but the real 10-year yield did not bottom until the end of 2012. The Gold price bottomed at the end of 2015, but real yields did not peak until 2018.

Furthermore, Gold peaked in August 2020 before real yields bottomed in mid-2021. The gold market discounted the coming rebound in real interest rates, which was spurred by the Fed's tightening campaign.

The opposite occurred in recent years and in stark fashion. The Gold price bottomed in October 2022, roughly one year ahead of the peak in the real 10-year yield. The real yield rose by another 0.75%, but Gold had already bottomed.

The real 10-year yield is the best indicator for Gold, but we must evaluate the two together because Gold leads at turning points. From 2021 to 2023, the real 10-year yield gained over 3.50%. This was an even stronger rise than in 2012-2013 and 2008, when the Gold price declined 35% and 30%, respectively. Yet, the Gold price held up much better, declining only 22%, and that was a hint of what was to come in 2024. The market was discounting that the huge rise in real interest rates was not sustainable and would reverse course.

Finally, the impact of the new secular bear market in Bonds, which we will analyze in Chapter 3, provides a new context for Gold's relationship with real interest rates. There are points in time when Bonds sell-off (and yields rise) because of inflation or solvency worries rather than an overheating economy. The result is strength in Gold amid temporarily higher real interest rates. This transpired at times during the 1970s and could be what we have seen very recently.

We will discuss additional fundamental drivers for Gold. Still, the overarching reality is that the US (and the Western world) has a debt problem that can only be solved through ongoing negative real interest rates and high inflation. Over time, this will devalue interest payments to more manageable levels.

Yield Curve

The yield curve or yield spread is the difference between short-term and long-term yields. It is also a driver of the price of Gold. The most common spread is the difference between the 2-year yield (a proxy for the Fed Funds Rate) and the 10-year yield.

A flattening yield curve (a shrinking or decreasing difference between the two yields) usually accompanies the middle part of an economic expansion and stock market boom. The curve flattens because the Federal Reserve raises short-term rates, which rise faster than long-term yields. This results in disinflation (a decrease in the inflation rate), which is bearish for Gold.

On the other hand, a steepening curve (or widening of the yield spread) is bullish for Gold. This can happen in one of two ways. Long-term bond yields rise faster than short-term rates (implying an increase in inflation expectations), or short-term rates decrease faster than long-term yields. That implies risk aversion and a loss of confidence in the economy and capital markets.

The yield curve will move from flattening or inversion (short-term rates are higher than long-term rates) to steepening when the Federal Reserve starts cutting interest rates and the economy slows toward recession.

In Figure 1.3 on the next page, we plot Gold and the yield curve (10-year yield and 2-year yield). We highlighted in yellow periods when Gold performed well and the yield curve steepened.

As you can see, the flattening curve in the late 1990s and from 2014 to 2018 coincided with Gold's decline and lack of performance. The flattening curve since early 2021 also coincided with a stagnant Gold market.

On the other side, the steepening of the curve into 2001 coincided with the major bottom in Gold. The steepening continued after the depths of the financial crisis, and Gold continued to rise alongside. The steepening of the curve in 2007 preceded Gold's surge above $700/oz and to $1000/oz.

At present, the yield curve has steepened from deep inversion to positive territory as the Federal Reserve has begun cutting interest rates. The price of gold has already broken out to a new all-time high. If the steepening continues, it indicates that the US economy is in recession, which necessitates further rate cuts. If the yield curve meanders around zero or slightly positive territory (as it did in the mid-1990s and late 1990s), it could indicate a soft landing or temporary soft landing, which is negative for Gold.

Figure 1.3: Gold & Yield Curve

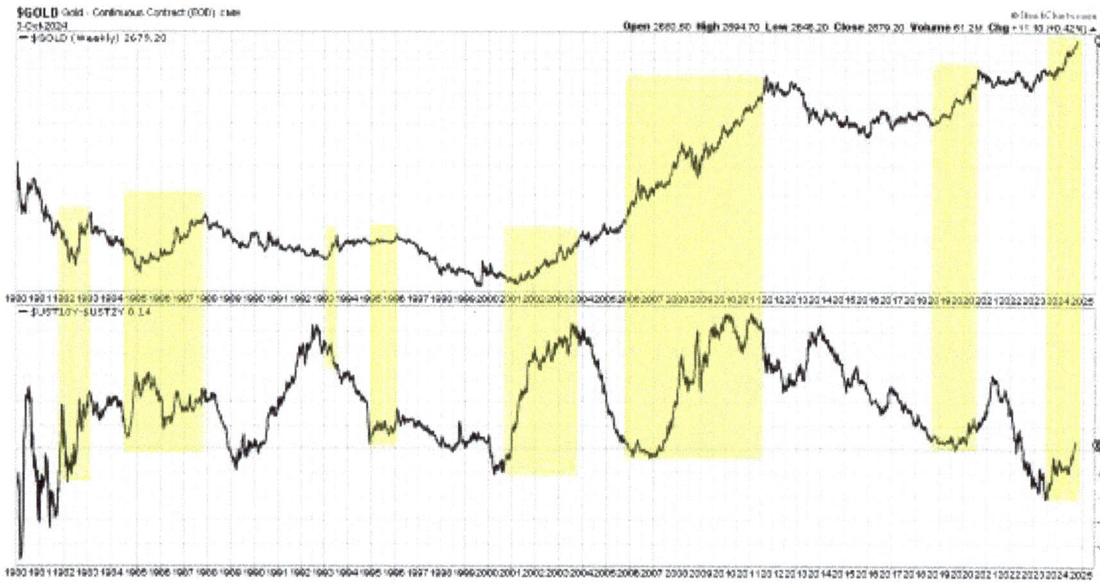

US Dollar Index

The US dollar trend is an important factor in determining the trend of the Gold price because Gold is priced in US Dollars. Gold is an alternative to the US dollar because it is the global reserve currency. While Gold is negatively correlated with real interest rates, the US dollar tends to be positively correlated with real interest rates. However, it is important to note that the negative correlation between the two is imperfect, and there is some evidence that the correlation has weakened in recent years.

In Figure 1.4 on the next page, we plot Gold and the US Dollar Index. The blue vertical lines mark important turning points favoring Gold, and the red vertical lines mark turning points favoring the US Dollar.

Figure 1.4: Gold & US Dollar Index

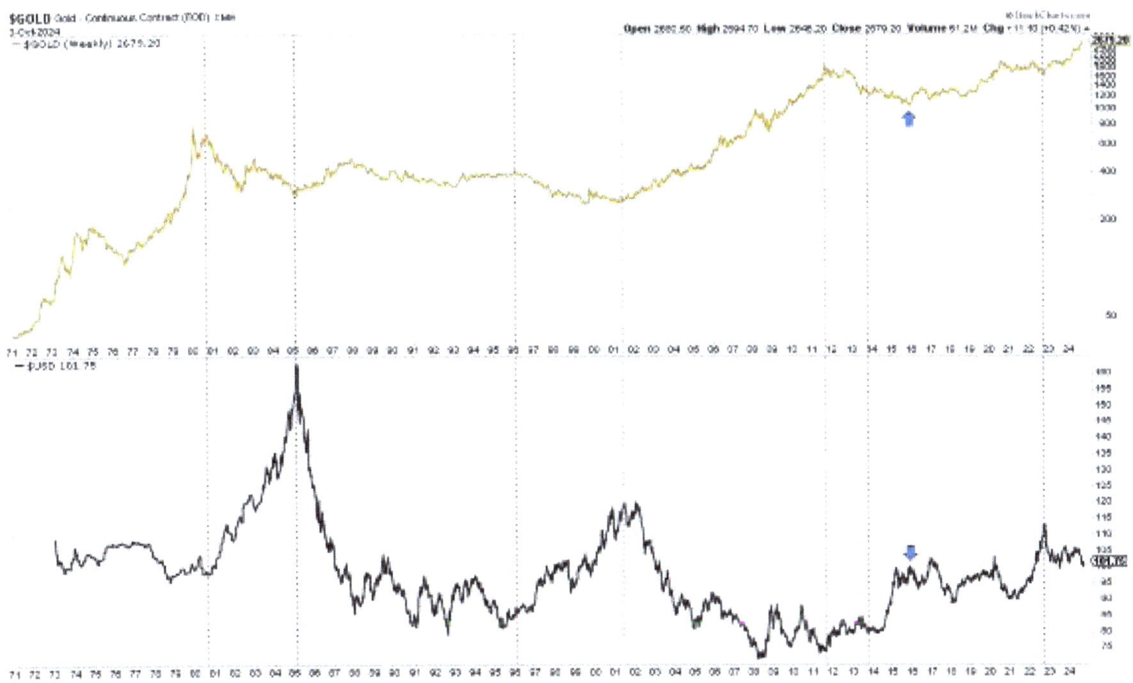

We have several important observations in the history of Gold and the US dollar.

1. First, the US dollar cannot sustain a real secular bull market if the gold price rises. However, there are certain periods when the two can trend together. The 2016 to 2020 period and the August 2018 to August 2020 period show that Gold can perform well even if the US dollar is stable and not falling. Ultimately, a secular bull market in Gold requires a relatively weak dollar over a long period.
2. Second, the negative correlation between Gold and the US dollar is less than normal on a longer-term basis. For example, the Dollar's all-time high was in 1985, but Gold's post-1980 low did not occur until 1999. The Dollar's all-time low was in 2008, but the Gold price is much higher today than in 2008. Gold is roughly 150% higher today than in December 2015, while the Dollar is at the same level. Here are a few other examples. The Dollar's worst decline was from 1985 through 1987, but Gold experienced only a modest cyclical bull market. In the 1970s, the Dollar's decline was modest, but Gold's run was historic.
3. Third, Gold performed much better during the recent secular advance in the Dollar than during previous secular advances. The Dollar gained 56% from 2011 to the peak in 2022. Gold declined 16% during that period. The uptrend from the Dollar in 1980 to 1985 and 1995 to 2001 coincided with some of the worst declines in Gold, 60% in the first half of the 1980s and 40% in the back half of the 1990s. Moreover, from August 2011 to October 2024, the Dollar and Gold each gained around 40%.

4. Finally, in studying the recent history between the two currencies, I have noticed the tendency for Gold to lead the US Dollar at key turning points. In other words, Gold can bottom before peaks in the US Dollar and peak before troughs in the US Dollar.

There are numerous examples. During its historic bottom in 2001, Gold bottomed more than several months before the US Dollar peaked. In the second half of 2005, Gold began a significant increase, yet the US dollar rose during the early part of Gold's move. After correcting over 30% during the financial crisis, Gold bottomed in October 2008, yet the US Dollar would not peak until several months later. Gold bottomed in August 2018 and would rise roughly 80% over the next two years. The US Dollar did not peak until March of 2020! It trended alongside Gold for much of 2019.

This leadership also works in reverse. Gold peaked in the summer of 2016, and the US Dollar declined below its 2016 low in 2017. It reached a new low, yet Gold could not surpass its 2016 high. Also, Gold peaked in August 2020, but the US Dollar did not bottom until January 2021.

One way to analyze Gold's performance in real terms is to chart it against foreign currencies or the inverse of the US Dollar Index. A simple way to calculate this is to multiply Gold by the US Dollar Index. Figure 1.5 below plots Gold (bottom) and Gold against foreign currencies (top).

Figure 1.5: Gold & Gold vs. Foreign Currency Basket (Gold/FC)

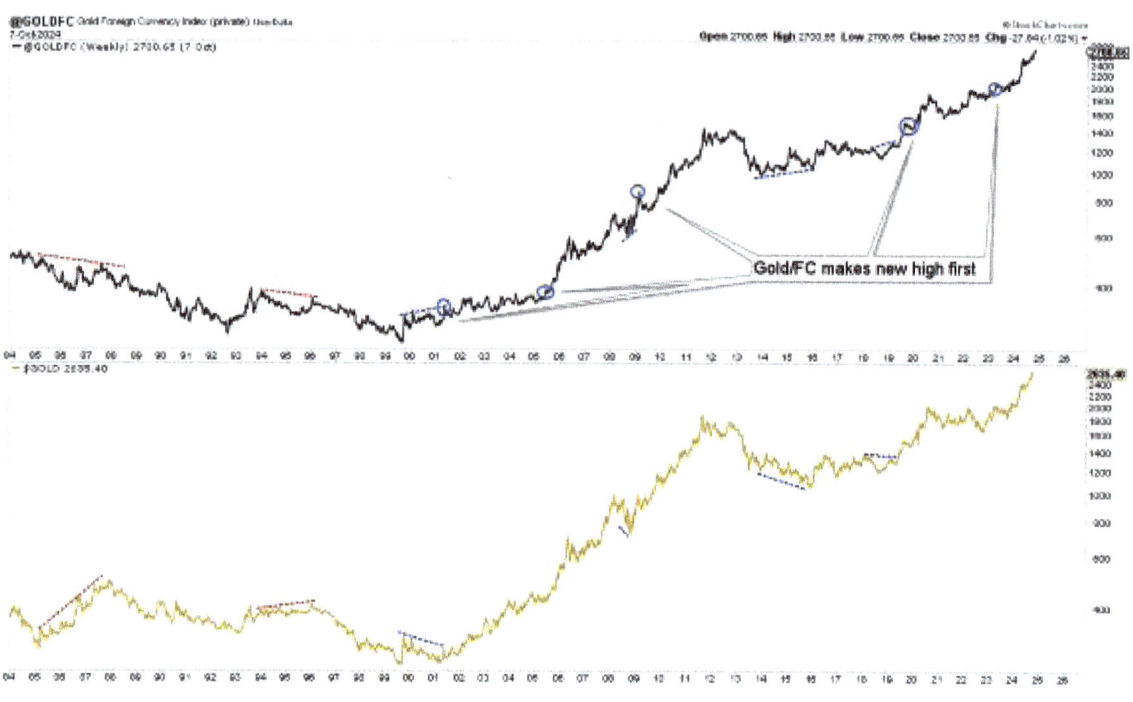

There are a handful of examples over the past few decades of Gold/FC leading the Gold price at key turning points. In the early 2000s, Gold/FC made a new 52-week high in the spring of 2001, just as Gold emerged from its double bottom.

Several years later, in the middle of 2005, Gold/FC made a major breakout to the upside. Gold followed several months later. Gold/FC provided another important divergence during the financial crisis. It bottomed a few months before Gold bottomed in late October 2008. Gold/FC broke out to a new high in early 2009, months before Gold did. Finally, Gold/FC broke to a new all-time high in August 2019, a year before Gold, and the same occurred when Gold/FC made a new all-time high in March 2023, a year before Gold did.

There are also examples of Gold/FC lagging the Gold price and not confirming its strength. Note the red arrows in the mid-1980s and mid-1990s. Gold made higher highs during these periods, yet Gold/FC did not. In 2017 and into early 2018, the Gold price was making higher highs, but Gold/FC did not confirm that. Non-confirmations from Gold/FC can lead to declines in the Gold price.

Gold/FC reflects how Gold is performing without the impact of a falling Dollar. If Gold is rising, but Gold/FC is weak, then it is a sign of a weak US Dollar and not strength in Gold. If the Dollar is climbing but Gold/FC shows strength, it is a signal of strength in the Dollar more than weakness in Gold.

The US Dollar appreciated gradually from 2011 to 2022, but Gold held up far better than it did during past periods of US Dollar appreciation. The reason is that Gold/FC has been considerably stronger than in the 1980s and 1990s. In other words, Gold has been much stronger recently against all other currencies than in the 1980s and 1990s.

Supply & Demand

The supply and demand dynamics for Gold are entirely different from other commodities. The vast majority of Gold is not consumed as there is little industrial use for it. Therefore, its supply grows virtually in perpetuity.

The majority of demand comes from jewelry and investment demand, which drives the trend in the price of Gold. Jewelry demand trends inversely to the price of Gold. When the price of Gold rises, jewelry demand falls. Conversely, jewelry demand increases when the price of Gold declines.

Investment demand is the mirror image of jewelry demand. It correlates positively to changes in the Gold price. Figure 1.6 on the next page, from the precious metals consultancy firm CPM Group, reflects the importance of investment demand. Investment demand tends to increase in years of an increase in the Gold price.

Figure 1.6: Investment Demand & Gold Price Change

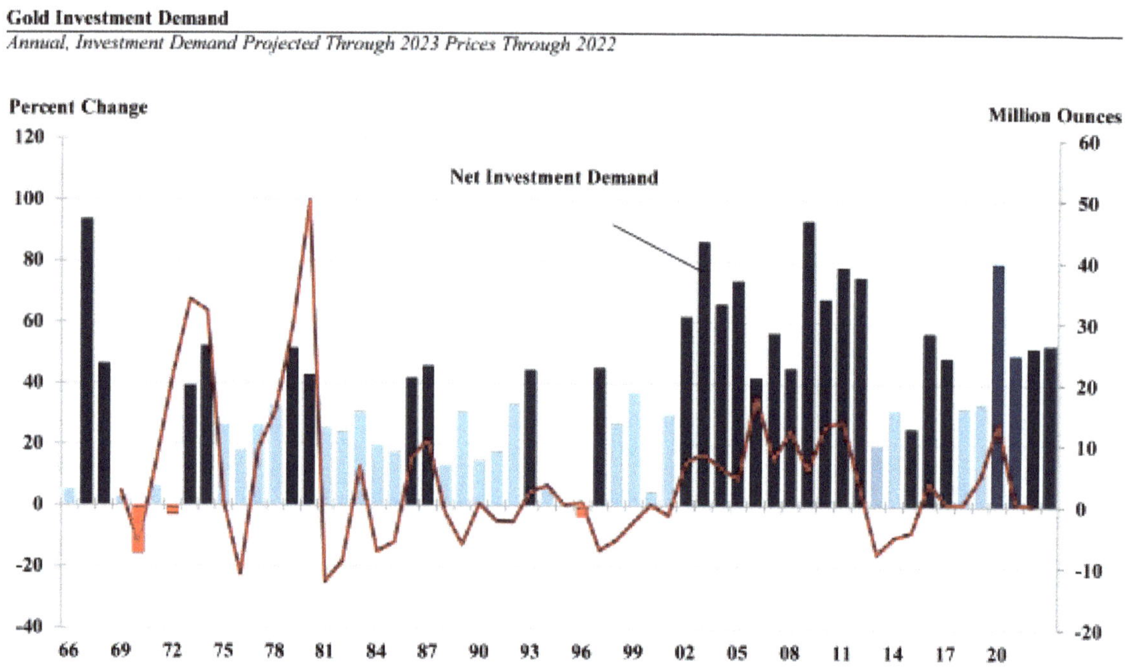

When Gold has bullish fundamentals, such as declining real interest rates and a steepening yield curve, investment demand increases materially, and the Gold price rises. If investors discount rising real interest rates and weaker fundamentals for Gold, investment demand declines, and so does the Gold price.

Central Bank Buying

Other categories of demand include investment and jewelry demand, technological demand, and central bank demand, whose impact is far different today than in decades past.

Central banks were net sellers during most of the 1970s to 1980s and 2001 to 2011 bull markets. They became net buyers only at the very end of those bull markets. As shown in Figure 1.7 on the next page, central bank demand has historically been somewhat inversely correlated to the Gold price. The boxes signal the previous secular bull markets, during which central bank demand was sparse.

However, central bank demand has emerged as a major source of demand alongside investment demand and has transformed the Gold market. Since the major low in the Gold price at the end of 2015, the two most important price lows were around \$1045/oz in 2018 and around \$1620/oz in 2022. In 2018, central banks bought 651 tonnes of Gold, the second-highest amount in history.

Central bank demand exploded higher in 2022 to over 1,000 tonnes, putting a floor in the Gold market as it endured the impact of rising real interest rates. According to the World Gold Council, central banks bought 1,082 tonnes in 2022 and another 1,037 tonnes in 2023. Furthermore, demand through the first half of

2024 (483 tonnes) is only marginally lower than in the past few years.

Figure 1.7: Central Bank Gold Demand (1970-2022)

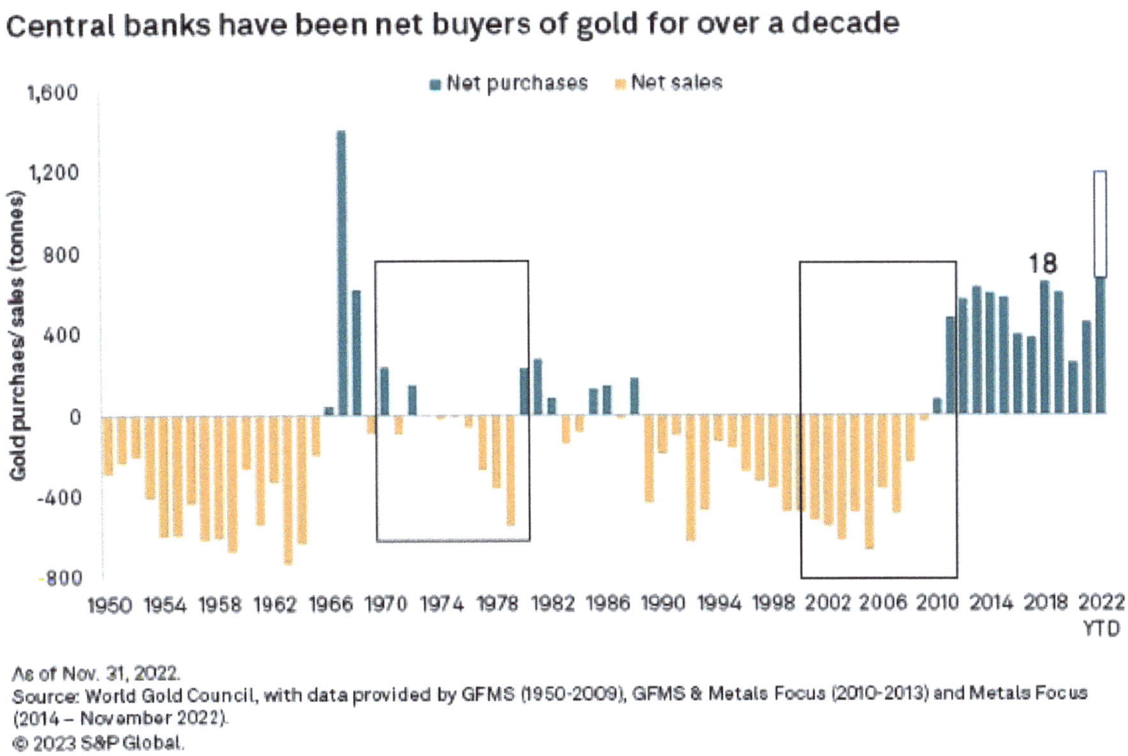

The fact that the level of central bank demand in 2022 continued in 2023 and in the first half of 2024 as the Gold price broke to a new all-time high signals an important change. Central banks were net sellers during the strongest periods (1970s and 2000s) and the 1990s. They only began buying at the end of the previous secular bull, and that continued through the secular bear market (2011 to 2023). Their consistent buying in recent quarters speaks to something larger on the horizon.

Outside of the United States, the world is gradually moving away from the US Dollar as a reserve currency. The economic and financial reason is because the US fiscal position is increasingly concerning (which we will touch on in Chapter 6). The geopolitical reason is countries are reacting to Russia being cut off from the SWIFT payment system and the potential seizure of their assets in the United States by the United States. Gold protects sovereign nations from this type of geopolitical and counterparty risk. This kind of geopolitical development drives Gold far more than a flare-up in some hotspots in the Middle East.

After seeing Figure 1.8 on the next page from Gainesville Coins and @JanGold, we understand why central bank demand could be consistently strong over the years ahead. Gold's share of International Reserves has only begun to increase in recent years. It reached 18% in 2023 and 21% in late 2024. During the bull market in the 1970s, it increased from below 40% to nearly 65%.

Figure 1.8: Gold as Percentage of Reserves

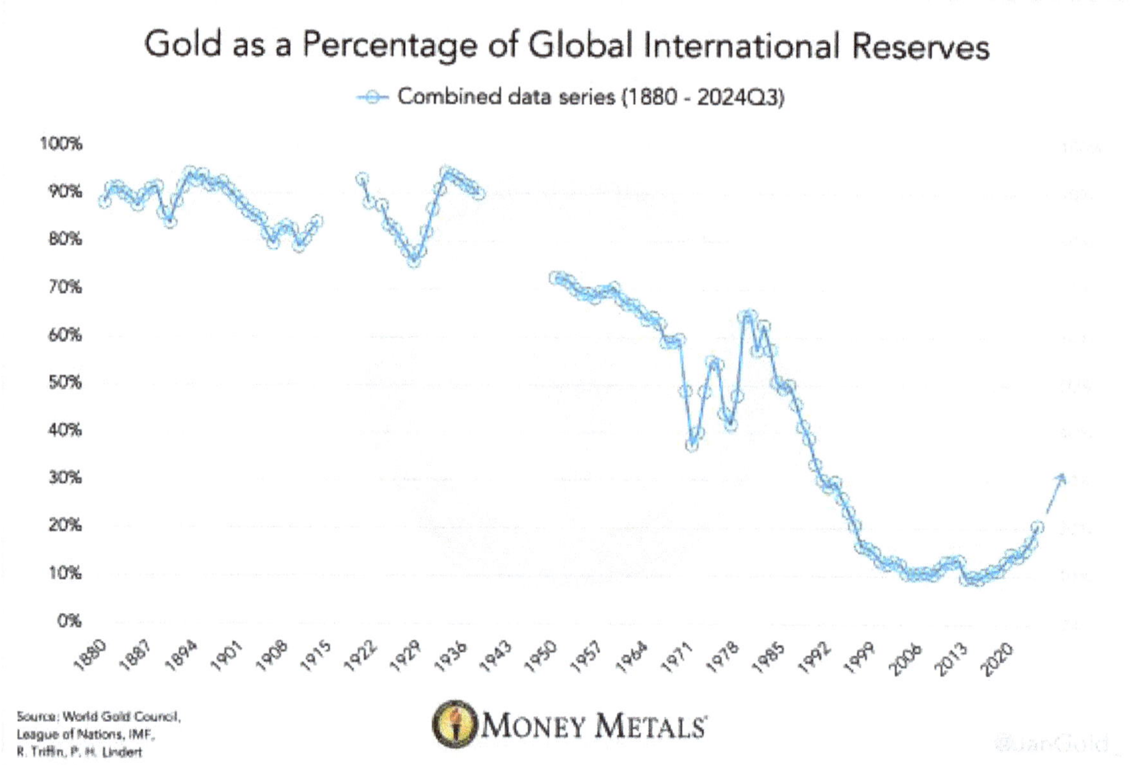

Global Gold Production

Gold is not consumed, unlike other commodities, so its supply grows perpetually. Gold moves on the margin due to monetary factors and investment demand. Broad supply and demand and production fundamentals for Gold do not impact the price.

Figure 1.9 on the next page shows the annual global output and demand for Gold. Demand consistently grows higher over time. Note that there was a growing deficit between demand and production from the mid-1980s until 2003. Gold remained in a secular bear market for the vast majority of that period.

Figure 1.9: Gold Production & Demand

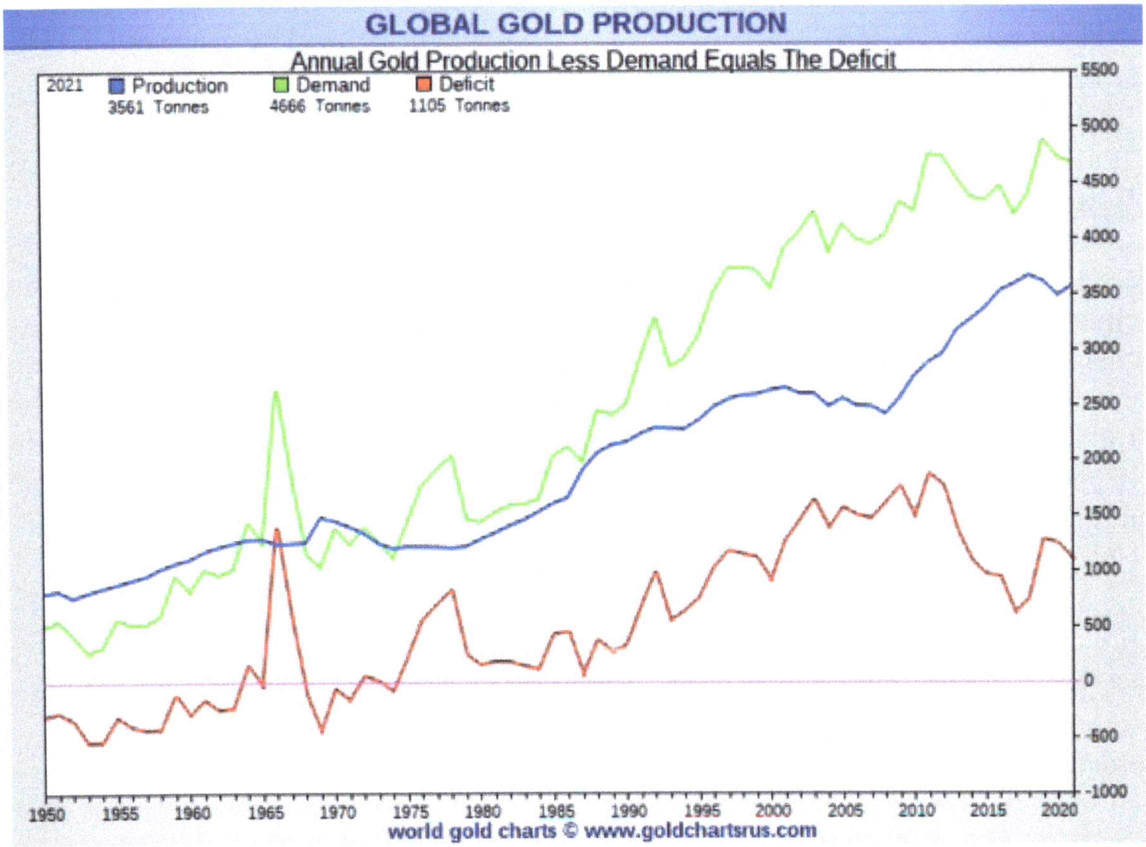

We can make one interesting observation regarding the global production of Gold. From the chart, one might think that production impacts the Gold price. It declines when the Gold price rises but rises when it falls. I credit the late Heinz Blasnik, who wrote under the pseudonyms Trotsky and Pater Tenebrarum, with a great explanation courtesy of Mike Shedlock.

According to Blasnik, mining companies are forced to "high grade" their mines during low Gold price environments. In other words, they mine the higher-grade portions of deposits, which results in lower unit costs. However, when the Gold price rises, mining companies can mine the lower-grade portions of their deposits, which results in higher unit costs.

In addition, the impact of the Gold price on future supply operates with a considerable lag. Gold bull markets lead to greater exploration spending, which leads to future production. However, the Gold bull market has run its course by the time those new mines are operating. Furthermore, the impact of a Gold bear market on future production is not realized until Gold is already back in a bull market.

The inverse relationship between global gold production and the Gold price has continued in recent years. Production declined from 2018 to 2020, when the Gold price enjoyed a cyclical bull market, and increased in 2021, when the Gold price declined.

Chapter Summary

Gold is unique in the commodity complex because its drivers are related entirely to monetary factors and not typical supply and demand fundamentals. Gold is inversely correlated with real interest rates. Gold will rise in value when real interest rates decline to or below 0, and Gold will fall when real interest rates rise. The best indicator for real interest rates is the real yield on the 10-year Treasury Note as derived from the TIPS market.

It is important to note that the Gold price usually leads real interest rates at market turning points. It will bottom and rebound before real interest rates decline, as evidenced by the 2022-2023 period. Gold will also peak and decline before real interest rates bottom, as evidenced by the 2011-2012 and 2020-2021 periods.

Secondary drivers of the Gold price include the Yield Curve, the US Dollar Index, and central bank demand. Gold also leads the US Dollar Index at key turning points. It is important to chart Gold against foreign currencies (similar to Gold multiplied by the US Dollar Index) to determine Gold's performance in real terms. Gold against foreign currencies is also a leading indicator of the Gold price.

Central bank demand has become a new driver for Gold and helped the price to bottom in 2018 and 2022. There are multiple reasons why central banks are likely to continue buying Gold in the years ahead.

Chapter 2

Gold's Relationship with the Stock Market

Over very long periods, Gold (and commodity prices) have an inverse relationship with the US stock market. When Gold and commodity prices are in a secular bull market, the US stock market is in a secular bear market, and vice versa. A secular bull market entails a market or asset consistently trending higher and making higher highs for over a decade. A secular bear market entails a long period in which a market or asset does not make or sustain higher highs. It typically entails a sideways trend for over a decade.

However, over shorter periods, such as a few years, the relationship between these asset classes can take many forms. There have been multiple periods in which the stock market and hard assets have gained together, declined together, and trended in opposite ways. As a result, which is pertinent today, there are some periods in which the secular trends in hard assets and stocks overlap.

In Figure 2.1 on the next page, we plot and define the secular bull markets in stocks and Commodities. We show the S&P 500 Index and the CRB Index, which in this chart is an equal-weighted index of commodity prices. Most commodity price indices today are distorted by extreme weightings of energy commodities.

The boxes highlight secular bull markets, and BO signals a breakout. As we can see, stocks and commodities take turns. The economic reason for that is that rising commodity prices signal inflation. When inflation rises and inflicts damage, stocks cannot be in a secular bull market. When inflation is under control, it is negative for commodity prices but good for stocks.

There were two major overlaps between stocks and commodity prices, the first from 1942 to 1951. Commodities were in a secular bull market until 1951. Although stocks did not begin a secular bull market in real terms until 1949, the bottom in 1942 was hugely significant, as stocks trended higher with little interruption until 1949. The image makes it difficult to see, but some metals prices and mining stocks in the 1960s performed quite well alongside the stock market.

Figure 2.1: S&P 500 & Commodity Prices

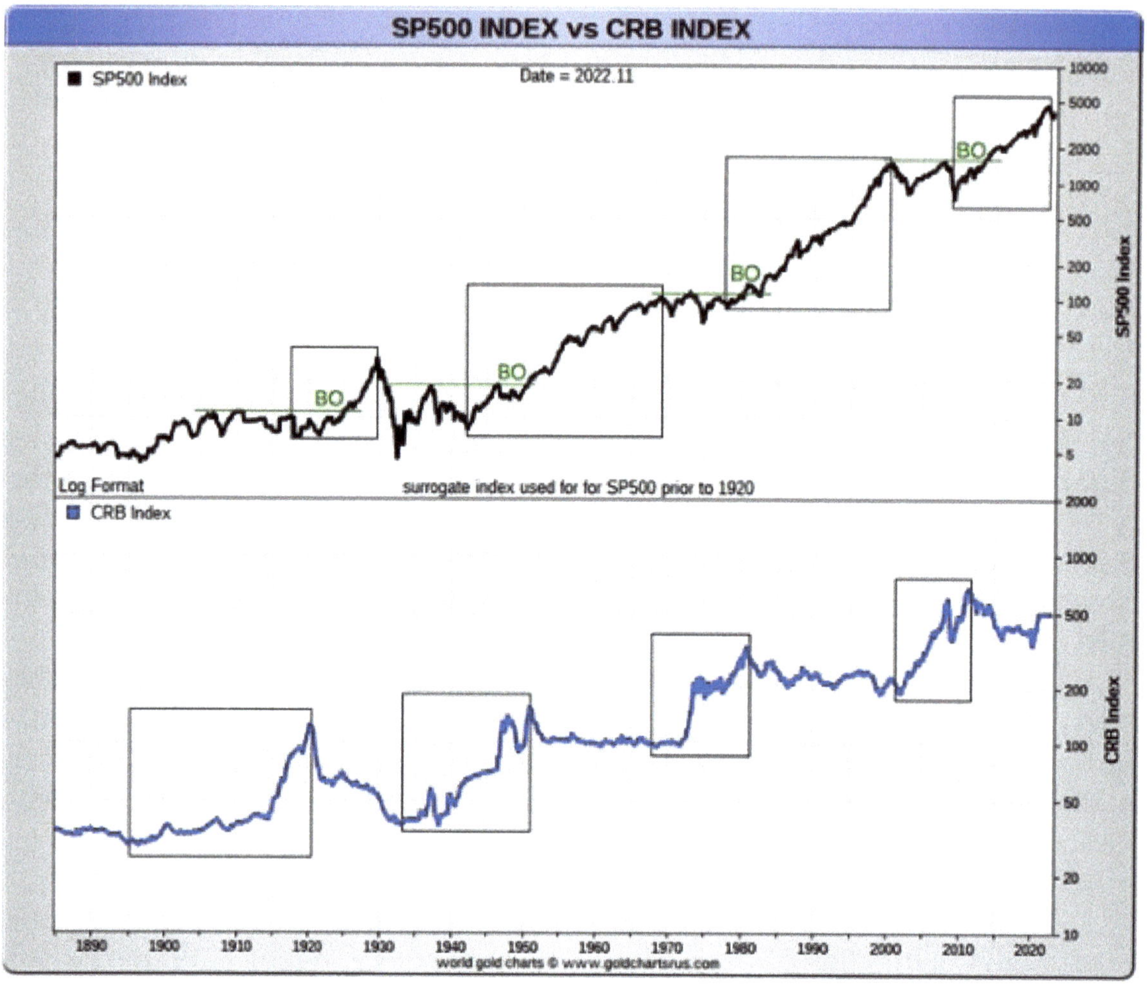

We are in the middle of the third overlap. The S&P 500 has continued to make higher highs and new all-time highs. Figure 2.2 on the next page shows the Bloomberg Spot Commodity Spot Index, which surpassed its 2008 and 2011 highs in late 2021, onto an all-time high in early 2022. Gold broke out to a new all-time high in March 2024.

Figure 2.2: Bloomberg Commodity Spot Index

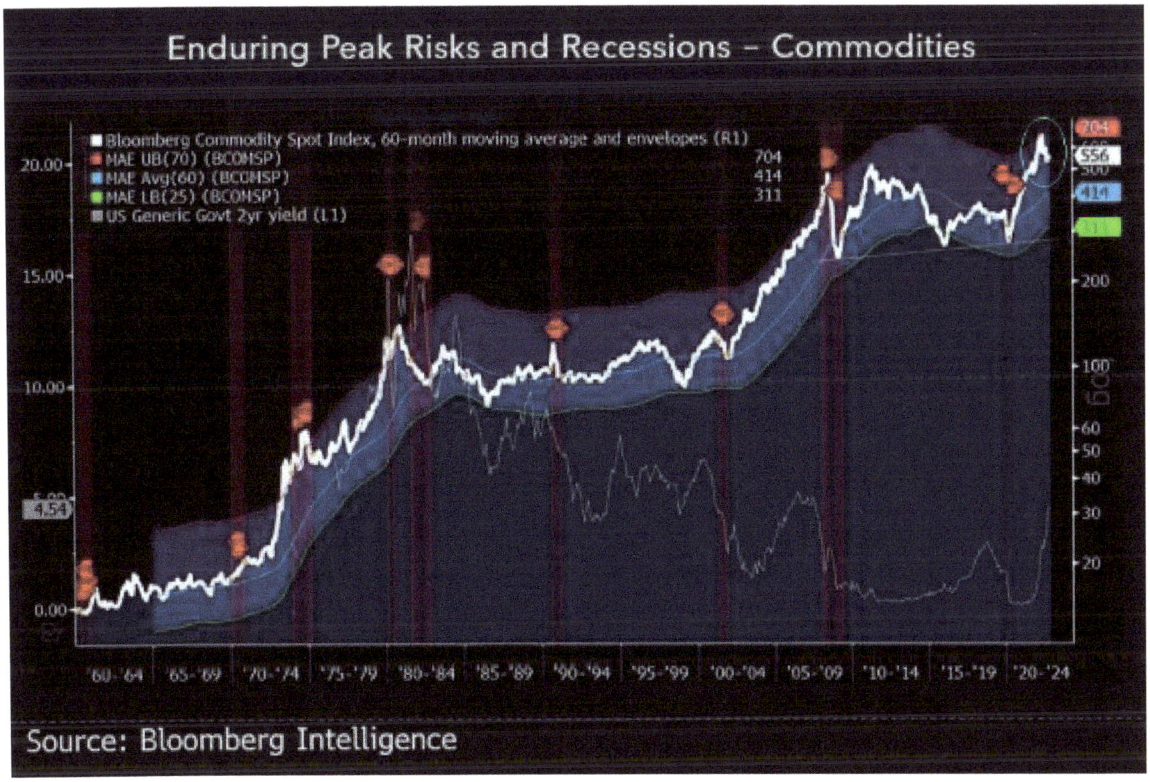

Let me diverge for a moment and circle back to the secular relationship between Gold and the S&P 500, as discussed at the beginning of this chapter. There is a sharp distinction between the secular trends of each. In Figure 2.3 on the next page, we can see that the breakout in each market occurred around the time the other market made a secular peak. Note how the few major breakouts in each market occurred soon after the other market made a secular peak.

There are several examples. The US stock market's epic breakout in 1982 occurred shortly after Gold's historic peak in 1980. The S&P 500 broke out from a 13-year base in 2013, two years after Gold's peak in 2011. Gold's historic move in 1971 began a few years after the S&P 500 peaked at the end of the 1960s.

Figure 2.3: S&P 500 & Gold Historical Breakouts

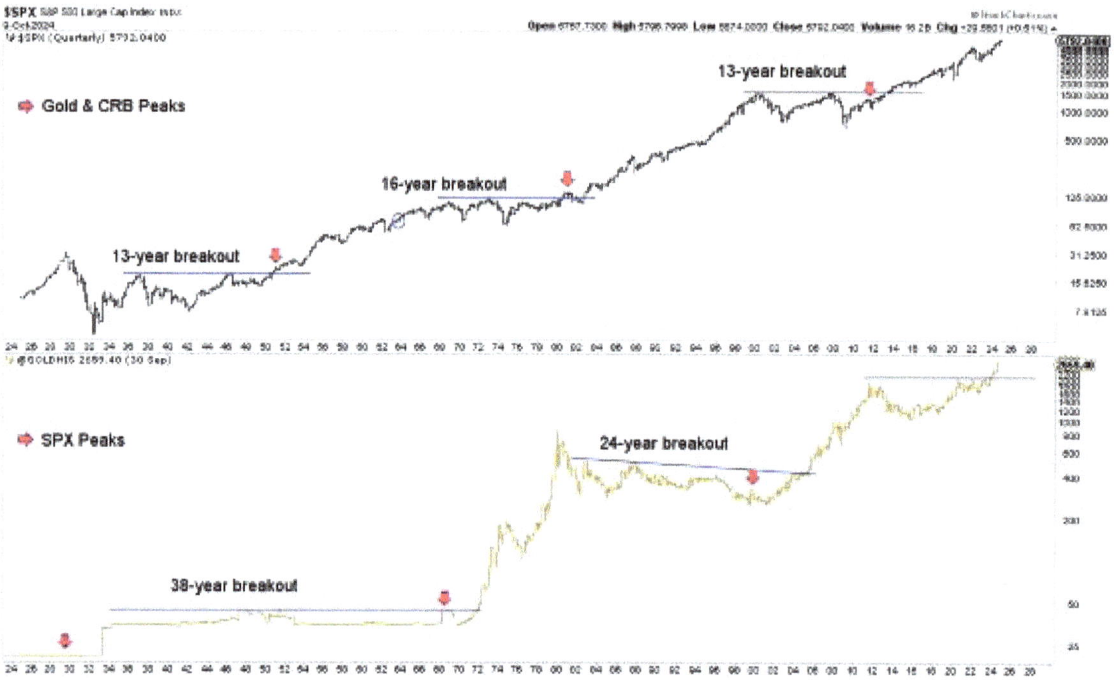

However, months ago, Gold broke out to a new all-time high from its super bullish 13-year cup and handle pattern, but the secular bull in the S&P 500 remains intact. This is a major overlap. How do we explain this, considering their well-defined inverted secular relationship?

Figure 2.4 on the next page plots the S&P 500 and Barron's Gold Mining Index (BGMI), a historical index for gold stocks, Silver, and Gold. This chart explores the precious metals sector more deeply while explaining the context of the current overlap in secular trends.

First, you can see that precious metals markets performed best during the secular bear markets in US stocks, highlighted in yellow. Within the yellow periods, there are periods in which US stocks enjoyed cyclical bull markets. These were periods in which precious metals and US stocks trended together. Those include 1932-1937, 1971-1973, and 2002-2007.

The major outlier and overlap in the secular relationship between US stocks and precious metals was the 1960s, during which gold stocks broke out of a three-decade-long base in late 1964 and enjoyed one of their strongest cyclical advances in history. Similarly, Silver also moved to new all-time highs (excluding a pop during the Civil War), but its advance was not as strong.

Figure 2.4: S&P 500, Gold Stocks, Silver, Gold

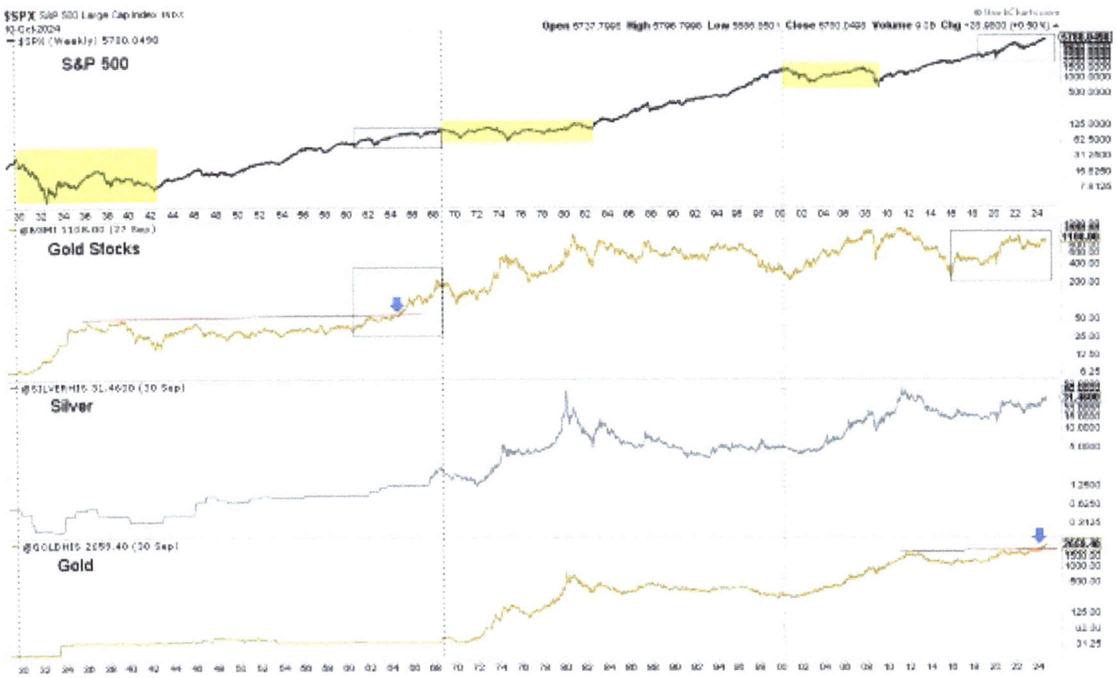

The S&P 500 did not begin a secular bear market until its peak in 1968, but its bull market began to slow considerably in the early 1960s. From its peak at the very end of 1961 to its secular peak at the end of 1968, the S&P 500 gained only 50%, and the Dow Jones Industrial Average, which peaked in 1966, gained only 34%. During those seven years, the gold stocks gained over 300%.

The massive breakout in gold stocks in late 1964 equates to the breakout in Gold today. See the blue arrows in Figure 2.4. Investors could not buy Gold until late 1971, so gold stocks in the 1960s functioned as Gold does today. From November 1963 to their respective peaks in 1968, the BGMI surged 373% while the S&P 500 gained only 56%.

While the current and most recent period has been similar to the 1960s, precious metals have not performed as well as before. A major reason is that the US stock market has remained in a secular bull market and has yet to slow down today the way it did after the early 1960s. Another reason is that Gold today faces far more competition for investor capital than gold stocks 60 years ago. Investors can buy emerging markets, foreign currencies, dividend ETFs, and TIPS. None of these options were available 60 years ago.

Figure 2.5 on the next page is a very important chart as it explains the difference in relative performance between gold stocks in the 1960s and Gold today. Note the two lines showing the breakout in gold stocks in late 1964 and the breakout in Gold in March 2024. The gold stocks immediately outperformed the S&P 500 after their breakout in late 1964, and that continued for another three years. While today Gold has risen from $2100 to as high as $2700, it has struggled to outperform the stock market.

Figure 2.5: S&P 500, Gold Stocks vs. S&P 500, Gold vs. S&P 500

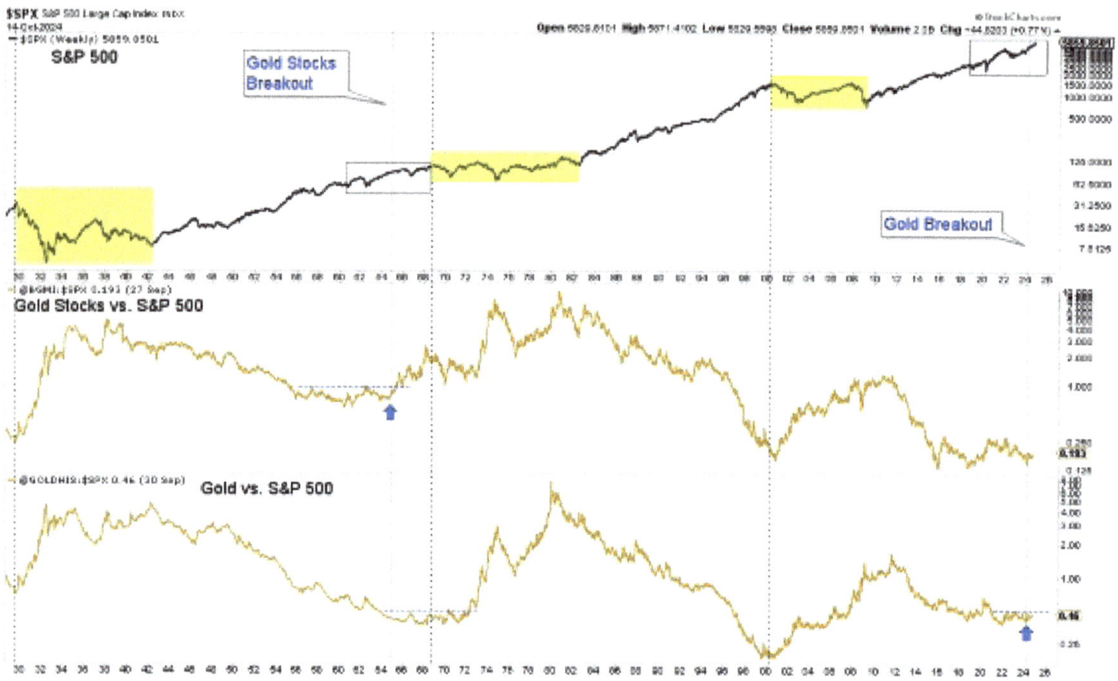

Gold breaking out of its 13-year cup-and-handle pattern and surging past $2100 signals the beginning of a new secular bull market, but this has yet to be confirmed because Gold is not outperforming the stock market and the conventional investment portfolio.

In Figure 2.6 on the next page, we show what we consider to be "The Most Important Chart in Gold." We plot Gold at the top and a ratio of Gold against the total return of the 60/40 conventional investment portfolio. This expounds upon the Gold-to-S&P 500 ratio by showing Gold against the total return (including dividends) of a portfolio of 60% Stocks and 40% Bonds.

The blue lines represent the nominal bottom in Gold and the start of its breakout moves against the 60/40 Portfolio above the red resistance lines. See the blue arrows. The vertical red lines mark the end of the secular bull markets.

As we can see, the strongest moves in Gold occurred in tandem with Gold, outperforming the 60/40 Portfolio. This makes complete sense, as Gold and the 60/40 Portfolio compete for investor capital. After the ratio broke above the red lines, the secular bull market in Gold continued for another eight years (1972-1980) and nine years (2002-2011), respectively.

Gold is very close to breaking out of a nearly 10-year-long base against the 60/40 Portfolio. If the secular bull market in Stocks ends in the next year or two, the ratio could explode higher out of its base, as it did in 1972 and 2002.

Figure 2.6: Gold vs. 60/40 Portfolio

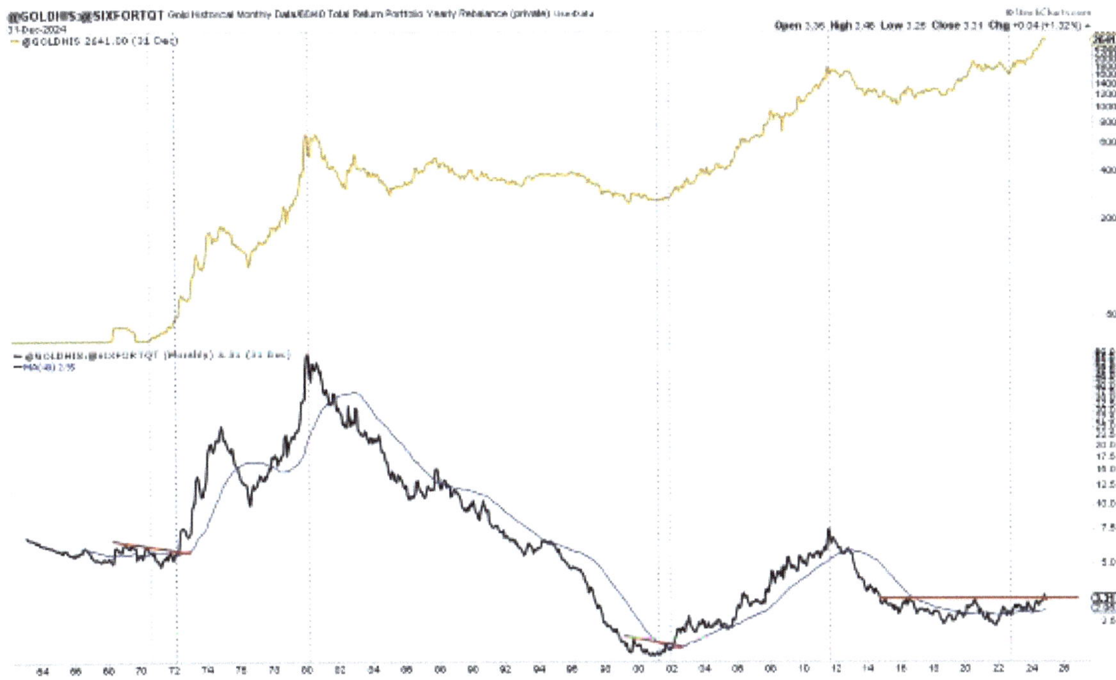

When I wrote the first version of my book in 2015, my conclusion, which proved to be incorrect, was that the US stock market could be in a secular bear market and that Gold would have a blowoff move like the one in the late 1970s to end its secular bull market. In the second version, written in 2019, I realized that US equities were in a secular bull market and that there were quite a few similarities to the 1960s.

I continue to hold that view, and the evidence argues that US equities are in the mature phase of a secular bull market that could end within the next few years.

Figure 2.7 on the next page, courtesy of Fidelity's Jurien Timmer, shows the cumulative real return from the S&P 500's four secular bull markets of the past 100 years. It is an excellent chart because, unlike a price-only comparison, it includes dividends and is adjusted for inflation. The previous two secular bull markets peaked in 2026 and 2028 on the current scale, with the 1966 peak in stocks in 2025 on this scale.

Figure 2.7: Secular Bull Market Analogs

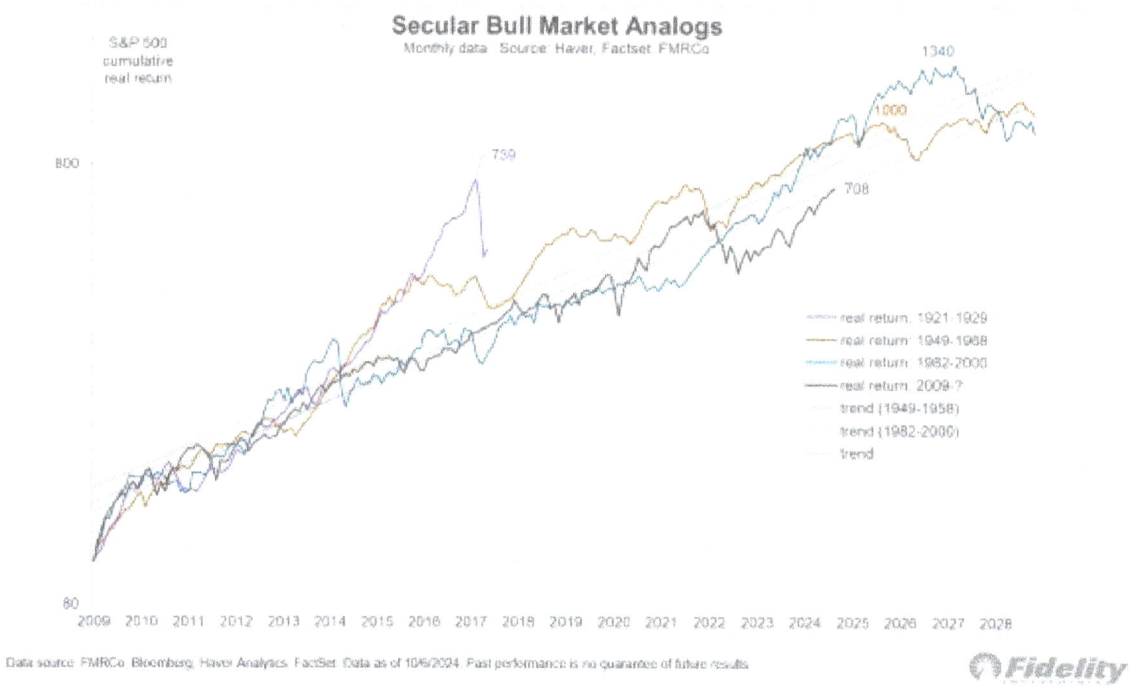

Let me step back and explain the driving forces behind these major trends so we can understand the causes of secular trends and trend changes.

Secular bear markets in equities usually begin with or are caused by extreme over-valuation, very high ownership of stocks, or rising long-term interest rates due to inflation. Policymakers decrease interest rates and increase government spending to combat the negative effects. Lower rates and particularly declining real interest rates help counteract recession by reducing the debt burden and encouraging more borrowing and consumption. Increased government spending also picks up the slack. These policies are inflationary and most favorable to Gold and hard assets, which are in a supply and demand imbalance due to the preceding secular bear market and years of low capital investment to create future supply.

Positive and rising real interest rates signify a healthy economic environment and usually coincide with secular bull markets in equities and often (but not always) in Bonds. They keep a lid on inflation but facilitate sustainable growth. Depositors, savers, and lenders can earn a real rate of return while providing capital for productive investment. The economy and financial system are healthy enough to withstand conventional monetary policy during these periods. At lows in the business cycle, policymakers will decrease rates and increase spending, but usually not to the degree seen recently as well as in the 1930s.

The trend in inflation mirrors that of commodity prices, and as a result, major turning points in commodity prices and the rate of inflation contribute to secular trend changes. Most notably, major peaks in commodity prices and the inflation rate (such as in 1920, the early 1950s, the early 1980s, and 2011) coincide with troughs in stock market valuations and the start of secular bull markets. On the other hand, as inflation begins to take hold (as it did in the mid-1930s, mid-1960s, and the wake of COVID-19), it leads to lower stock valuations and secular bear markets.

Figure 2.8 below shows the interplay between the stock market, valuation, long-term interest rates, and rate of inflation. We plot the Dow Jones Industrial Average, CAPE (10-year PE Ratio courtesy of Yale Professor Robert Schiller), the yield on the 10-year Treasury Note, and the CPI (consumer price index). The yellow highlights the secular bear markets in US stocks, including 1906-1921, 1929-1942, 1966-1982, and 2000-2009.

Extremely high valuations (most notably 1929 and 2000), inflation and rising rates (mid to late 1960s), or a combination (1906) can be the root cause of a secular bear market.

Although valuations are quite high today (CAPE ratio is in the 93rd percentile), the best comparison is to the early 1900s and mid to late 1960s. The 1929 and 2000 peaks were true bubbles during which Bonds remained in a secular bull market. Long-term rates are rising today, and Bonds are in a secular bear market, much like in the mid to late 1960s and early 1900s. The 10-year yield reaching and moving above 5% in 1966-1967 is said to have caused the secular peak in US Stocks. See the blue arrows. I would not be surprised to see a repeat over the next few years.

Figure 2.8: Stock Prices, CAPE Ratio, 10-Year Yield, CPI (Inflation)

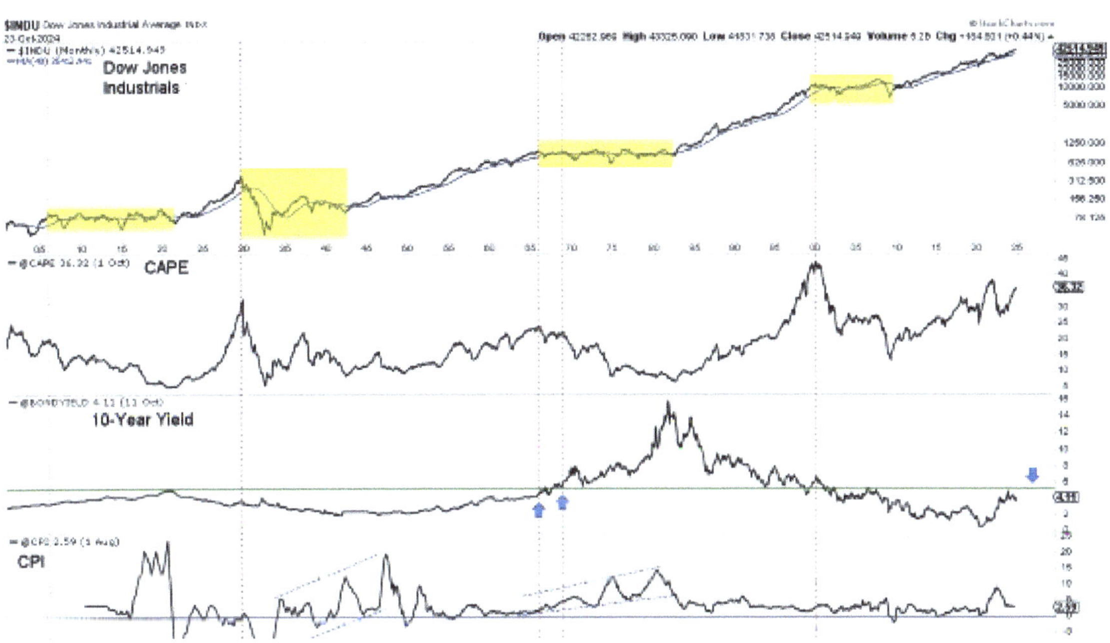

It is important to note that a secular bear market occurs quietly in an inflationary time such as the present, the late 1960s, or the early 1900s. The market loses value not from a major crash like in 1929 or 2000 but from ongoing inflation and lower valuations.

From the stock market peak in February 1966 to the peak in December 1972, the S&P 500 gained only 28%, while the CPI gained 33% during the same period. However, the S&P 500's total real return was 4.2% annualized over that nearly 7-year period due to strong dividends, which do not exist today.

Current estimates for future returns, as one would expect due to high valuations and heavy ownership of stocks, are in the low single digits. Goldman Sachs published its estimate in October 2024 that the S&P 500 will deliver a total return of 3% per annum and 1% per annum (inflation-adjusted) during the next 10 years. Barry Bannister, the Chief Equity Strategist at Stifel, estimates an inflation-adjusted annual return of 3% over the next 10 years. Savita Subramanian, the Chief of Equity Strategy at Bank of America, estimates a 1% to 2% return per annum over the next 10 years. These bode poorly for the S&P 500 as they are even lower when we remove dividends.

In Figure 2.9 on the next page, we plot the S&P 500 along with several data sets: the CAPE ratio, Household Equity Investments (as a percentage of all assets), and Professor Schiller's Excess Cape Yield, which is an estimate of total real return per annum over the next 10 years. That is presently at 1.83%. Many have observed that Household Equity Investments have an even stronger inverse correlation to future equity market returns than the CAPE ratio. It is currently at an all-time high, surpassing the peaks in 2000 and 2021.

The confirmation signal for a new secular bear market is when the S&P 500 convincingly falls below its 40-month moving average. The blue arrows signal how the stock market remains above the moving average during a secular bull market. The red arrows signal the first major break below the moving average, which all occurred the year after the secular peak.

Figure 2.9: S&P 500, CAPE Ratio, Household Equity Investments, Excess Cape Yield

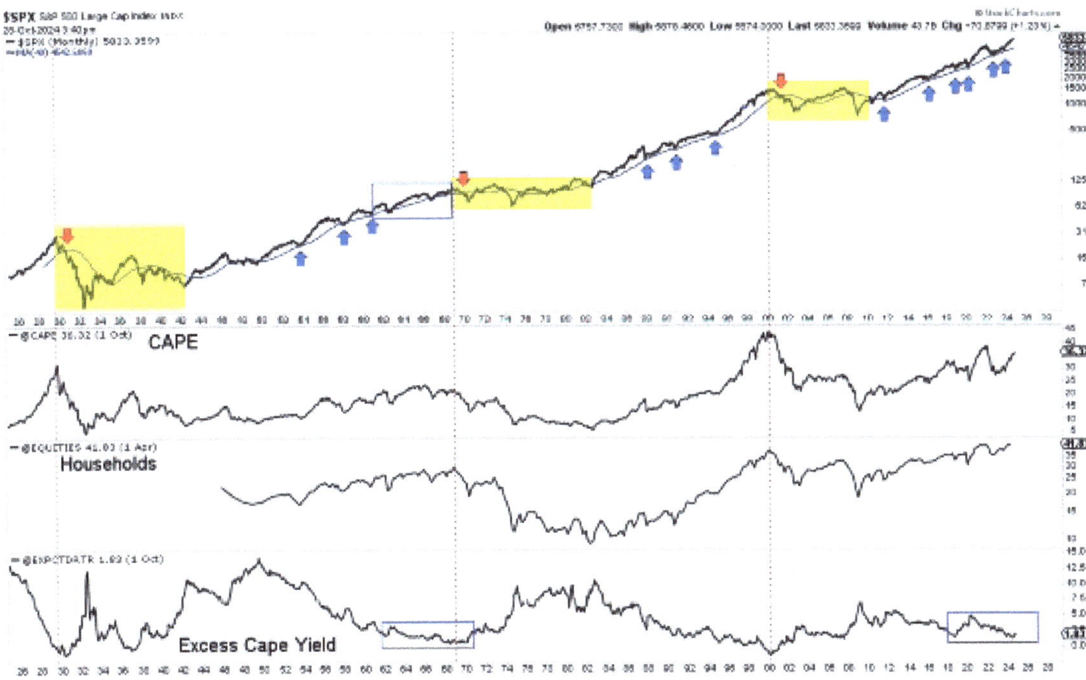

Finally, it is important to note that conventional stocks are not a hedge for a secular inflationary cycle. The modern world of finance does not know or understand this because there has been only one such cycle in the last 100 years! In Figure 2.10 on the next page, we plot an index showing the total real return of the stock market, dating back to 1900. The chart includes the rolling 20-year return and 15-year return. The vertical red line marks the start of the four secular bear markets.

The inflationary secular bear markets of 1906-1921 and 1968-1982 ended worse than those of 1929-1942 and 2000-2009. Stocks can initially rise during a secular inflationary period. Still, persistent inflation eventually eats away at corporate margins, forcing capital into alternative investments and resulting in lower and lower valuations for conventional stocks.

Consider the total real return roughly 13 years after each secular peak. After the 1906 and 1968 peaks, the total real return was materially lower. However, 13 years after the 2000 peak, the total real return had already made a new high! In 1942, the total real return was relatively in line with that of 1919 and 1981, but that was only due to the near 90% stock market crash after the 1929 peak.

In the latter stages of inflationary secular bear markets, the total real return drops to a level similar to 20 years ago. It made no progress from 1902 to 1921 and from 1906 to 1923. During the 1960s and 1970s, there was no progress from 1962 to 1982 and from 1965 to 1984.

Figure 2.10: S&P 500 Total Real Return, 20-Year & 15-Year Rolling Returns

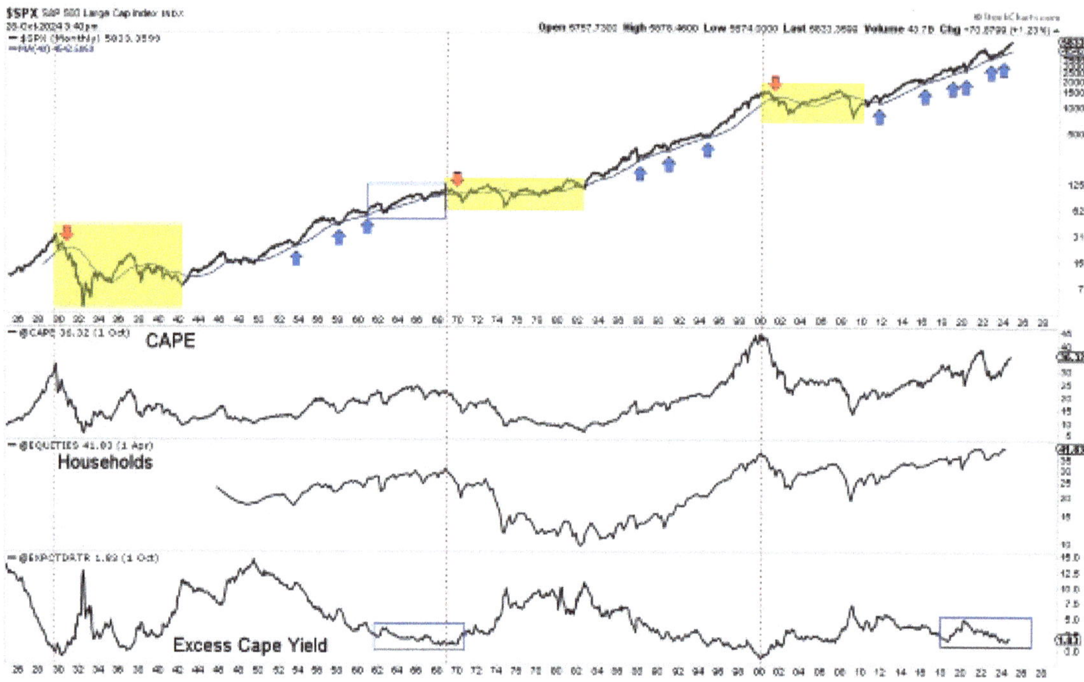

Chapter Summary

The secular trend between stocks and commodities (and Gold) alternates. When one is in a secular bull market, the other is in a secular bear market. Rising commodity prices are inflationary and negative for conventional stocks. Major peaks in commodity prices lead to secular bear markets in hard assets and periods of lower inflation, which is very positive for the stock market.

The two asset classes can and often will trend together for multi-year periods, and there is some history of secular trends overlapping. The 1940s is one case of overlap, in which the stock market made an epic low in 1942 in the middle of a secular bull market in commodities. Another case of secular overlap was in the 1960s, during which Silver trended higher, and gold stocks exploded out of a 37-year base in 1964, two years before the peak in the Dow Jones Industrial Average and four years before the peak in the S&P 500.

We see another overlap today, which is much like the 1960s. The secular bull market in US stocks continues even as Gold broke out of its 13-year cup and handle pattern in March 2024. Bonds fell into a secular bear market in 1965 and after COVID-19. The secular bull market in US stocks slowed down after the mid-1960s but did not end until 1968. History, valuations, and household positioning argue the secular bull market in US stocks, while likely to continue for another year or more, is in its later innings.

The breakout in Gold to new all-time highs, coupled with rising inflation expectations and a new secular bear market in Bonds, argue that the coming secular bear market will be inflationary and similar to 1968-1982 or 1906-1921. These secular bears did not begin with crashes like the 1929-1942 and 2000-2009 because Bonds were no longer in a secular bull market.

An inflationary secular bear market is deceptive because US stocks can initially hold up and perform okay, lulling investors into a false sense of security. As inflation persists, it slowly wreaks havoc on stocks, steadily eroding real value over time. In its latter stages, the total real return index will reach a level showing no progress over the previous twenty years.

Figure 2.6 shows two signals for a full secular transition from US stocks to Gold. First, as shown in Figure 2.6, Gold needs to break out and away when measured against the total return of the 60/40 Portfolio. This occurred in 1972 and 2002, confirming a new secular bull market in Gold that lasted another eight and nearly ten years, respectively. The second signal is the S&P 500 falling below its 40-month moving average.

Chapter 6 will discuss the macroeconomic reasons for higher and persistent inflation. There are several. COVID-19 and the Ukraine War have been major catalysts for reshoring supply chains. Global trade, which increased as a share of GDP from 35% in 1985 to 61% in 2008 and kept a lid on inflation, is past its peak. According to a Gallup poll, Americans' approval of labor unions is now the highest since 1965.

The factors that have contributed to low and stable inflation for decades (increasing globalization and global trade, labor losing power, and economic neoliberalism) are reversing course, impacting corporate profits and record profit margins.

Chapter 3

Gold's Relationship with Bonds & Currencies

The secular relationship between Gold and Bonds is not as uniform as that between Gold and the stock market. Secular bull markets in precious metals have occurred during both secular bulls and secular bears in Bonds. For example, Bonds were in a secular bull market during the 1930s and 2000s, when precious metals were in a secular bull market. However, Bonds were in a secular bear market in the last half of the 1960s and the entire 1970s, and this played a significant role in the secular bull market in precious metals.

There is a fundamental explanation for the changing correlation between Bonds and Gold. A weak economic environment with low growth, recession, and deflation risk is bullish for Bonds and Gold. See the 1930s and the 2000s. However, an environment of rising inflation, rising inflation expectations, and low or no growth is bullish for precious metals but bearish for Bonds. Consider the late 1960s and 1970s and recent years, but to a lesser extent.

Gold and Bonds are often more correlated than not around cyclical economic turning points. When the economy slows considerably or enters a recession, the rate of inflation declines, and capital moves out of stocks and into Bonds for their security and yield. Bond prices rise. As bond yields fall, the Federal Reserve elects to cut interest rates. Real interest rates decline, and Gold climbs. Hence, Gold and Bonds can perform similarly before and during recessionary and potentially recessionary environments.

Circling back to secular trends, we should note that the secular trend in Bonds and bond yields lasts much longer than in equities and Commodities. Since the start of the Great Depression, Stocks and Commodities have had six different secular trends, while Bonds and bond yields have had only three in the last 120 years!

In the last chapter, we argued that the current macroeconomic environment is similar to the mid-to-late 1960s. Part of our case included the recent awakening of inflation, which also occurred in the mid-to-late 1960s. Bond yields are positively correlated to inflation, while Bond prices are negatively correlated to inflation. If inflation has made a secular turn, then so has the bond market.

The COVID-19 crash in 2020 marked the end of the secular bull market in Bonds (and the decline in yields) that began in late 1981. This will have hugely bullish implications for Gold and hard assets. It has already helped push Gold higher.

As shown in Figure 3.1 below, bond yields have only experienced one secular uptrend in the last 100 years. This uptrend coincided with a secular bear market in the S&P 500 and the best secular bull market in Gold and precious metals. Unlike in the 1930s and 2000s, Bonds were in a secular bear market.

Bond yields began to rise earnestly in the second half of the 1950s, and bond returns diminished before equity returns slowed in the 1960s. Higher inflation leads to higher interest rates, which are negative for consumers and corporations. These economic factors face a higher borrowing cost, which impacts consumption, the cost of maintaining debt, and, ultimately, corporate profits.

Figure 3.1: Gold, S&P 500, Bond Total Return & 10-Year Yield

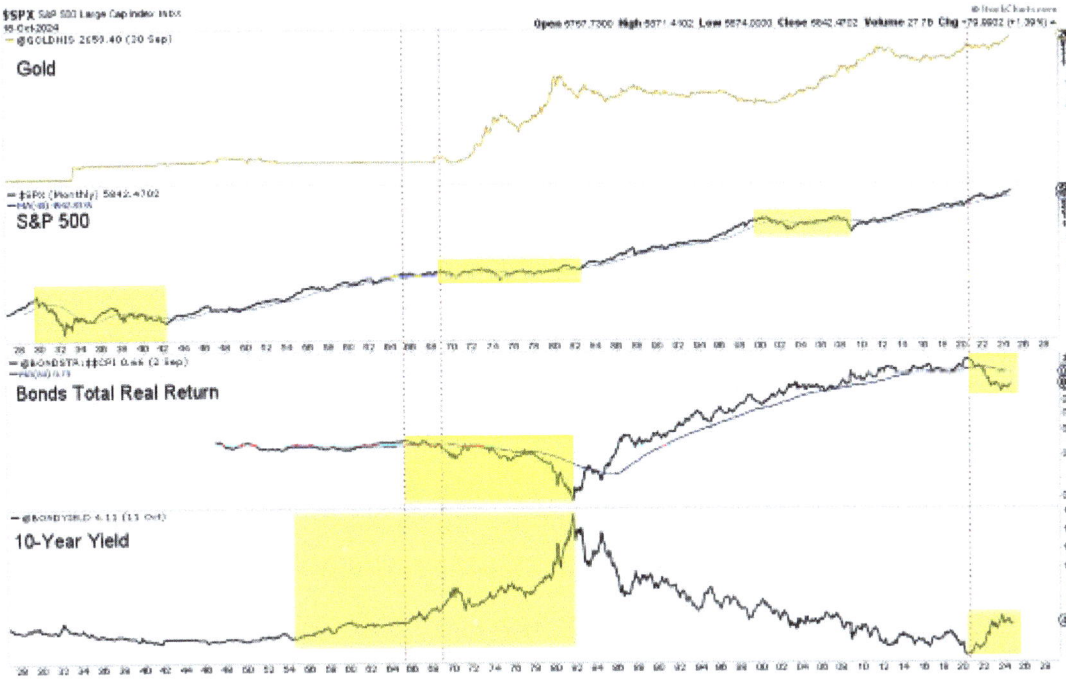

The difference between today and the 1960s (the last period inflation began to increase after many years) is that there is dramatically more debt today. According to MacroTrends, debt to GDP is three times higher today than in the mid-1960s. Also, according to RBC Wealth Management and Federal Reserve Data, corporate debt to GDP is twice as high as in the mid-1960s.

In Figure 3.2 on the next page, we plot Gold against Bonds' Total Return (of the 10-year Treasury) and Gold against the price of the 30-year Bond. Both have made major breakouts in recent years. Gold against Bonds' Total Return broke out in March 2024 and is now at a 35-year high. Meanwhile, Gold against the price of the 30-year Bond broke out at the end of 2022, surpassing its 2011 and 1980 peaks.

These ratios signal that capital is already fleeing Bonds in favor of Gold. As inflation ticks higher, bondholders and income-focused investors will slowly move out of Bonds in favor of Gold. The weakness in Bonds in recent years is a significant reason why Gold was able to break out from its cup-and-handle pattern amidst an ongoing secular bull market in Stocks.

Figure 3.2: S&P 500, Gold, Gold vs. Bond Total Return, Gold vs. 30-Year Bond

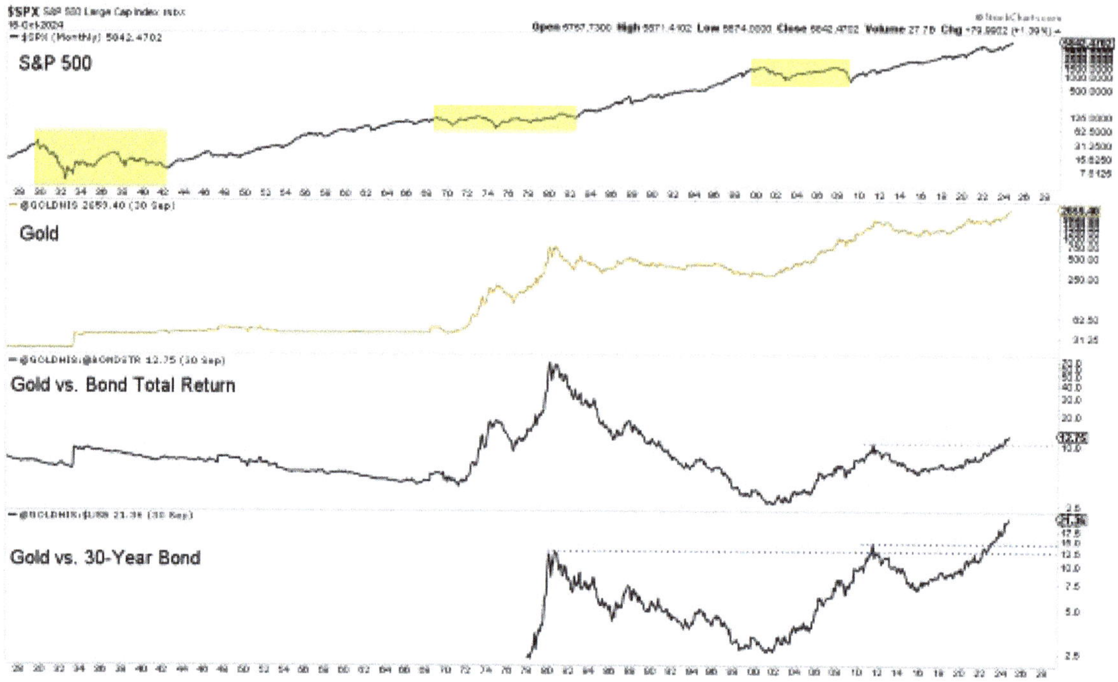

Because of the debt incurred at historically low interest rates, the federal government and indebted corporations will have difficulty absorbing and enduring higher interest rates. As we noted in Chapter 2, higher long-term rates are likely to end the secular bull market in Stocks. The money printing and debt binge becomes a major drag on the economy and corporations only when bond yields reach a certain threshold.

The likely policy option to mitigate the impact of higher bond yields is very bullish for precious metals. Many economists and investment professionals see yield curve control in our future. Under such a policy, the central bank buys long-term bonds to keep bond yields at a specific level. (This is in addition to their normal manipulation of short-term interest rates.)

The US last employed yield curve control from 1942 to 1951. Over those nine years, inflation averaged 5.5% per year, a boon for Stocks and Commodities. However, unlike in the 1940s, Stocks today are not cheap and are not coming out of a nasty secular bear market. But I digress.

Japan has used yield curve control since 2016. The Gold price in Japanese Yen terms has nearly tripled since the policy started in September 2016, outpacing Gold's performance in US Dollars (a double). The Yen declined 37% against the US Dollar from September 2016 to July 2024.

Although the secular trend in Bonds has shifted to bearish, be aware of counter-trend moves. If the economy enters a recession in 2025 or after a period of stagflation, Bonds will rally, and bond yields will decline, temporarily.

We move along to the US Dollar.

Chapter 1 briefly covered Gold's relationship with the US Dollar. In this lesson, we will expand on that by focusing on the relationship between Gold and the dollar in the context of the other asset classes.

First, let me remind you of the important conclusions from that lesson. Gold leads the US dollar at key turning points, and as a result, Gold against foreign currencies is a leading indicator of the Gold price in dollars. Finally, Gold has never been in a secular bull, while the US Dollar has been in a secular bull. Until now.

In Figure 3.3 below, we examine the US Dollar index again, this time with the important context of the other asset classes.

Figure 3.3: S&P 500, US Dollar Index, Bonds Total Return, Gold

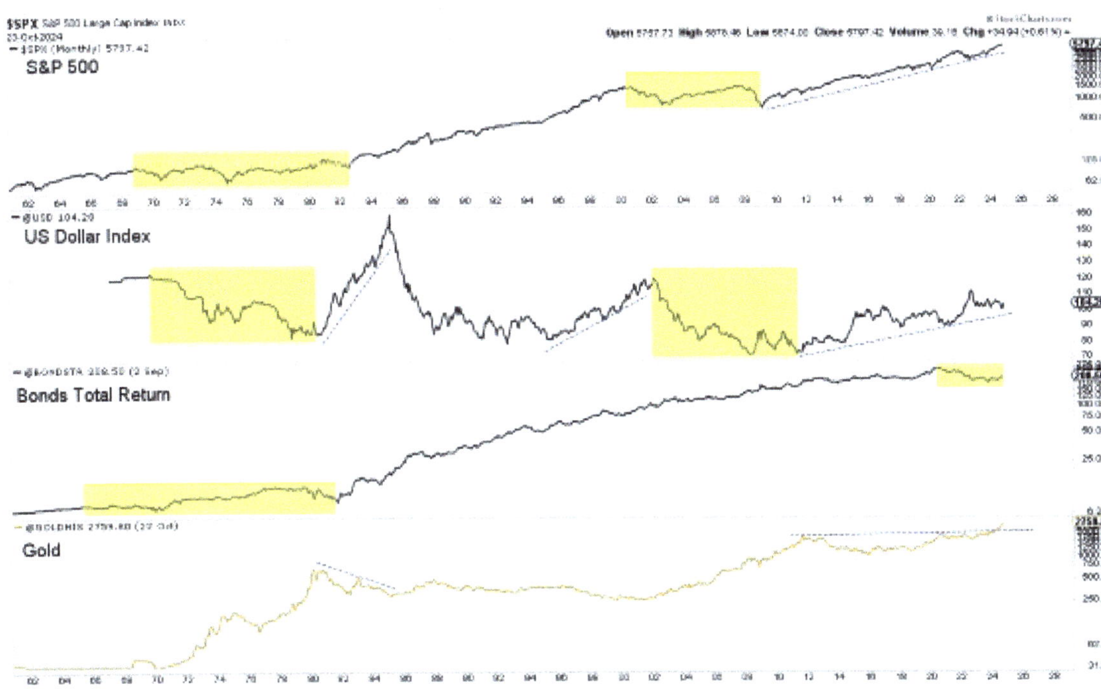

The two secular bear markets in US stocks (1968-1982 and 2000-2009) coincided with two secular bear markets in the US Dollar Index (and secular bulls in precious metals). Similarly, most of the secular bull market in US stocks from 1982 to 2000 coincided with a rising US Dollar. The same is true in the current cycle, as the secular bull in US stocks has coincided with a secular bull in the US Dollar.

Gold does not respond too well to cyclical declines in the US Dollar index during secular bull markets in US equities. The US Dollar Index was cut in half from 1985 to 1992 (its worst decline in history), and Gold mustered only a cyclical bull market from 1985 to 1987. The dollar declined sharply in 2017, and Gold could not surpass its 2016 high.

The 2022 peak in the US Dollar coincided with a bottom in Gold. However, due to its broad strength against all currencies, Gold broke out earlier this year.

Gold against foreign currencies has been stronger than Gold since 2014 and 2018. Its strength in recent years was an earlier signal that the new secular bull market would be global and much less dependent on a weak US Dollar.

In Figure 3.4 below, we highlight the breakout and leading performance of Gold against foreign currencies (Gold/FC) from 2021 to 2023. It broke out to new all-time highs before Gold, while the US Dollar enjoyed a strong rise.

Figure 3.4: S&P 500, US Dollar Index, Gold/FC, Gold

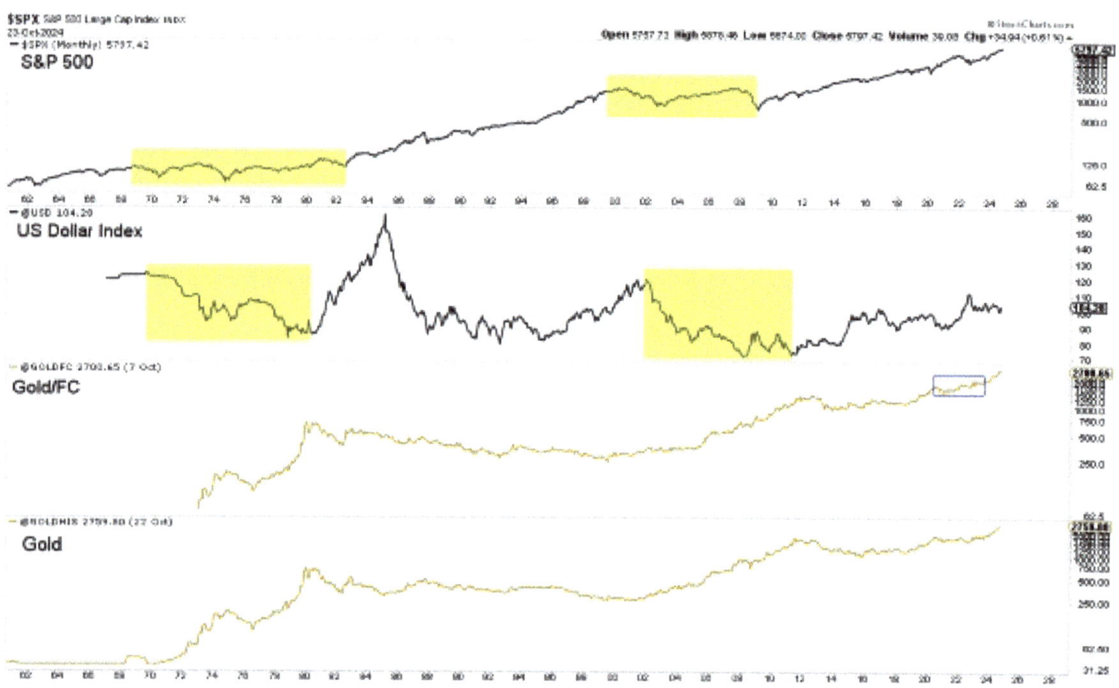

Chapter Summary

The secular relationship between Bonds and Gold is not as uniform as that between Stocks and Gold. Because Bonds can trend for 30 to 40 years, they have been secular bulls and secular bears during Gold's secular bull markets.

This is only the second time Bonds have been in a secular bear market in the last 100 years. The last time they fell into a secular bear market, as they did after COVID-19, was in the mid-1960s. The secular bear market began in concert with the aforementioned massive breakout in gold stocks. The current secular bear market in Bonds began after COVID-19 and helped stabilize Gold in 2022, which helped it break out earlier this year.

A secular bear market in Bonds and rising bond yields will eventually hurt the stock market and the economy. Initially, income-focused investors will move capital to dividend-paying stocks and, secondarily, TIPS and Gold. As the bear market and inflation intensify, stocks and the economy are negatively affected. Capital then moves out of Stocks and to TIPS, Gold, Silver, and other Commodities.

Inflation and higher bond yields have yet to hit the threshold that damages the economy and Stocks. Hence, Stocks and the US Dollar remain in secular bull markets. The US Dollar and the stock market trended higher together in the mid-to-late 1990s and have again since 2011. Therefore, the secular bull markets in both could continue until higher bond yields hit that threshold. Do not expect the US Dollar to decline significantly if the US stock market remains in a secular bull market.

Gold's strength against foreign currencies over the past ten years has recently signaled the global nature of the new secular bull market in Gold. As a result, Gold is much less reliant on the weakness of the US dollar than it has been in the past.

Chapter 4

What Really Drives Silver

Silver has long been considered "the poor man's Gold" or "Gold's little brother" because historically, it was money but much less valuable than Gold. According to Wikipedia, Silver was far more common than Gold as the monetary standard from 3000 BC until the late 19th century. The United States mandated a Silver Standard with the Mint and Coinage Act of 1792 and a value of Silver of roughly 15 times that of Gold. However, the Silver Standard officially ended under the Coinage Act in 1873, in which Silver was demonetized.

Figure 4.1 on the next page, from Sharelynx.com, plots the Gold/Silver ratio dating back 300 years and includes my annotations. The ratio has consistently hovered around 15, reflecting the historic supply differential (and often the legally mandated value) between the two metals.

Since the demonetization of Silver (under the Coinage Act of 1873), the ratio has ranged from 15 to over 100. It fell to 15 during the commodity peak in 1920, the Gold bubble peak in 1980, and in 1968 due to Gold's artificially low price due to the Gold Standard. The ratio fell to 32 when Silver spiked to $50 in 2011.

As we publish, the Gold/Silver ratio stands at 80. If we are in a secular bull market that will last another 10 to 15 years, then 15x to 20x is a reasonable target, but only for the end of the bull market.

Figure 4.1: Gold/Silver Ratio

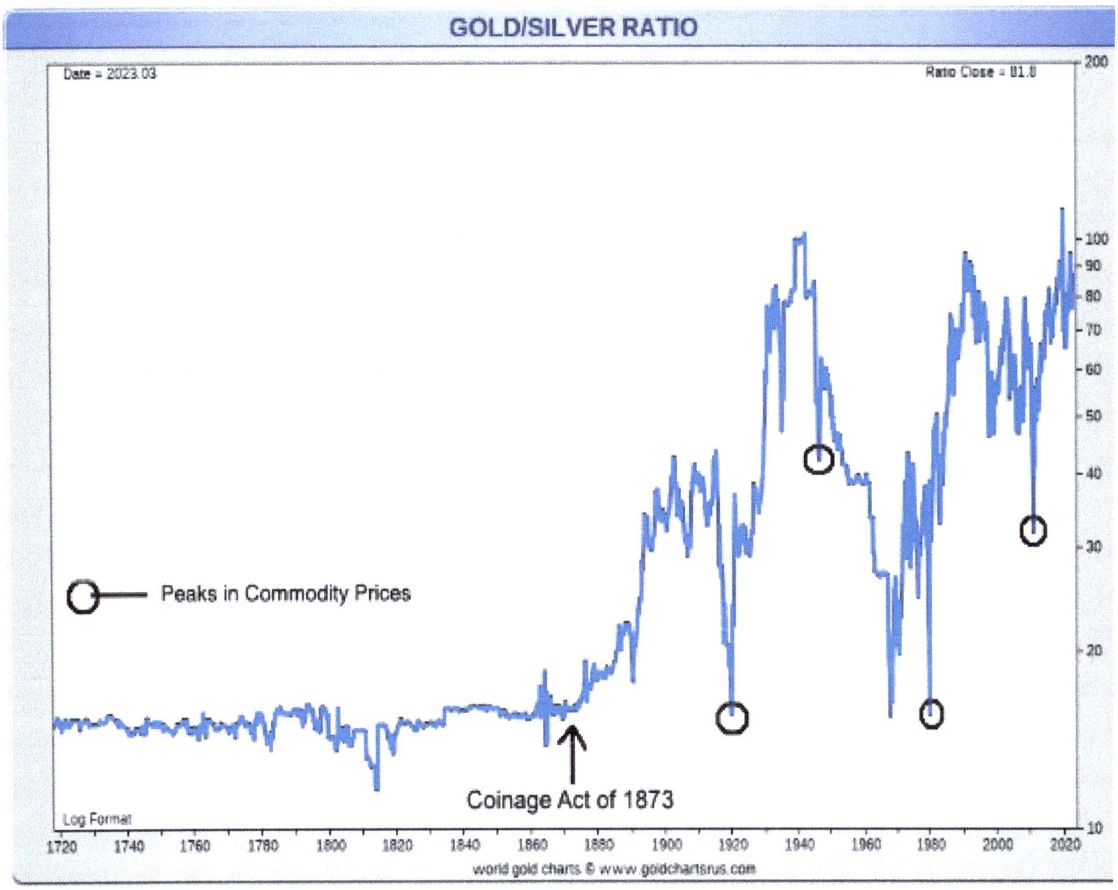

Although Silver is consumed like a commodity or base metal, its driving forces are quite similar to Gold. In terms of demand, that means investment demand.

While Gold demand is almost entirely composed of jewelry, investment demand, and central banks, Silver demand is mostly industrial, jewelry, photography, and silverware. However, as with Gold, investment demand drives Silver on the margin. In Figures 4.2 and 4.3, we share screenshots of data from Metals Focus and GFMS, courtesy of The Silver Institute.

Figure 4.2 on the next page shows a screenshot of the supply and demand data from 2007 through 2016. The strongest gains in the Silver price correspond with the strongest inventory builds in the ETPs or exchange-traded products. The only year that was different was 2008. Note the data from 2009 and 2010, two of Silver's three strongest years in recent decades. In addition, the changes in ETP inventories in 2013, 2014, and 2015 should be noted. These were bad years for Silver despite huge supply deficits.

Figure 4.2: Silver Supply & Demand Statistics 2007-2016

TABLE 1 - WORLD SILVER SUPPLY AND DEMAND

(million ounces)	2007	2008	2009	2010	2011	2012	2013	2014	2015	2016
Supply										
Mine Production	667.7	684.7	717.3	753.0	758.3	791.7	823.7	868.6	890.8	885.8
Net Government Sales	42.5	30.5	15.6	44.2	12.0	7.4	7.9	-	-	-
Scrap	203.7	200.4	200.1	226.4	260.1	253.8	191.0	165.3	141.1	139.7
Net Hedging Supply	-24.1	-8.7	-17.4	50.4	12.2	-47.1	-34.8	16.8	7.8	-18.4
Total Supply	**889.8**	**907.0**	**915.6**	**1,074.1**	**1,042.7**	**1,005.8**	**987.8**	**1,050.7**	**1,039.7**	**1,007.1**
Demand										
Jewelry	182.3	177.6	176.9	190.0	191.5	187.4	221.8	227.9	228.3	207.0
Coins & Bars	61.6	196.6	92.9	147.7	208.4	159.2	240.6	234.0	290.7	206.8
Silverware	60.2	58.4	53.2	51.6	47.2	43.7	58.8	60.7	62.9	52.1
Industrial Fabrication	646.0	641.8	528.2	633.8	661.4	600.0	604.5	595.7	569.6	561.9
....of which Electrical & Electronics	262.5	271.7	227.4	301.2	290.8	266.7	266.0	263.4	245.9	233.6
...of which Brazing Alloys & Solders	58.6	61.8	53.8	61.2	63.2	61.1	63.7	66.7	61.5	55.4
...of which Photography	117.0	98.2	76.4	67.5	61.2	54.2	50.5	48.5	46.6	45.2
...of which Photovoltaic*	-	-	-	-	75.8	58.2	55.9	51.8	57.2	76.6
...of which Ethylene Oxide	7.9	7.4	4.8	8.7	6.2	4.7	7.7	5.0	10.2	10.2
...of which Other Industrial*	200.0	202.7	165.8	195.2	164.1	155.0	160.8	160.5	148.4	141.0
Physical Demand	950.2	1,074.5	851.1	1,023.1	1,108.5	990.2	1,125.8	1,118.3	1,151.5	1,027.8
Physical Surplus/Deficit	**-60.3**	**-167.5**	**64.5**	**50.9**	**-65.8**	**15.6**	**-137.9**	**-67.6**	**-111.8**	**-20.7**
ETP Inventory Build	54.8	101.3	156.9	129.5	-24.0	55.3	2.5	1.5	-17.7	47.0
Exchange Inventory Build	21.5	-7.1	-15.3	-7.4	12.2	62.2	8.8	-5.3	12.6	79.8
Net Balance	**-136.6**	**-261.7**	**-77.2**	**-71.1**	**-54.0**	**-101.9**	**-149.2**	**-63.8**	**-106.7**	**-147.5**
Silver Price, $ per oz.	13.38	14.99	14.67	20.19	35.12	31.15	23.79	19.08	15.68	17.14

*Photovoltaic demand included in "Other Industrial" prior to 2011

In recent years, the strongest gains in the Silver price occurred in 2016, 2019, and 2020, as seen in Figure 4.3 on the next page, which included the strongest investment in Silver exchange-traded products.

After 2021, the Silver price declined for two years as investment demand declined. The supply-demand imbalances, which were some of the biggest on record, did not impact the Silver price.

Figure 4.3: Silver Supply & Demand Statistics 2015-2024

Silver Supply and Demand

Million ounces	2015	2016	2017	2018	2019	2020	2021	2022	2023	2024F	Year on Year 2023	Year on Year 2024F
Supply												
Mine Production	896.8	899.8	863.6	850.6	837.2	783.4	829.0	836.7	830.5	823.5	-1%	-1%
Recycling	147.0	148.7	147.2	148.7	148.2	164.3	173.7	176.9	178.6	178.9	1%	0%
Net Physical Disinvestment	0.0	0.0	0.0	0.0	0.0	0.0	0.0	0.0	0.0	0.0	na	na
Net Hedging Supply	2.2	0.0	0.0	0.0	13.9	8.5	0.0	0.0	0.0	0.0	na	na
Net Official Sector Sales	1.1	1.1	1.0	1.2	1.0	1.2	1.5	1.7	1.6	1.5	-6%	-9%
Total Supply	**1,047.0**	**1,046.5**	**1,011.8**	**1,000.5**	**1,000.3**	**957.4**	**1,004.3**	**1,015.4**	**1,010.7**	**1,003.8**	**0%**	**-1%**
Demand												
Industrial (total)	457.1	489.5	526.4	524.2	523.5	509.7	561.3	588.3	654.4	710.9	11%	9%
Electrical & Electronics	272.3	308.0	330.7	331.0	327.3	322.0	361.2	371.3	446.1	485.6	20%	9%
...of which photovoltaics	59.6	*81.6*	99.3	*87.0*	*74.9*	*82.8*	88.9	*118.1*	*193.5*	*232.0*	64%	20%
Brazing Alloys & Solders	51.1	49.1	50.9	52.0	52.4	47.5	50.5	49.2	50.2	51.8	2%	3%
Other Industrial	133.7	131.5	135.8	141.2	143.8	140.2	159.6	167.8	159.0	173.5	-5%	9%
Photography	38.2	34.7	32.4	31.4	30.7	26.9	27.7	27.5	27.0	26.1	-2%	-3%
Jewelry	202.5	189.1	196.2	203.2	201.6	150.9	182.0	234.5	203.1	211.3	-13%	4%
Silverware	58.3	53.5	59.4	67.1	61.3	31.2	40.7	73.5	56.2	58.8	-25%	7%
Net Physical Investment	309.3	212.9	155.8	165.9	187.4	208.1	284.3	337.1	243.1	212.0	-28%	-13%
Net Hedging Demand	0.0	12.0	1.1	7.4	0.0	0.0	3.5	17.9	12.2	0.0	-32%	na
Total Demand	**1,065.4**	**991.8**	**971.3**	**999.2**	**1,004.4**	**926.8**	**1,099.6**	**1,278.9**	**1,195.0**	**1,219.1**	**-7%**	**2%**
Market Balance	-18.4	54.7	40.5	1.3	-4.1	30.6	-95.4	-263.5	-184.3	-215.3	-30%	17%
Net Investment in ETPs	-17.1	53.9	7.2	-21.4	83.3	331.1	64.9	-125.8	-42.1	50.0	-67%	na
Market Balance less ETPs	**-1.3**	**0.8**	**33.3**	**22.7**	**-87.4**	**-300.5**	**-160.3**	**-137.7**	**-142.2**	**-265.3**	**3%**	**87%**
Nominal Silver Price (US $/oz, London price)	15.68	17.14	17.05	15.71	16.21	20.55	25.14	21.73	23.35	-	7%	na

Source: Metals Focus

Although investment demand drives Silver on the margins, industrial demand is heating up and could play a more important role in the years ahead. It has risen in each of the previous three years and is projected to rise to a record 710.9 million ounces in 2024. Historically, industrial demand made up half of all silver demand. Now, it accounts for 64% of all demand.

Many analysts project industrial demand will continue to grow over the next decade due to the ongoing energy transition. Silver is needed in solar panels and electric vehicles, which require 1.5 to more than twice as much as silver used in cars with internal combustion engines. Analysts project that as many as 90 million ounces of Silver will be needed for automobiles in 2025. However, solar panels are a game-changer. Sprott estimates that solar demand could grow 170% to 273 million ounces in 2030, representing one-fifth of all silver demand.

The recent increase in industrial demand did not and has not impacted the price of Silver because (investment demand is paramount) but also because above-ground stockpiles are plentiful. London Bullion Market Association vaults have ~900 million ounces of Silver, while COMEX vaults carry ~300 Million ounces. (COMEX stands for the Commodity Exchange, a division of the Chicago Mercantile Exchange).

Above-ground stockpiles of Silver have decreased, but there is a cure for that. Higher silver prices will draw out more above-ground Silver held outside of the COMEX and LBMA and induce more silver production. Most Silver is mined as a byproduct of base metals (Lead, Zinc, Copper) and Gold. Higher base metals prices will be required to induce greater production of Silver.

Although the industrial demand for Silver is growing sharply, history shows that the trend in Gold remains the most important driver of Silver. Figure 4.4 below compares Silver with Gold and Copper. Historically and recently, Silver has aligned more with Gold than Copper.

Figure 4.4: Gold, Silver, Copper

Historically, Silver has acted as a highly leveraged play on Gold. It greatly outperformed Gold during the two secular bull markets (in yellow) and underperformed badly during the two secular bear markets (1980 to 2001 and 2011 to 2023).

Silver has also followed Gold more closely than Copper on a shorter-term and more cyclical basis. Consider the following examples. Copper performed reasonably well from the mid-1980s to the mid-1990s. It even retested its 1980 peak in 1989 and 1995. Gold trended down during this period, while Silver, by 1993, was trading at around a 20-year low. Each market performed well in the early to mid-2000s, but Gold and Silver strongly outperformed Copper from 2006 to 2011.

The outlier in Silver's history was the price increase in 1997 due to Warren Buffett's huge investment. Silver resumed its downtrend in 1998. Buffett sold it in 2006.

Most recently, Silver has remained strongly tied to Gold. The vertical line shows the Gold peak in August 2020. Copper surged higher into 2021, which temporarily helped Silver. However, copper did not peak until early 2022, when Gold and Silver were trading below their August 2020 peaks. In 2024, Gold exploded above its previous peak of $2100, and Silver followed by surpassing $29-$30. Copper remains below its 2021 and 2022 peaks.

In Figure 4.5 below, we plot Gold, Silver, and the Consumer Price Index (CPI) to compare Silver's performance around important breakouts in the Gold price and rising inflation. The vertical blue lines mark the most important breakouts in Gold, and the lighter ones mark the other breakouts in Gold.

The biggest moves in Silver occurred after the most important breakouts in Gold. Breakouts in Gold usually occur before and lead to breakouts in Silver. Most notably, Gold broke out first in 1978, 2003, and 2019 and did so again in March of 2024, a few months before Silver's breakout.

Gold usually leads inflation, and Gold also leads Silver. The three most significant breakouts in Gold and ensuing advances in Silver occurred amid rising inflation. Here is how to think of the relationship between Gold, Silver, and inflation and how Silver might perform. Silver will outperform if Gold breaks out to the upside and inflation rises. If Gold breaks out to the upside but in a deflationary and recessionary environment, then Gold will outperform Silver.

Figure 4.5 Gold, Silver, CPI

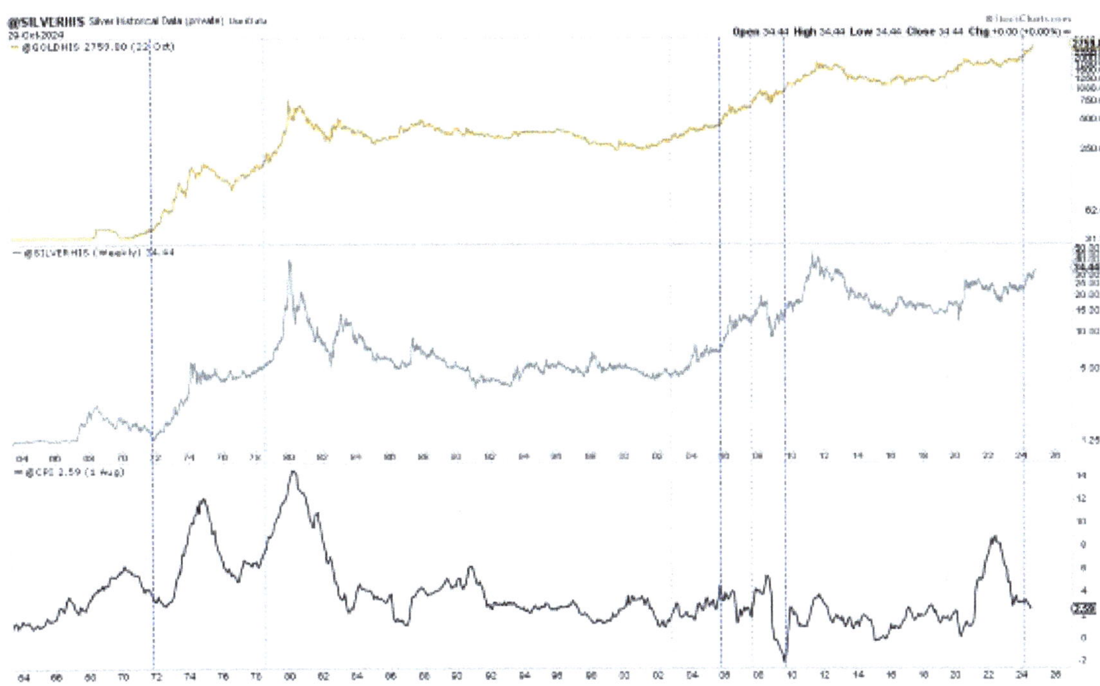

In 2024, Gold and Silver made significant breakouts but Silver underperformed for two reasons.

1. First, the rate of inflation has not increased statistically. The larger narrative of economic weakness, recession, and Fed rate cuts supports Gold more than Silver until inflation expectations rise.
2. Second, the technical setup is conducive to Gold outperforming until Silver moves beyond the $35/oz to $37/oz resistance level. Gold broke out from a 13-year cup and handle pattern to a new all-time high. It is in blue sky territory, facing little long-term resistance. Although Silver broke past four-year resistance at $28-$30/oz, it still needs to chew through

supply at $35 to $37. When Silver breaks past $37, it will be in a position to outperform Gold.

Chapter Summary

Silver is the most unique commodity because of its long history as money and modern history as an industrial metal. Industrial demand now amounts to 64% of the total demand for Silver, but it continues to trade mostly as a leveraged play on Gold.

History shows that greater industrial demand or a significant supply deficit has not impacted the Silver price. The trend in the Gold price remains the exclusive driver. When Gold is in a secular bear market, Silver is a complete afterthought and trades as such. However, when Gold is in a secular bull market, Silver becomes a precious metal and will outperform Gold significantly as the bull market matures.

With Gold in a new secular bull market, the outlook for Silver over the years ahead is quite promising. The potential acceleration of growth in industrial demand over the years ahead adds a new wrinkle to the picture. This could cause Silver to trade as more of a base metal or perhaps provide it with more support during periods of weakness. Nevertheless, we should assume Gold will remain the primary driver.

Chapter 5

Technical Analysis of Gold & Silver

In 2024, Gold crossed what could be a very important turning point in its history. In March, Gold broke out from a 13-year-long cup and handle technical pattern by clearing $2100/oz convincingly. Cup-and-handle patterns are among technical analysis's most reliably bullish patterns. Furthermore, multi-decade-long bases, which this pattern in Gold was, tend to give way to multi-year and multi-decade rises. The setup is in place for a very exciting Gold market over the years and decades ahead.

In past lessons, I explained the importance of intermarket analysis for Gold and the entire precious metals sector. Gold must outperform the stock market and other asset classes to be in a secular bull market.

Although Gold has trended higher in recent years and broke out from its cup-and-handle pattern, it has yet to outperform the stock market and the conventional 60/40 portfolio. This explains why recent strength has had a different feel to many investors and why the precious metals sector (mining stocks and Silver, especially) remained in a secular bear market until March 2024. Capital has yet to move out of conventional assets in favor of Gold.

As you can see in Figure 5.1 on the next page, while Gold has broken out from a 13-year-long cup-and-handle pattern, it has yet to confirm a new uptrend when measured against the S&P 500 and the total return of the 60/40 Portfolio (60% in stocks and 40% in bonds). However, as the blue arrows indicate, the impending breakout could be only months away.

Figure 5.1: Gold, Gold vs. S&P 500, Gold vs. 60/40 Portfolio

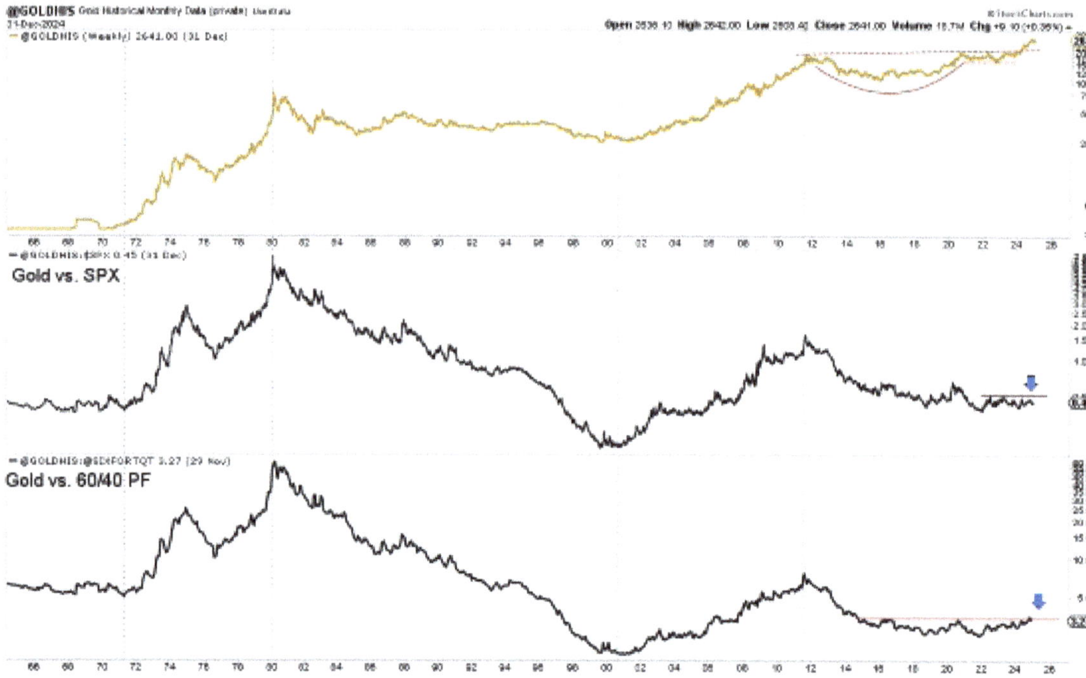

Let's cover the history and importance of "cup and handle" patterns.

A cup and handle pattern is a bullish continuation pattern. That means it develops following an uptrend, and that uptrend resumes after the pattern is complete. The pattern begins as a market declines in the shape of a U more so than a V. When the market rebounds and reaches its previous peak, the cup is complete. The handle is a small correction that retraces no more than 50% of the rebound (usually around 38%). In terms of time, the handle is brief compared to the time it takes for the cup to develop.

The upside targets are triggered when the market breaks out of the pattern and advances to a new high. Measuring the depth of the cup and adding it to the previous high gives the arithmetic target. The rarely mentioned log target is achieved by measuring the percentage move from the bottom of the cup to the previous high and then measuring it forward of the prior high.

Technical patterns sometimes fail, but cup and handle patterns are among the most reliable. When the pattern develops as stated and the market trades close to the high during the handle consolidation, the odds of a successful breakout are very high. Hence, it was no surprise that Gold was able to break out from its pattern.

Cup and handle patterns typically occur in shorter time frames, making perfect comparisons difficult. Nevertheless, we will share some historical examples that can provide context for Gold's recent breakout.

The best comparison might be the stock market from 1937 to 1950. Figure 5.2 below plots the S&P 500. The highlighted portion shows the duration of the pattern.

The cup lasted nine years, while the handle lasted four, and retraced slightly more than 38% of the preceding advance. The market reached its arithmetic target in four years and its log target one year later. Although it took some time for the market to hit the upside targets, 1949 to 1957 was one of the strongest and smoothest periods in the stock market's history.

Figure 5.2: Stock Market 1937-1950

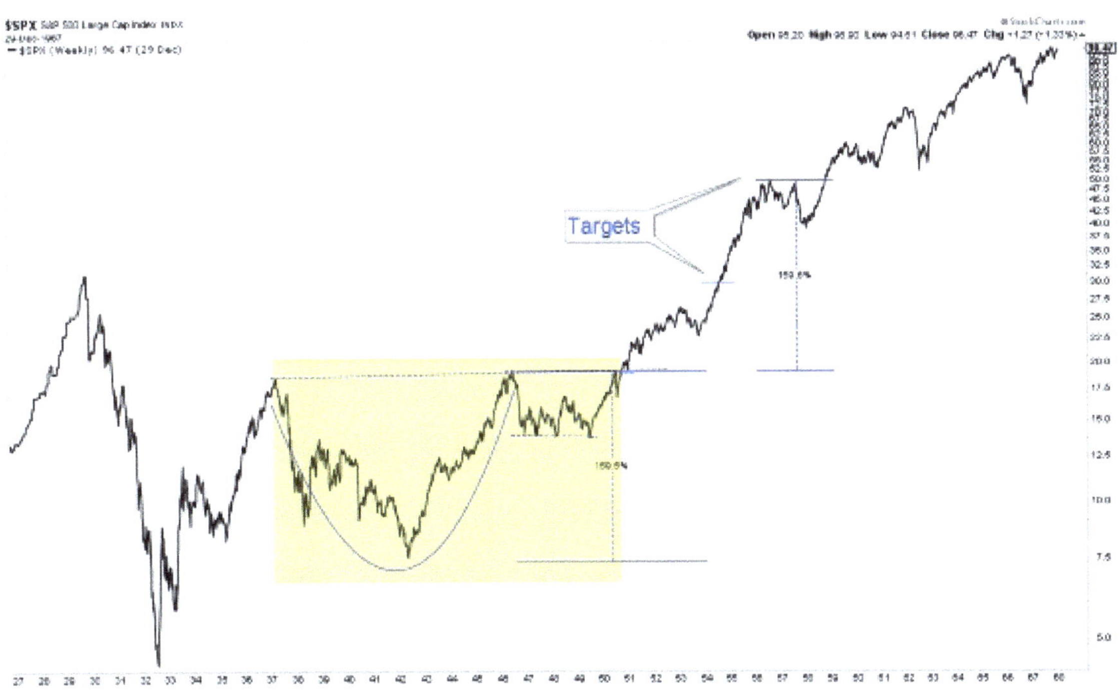

Figure 5.3 on the next page plots Gold at the turn of the century and highlights its unconventional cup and handle pattern from 1996 to 2005.

This pattern is technically a saucer bottom pattern because it is not a bullish continuation pattern. That technicality aside, the pattern formed a super bullish handle consolidation in 2004-2005 and then exploded higher. Although Gold endured significant corrections in 2006 and 2008, it followed the outcome of a cup and handle pattern by gaining roughly 300% in six years.

Figure 5.3: Gold 1996-2005

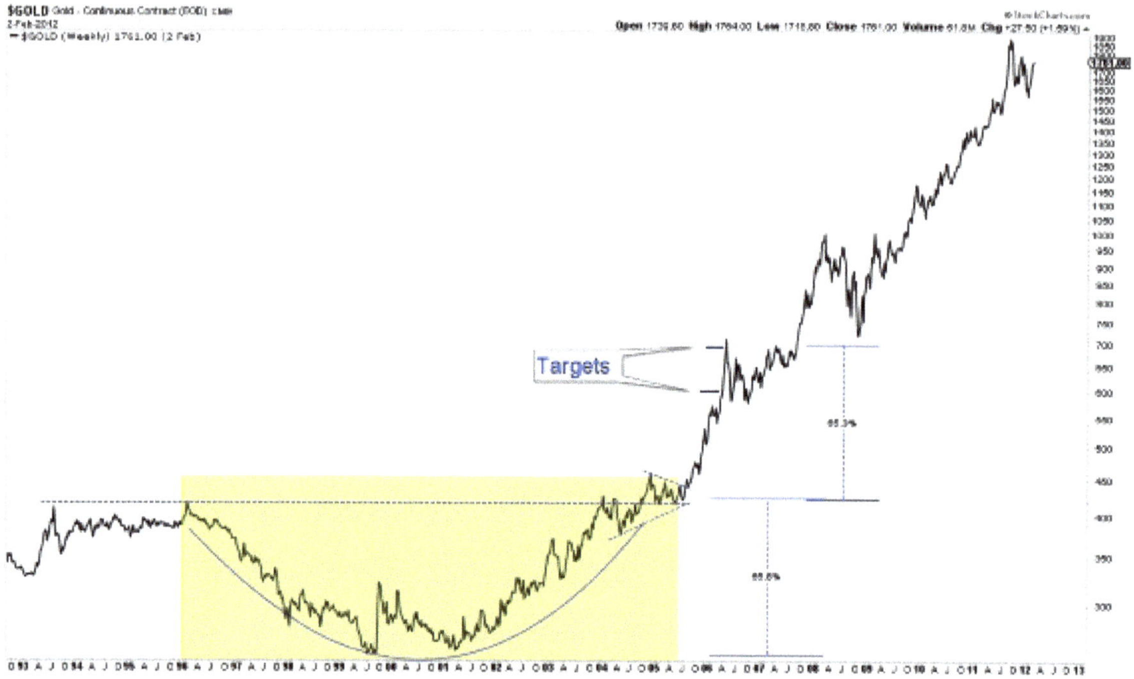

Figure 5.4 below plots the Japanese Nikkei Index in the 1960s and 1970s.

Figure 5.4: Japan 1961-1969

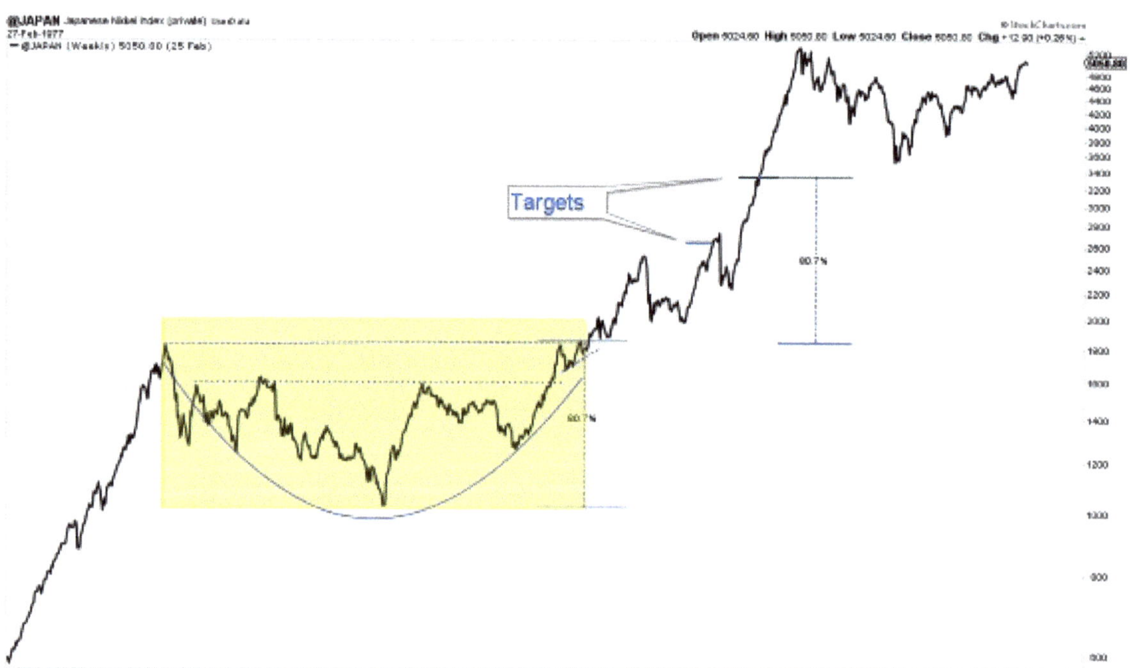

After eight years, a somewhat unconventional cup (yellow), and an extremely tiny handle at the end of 1968, the Nikkei exploded to the upside over the next four years. From 1961 to 1969, the market traded between roughly 1,800 and 1,000. Four years after the breakout, the market surged almost 200%, reaching 5,350.

Figure 5.5 below plots Hong Kong (Hang Seng Index) and highlights 1973 to 1986.

The Hang Seng broke out in 1986 from a 13-year base and two potential cup and handle patterns. The price action from 1981 to 1986 is its own cup and handle pattern but could also be the handle to the cup that formed from 1973 to 1981.

The Hang Seng immediately surpassed its arithmetic target (2,900) but did not reach its log target (from the 1981 to 1986 cup) for another five years due to the post-1987 stock market crash malaise. However, after the breakout in 1986, the Hang Seng gained roughly 575% over the next eight years. From 1973 to 1986, the market could not surpass 1,800. After it did, it surged to 12,000 over the next eight years.

Figure 5.5: Hong Kong 1973-1986

Although not a cup-and-handle pattern, the stock market before its historically significant 1982 breakout shares some similarities to Gold and bears mentioning. In Figure 5.6 on the next page, we plot the S&P 500 and Gold dating back to 1929 and show the similarities between Gold in 2023 and the S&P 500 in the early 1980s before it began its secular bull market.

The major similarity is the 1974 to 1982 period in the S&P 500 with 2016 to 2024 for Gold. Each market put in a major price low at the start of the period and then trended higher for over seven years but had yet to break away from its secular bear market. Although the stock market trended higher from the mid-1970s to the early 1980s, it underperformed hard assets, just as Gold trended higher since the end of 2015 but underperformed the stock market.

The two markets shared other, though less significant, similarities in the decades following their bubble peaks: the S&P 500 in 1929 and Gold in 1980. Following the bubble peaks, Gold did not make a new all-time high until 28 years later, and the S&P 500 did not make a new all-time high until 26 years later. Furthermore, at its 1974 low, 45 years after 1929, the S&P 500 was only 100% higher. Gold was only 30% higher than its 1980 peak 36 years later.

Figure 5.6: Gold & S&P 500 History

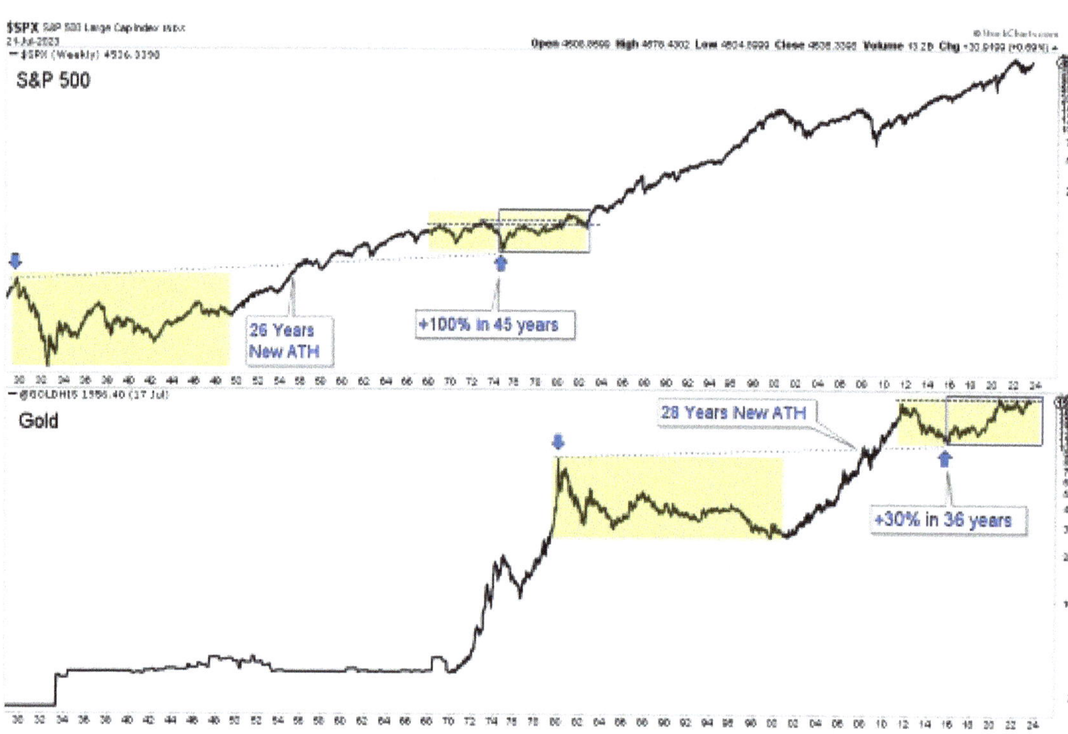

In Figure 5.7 on the next page, we highlight Gold since 1970 and mark its cup-and-handle pattern, which occurred from the 2011 peak through the breakout in March 2024.

This cup and handle pattern was stronger than typical because the right side of the cup, having reached ~$2050/oz in August 2020, is higher than the left side, the 2011 peak of $1920/oz. Also, the handle, for other than a few weeks, remained above its 38% retracement in the upper $1600s.

As we publish, Gold is trading around $2700/oz, some seven months after it broke above $2100/oz. The cup-and-handle pattern arithmetic target (or measured upside target) is around $3000/oz, while the log target is nearly $4,000/oz.

Figure 5.7: Gold Cup & Handle Pattern & Breakout

It is important to understand that these types of patterns and long bases have tremendously bullish implications beyond just a few years after the breakout. The S&P 500 broke out from its 13-year cup and handle pattern in 1950 and experienced a very strong advance into 1957, which continued into the 1960s. Gold's breakout from its cup and handle bottom formation in 2005 sparked a run that continued for another six years. The Japanese Nikkei's breakout from an eight-year cup surged higher for another four years before the next bear market. After breaking out of a huge 13-year base, Hong Kong's Hang Seng surged 575% over the next eight years.

Gold's breakout from its 13-year cup-and-handle pattern marks the start of a new secular bull market in which Gold and precious metals should trend higher for at least another decade.

Consider Gold's breakout in the context of secular peaks in the stock market and the Gold to 60/40 portfolio ratio, as shown in Figure 5.8 on the next page.

Gold peaked in 2011 and 1980, 11 years after the secular peak in the S&P 500. (Gold stocks peaked in 1937, more than seven years after the stock market peak in 1929.)

In addition, Gold peaked nine years after its impulsive advance against the 60/40 portfolio began in 1971 and 10 years after its impulsive advance began against the 60/40 portfolio in 2001.

The stock market has yet to reach a secular peak, and it remains questionable whether Gold has begun an impulsive advance against the 60/40 portfolio. Considering history, either case suggests the secular bull market in Gold and precious metals will continue well into the 2030s.

Figure 5.8: S&P 500, Gold vs. 60/40 Portfolio, Gold

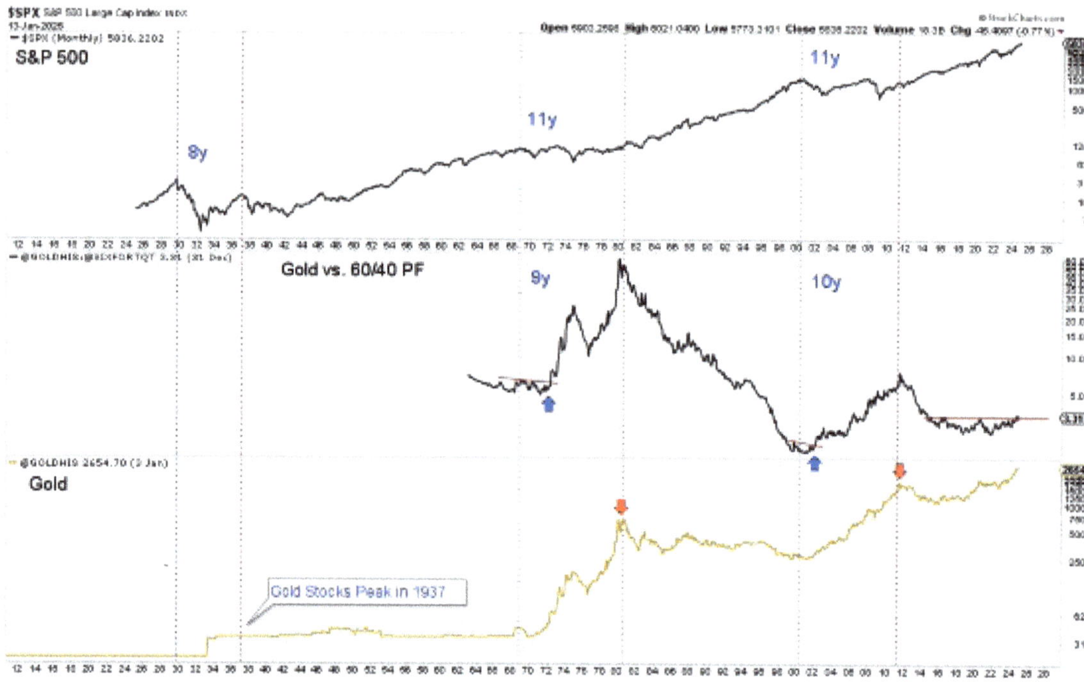

As explained in Chapter 4, Silver reliably follows strength in Gold and leverages moves in Gold. Therefore, the incredibly positive outlook for Gold is, of course, massively positive for Silver.

Regarding the technical outlook for Silver, we should keep two points in mind. First, Silver is set to have the biggest breakout in the modern history of capital markets when it surpasses $50/oz. The greatest breakout of all time was that of commodity prices in 1971. See Figure 11.6 later in the book. Second, Silver, like Gold, will be unleashed after Gold breaks out against the 60/40 Portfolio.

In Figure 5.9 on the next page, we plot Silver against the 60/40 Portfolio and Gold against the 60/40 Portfolio. The blue arrows mark the points where Gold began an impulsive breakout move against the 60/40 Portfolio: the beginning of both 1972 and 2002. Each point was incredibly close to epic bottoms in the price of Silver and Silver against the 60/40 Portfolio.

Silver is in a different position today as it has moved well off its 2022 and 2020 bottoms. However, for continued upside and explosive moves beyond $35/oz and $50/oz, Silver and Gold need to outperform the 60/40 Portfolio.

Figure 5.9: Silver, Silver vs. 60/40 Portfolio, Gold vs. 60/40 Portfolio

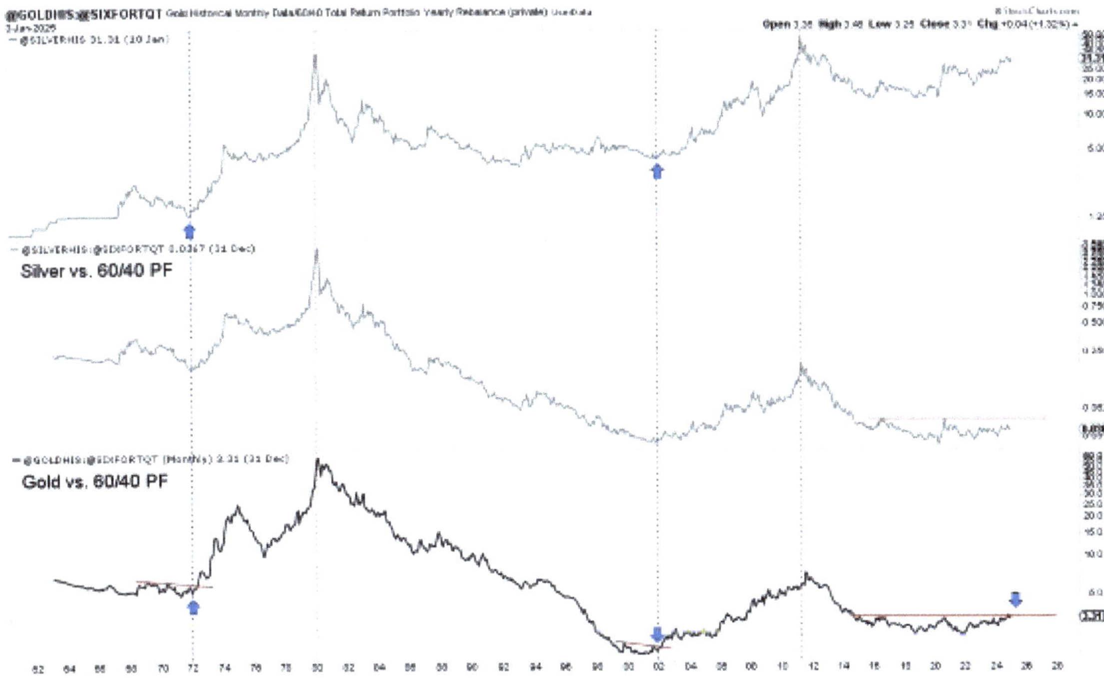

Figure 5.10 on the next page plots the chart of Silver. In nominal terms, Silver is sporting an incredible and historic multi-decade base back to its 1980 peak, 45 years in the making. This is unparalleled in the modern history of capital markets. When Silver reaches $50/oz, it will be the third test of $50 in a half-century.

Although Silver looks like a gigantic cup and handle pattern, it is technically not because the handle consolidation (2011 until present) retraced roughly 75% of the advance from $4/oz to $50/oz. As stated earlier, the handle consolidation retraces only 38% or 50% at the absolute most. Silver's price action since the 2011 peak has been much too weak to characterize it as a handle.

However, the huge 45-year base in Silver, like a cup and handle pattern, has extremely bullish implications once Silver is ready to break above $50/oz. Potential measured upside targets of $87/oz and $96/oz exist.

Figure 5.10: Silver's Huge Base

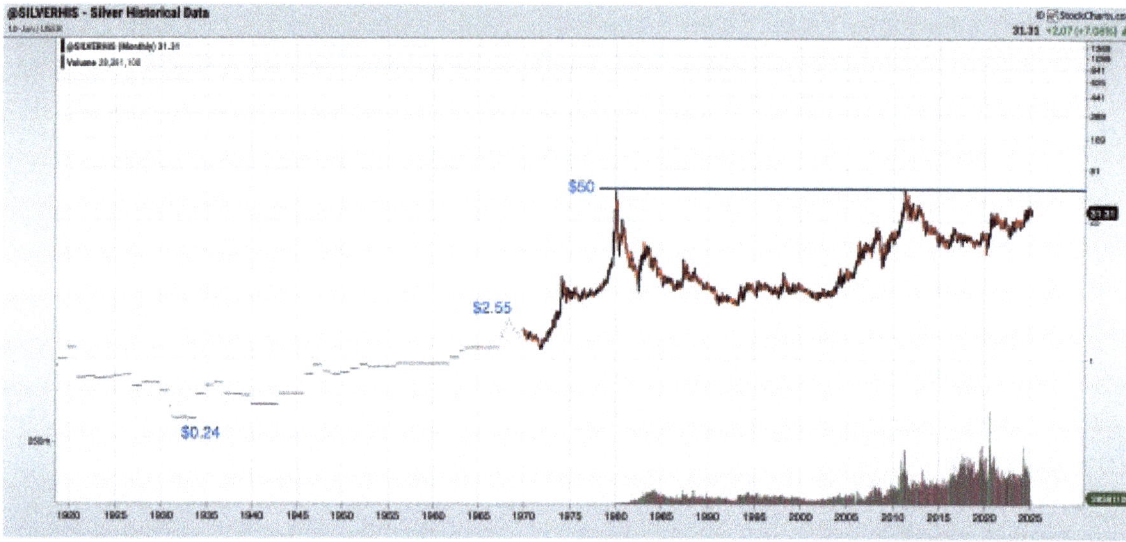

There are no other examples of individual commodities breaking out of bases of more than 40 years in the last 50 years. The closest and best comparison would be the breakouts in Copper and Oil in the 2000s and the ensuing upside, as shown in Figure 5.11 on the next page.

In 2005, Copper broke out from a 32-year-long base. From 1973 to 2005, the metal traded between $0.50/lb and $1.40/lb. After its breakout in 2005, it surged 170% to as high as $3.92/lb in only 12 months!

In 2004, Oil broke out from a 24-year-long base. Oil had traded between $10 and $40 per barrel from 1980 to 2003. Then, it broke above $40 per barrel (in 2004) and gained nearly 70% in 14 months and 95% in two years. Post-breakout, it ultimately gained 268% in the next four years.

Consider Silver's current 45-year-long base and the upside potential after it breaks $50/oz. Copper surged 170% 12 months after its breakout, while Oil gained nearly 70% 14 months after its breakout. Oil's path would put Silver above $80/oz, while Copper's path would put Silver well above $100/oz.

Figure 5.11: Copper & Oil

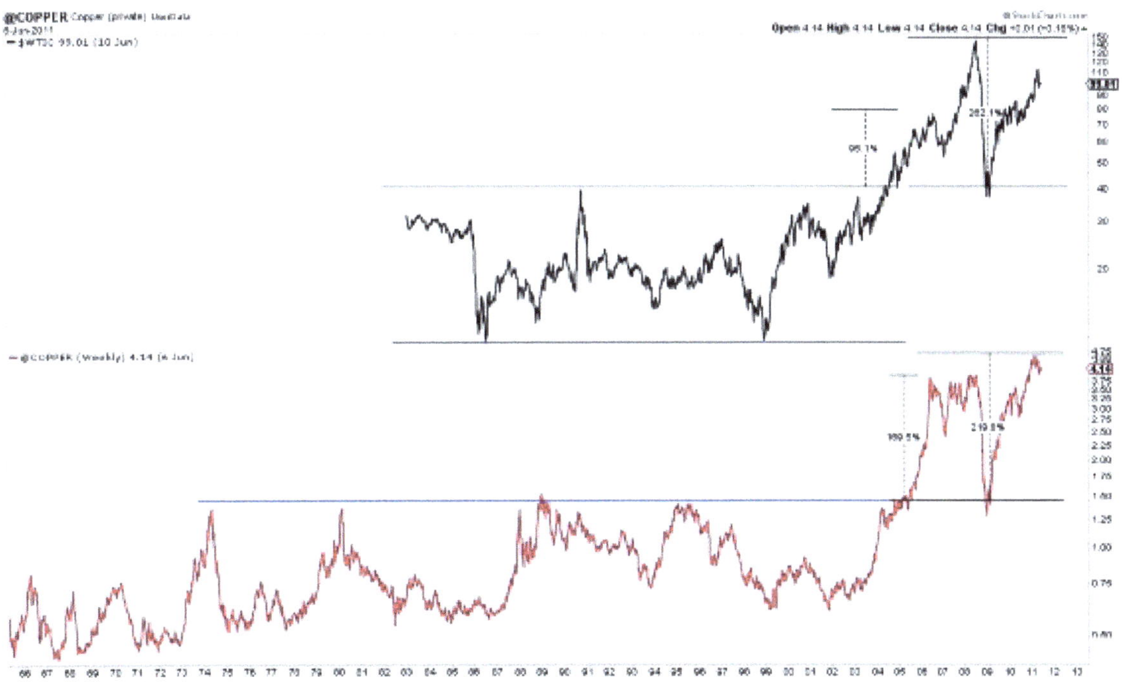

Finally, we close this Chapter by noting two very important technical similarities between this fledgling secular bull market and the secular bull market of the 1970s.

1. First, unlike in the 1930s and 2000s, both Bonds and Stocks were in a secular bear market during the 1970s. Bonds are currently in a secular bear market for the first time since 1965 to 1982. After 1968, Stocks began their secular bear market, setting the stage for an incredible 1970s in hard assets. Today, Stocks are near the end of a secular bull market and will later join Bonds in a secular bear market.
2. Second, Gold and Silver, as they were in the late 1960s and unlike in the 2000s, are in a position to make new all-time highs at the beginning of this secular bull market. In the 2000s, Silver never exceeded its 1980 price. Other than some time in 2008, Gold spent only the last two years of that secular bull market at a new all-time high.

In Figure 5.12 on the next page, we plot Gold and Silver and mark the breakouts to new all-time highs after many years with blue arrows. Gold's two biggest breakouts were in 1972 and March 2024, which followed a 13-year base. The unsustained breakout in 2008 and sustained breakout in 2009 occurred too late in that secular bull market. For Silver, we can mark the breakout in 1967 or 1973.

Figure 5.12: Gold & Silver Breakouts to New All-Time Highs

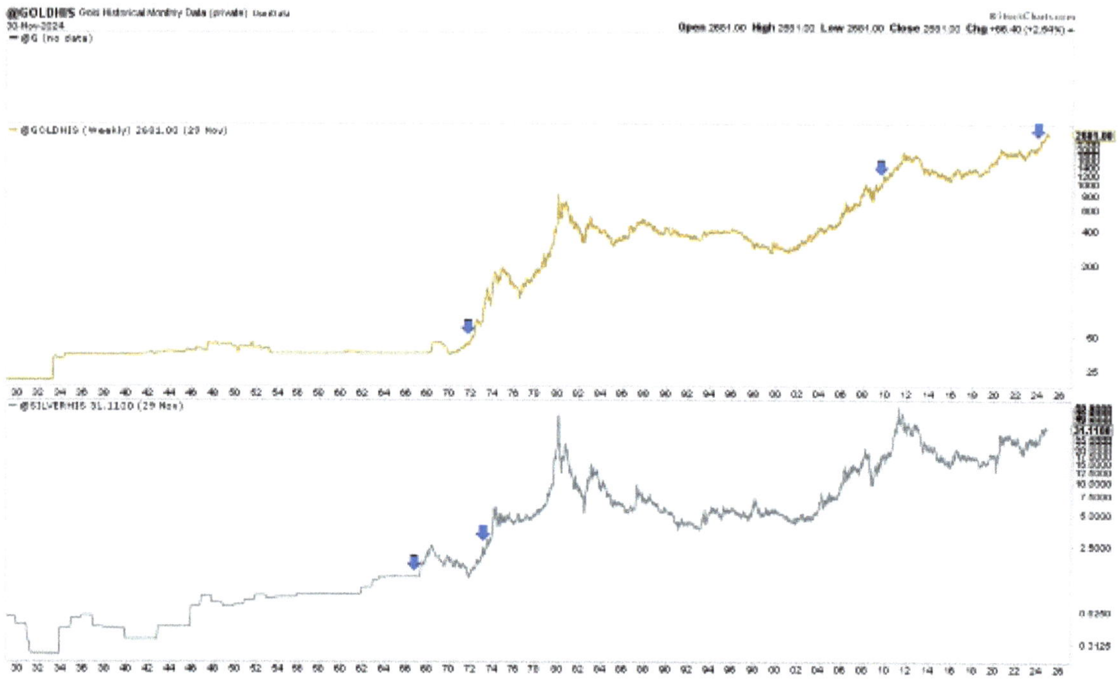

Once the stock market secular bull ends and Silver breaks $50, this precious metals secular bull market could mirror the 1970s, in which the gains dwarfed those in the 2000s. Using daily closing prices, we find that Gold surged 2300% from 1970 to 1980 but gained only 648% from 2001 to 2011. Silver exploded 3540% from 1971 to 1980 but gained only 1106% from 2001 to 2011.

In inflation-adjusted terms, Gold gained 879% in the 1970s to 448% in the 2000s, while Silver gained 1351% in the 1970s to 839% in the 2000s.

Chapter Summary

In March 2024, Gold broke out of its 13-year-long cup-and-handle pattern. It has upside targets of roughly $3000/oz and $4000/oz. This is the most significant breakout in Gold since the Gold Standard ended in 1971. The 2005 breakout was also substantial but did not occur at an all-time high. As the historical examples show, breakouts around an all-time high out of long bases lead to very significant moves for not only a few years but also, in some cases, over a decade.

The current position of the stock market and Gold against the 60/40 portfolio confirms that the cup-and-handle breakout is the start of a new secular bull market in Gold and precious metals. Once Gold can outperform the 60/40 portfolio and the stock market peaks, Gold's new secular bull market will be confirmed, and Gold, Silver, and gold stocks will accelerate to the upside. This is one of the most important pieces of information from this book.

Silver breaking out of a now 45-year-long base past $50/oz will mark the biggest breakout in capital markets over the last 50 years. The moves in Copper and Oil, after they broke out from 32-year-long and 24-year-long bases, respectively, argue that Silver could approach $100/oz after the first year of its breakout and trade above $100/oz after the first few years.

Finally, the bond market context and long-term technical setup put Gold and Silver in a position to move much like the 1970s rather than the 2000s or 1930s.

Chapter 6

Fundamental Drivers for Gold & Silver in 2020s & 2030s

In a previous chapter, we discussed the root fundamental drivers for precious metals, which include real interest rates, inflation, and secular trends in conventional financial assets such as Stocks and Bonds.

This chapter will discuss the fundamental drivers that will power a new secular bull market in precious metals into the 2030s. The three drivers are the US Government's debt and poor fiscal condition, new secular inflation drivers in the economy, and the rest of the world's move away from US Treasurys and into Gold as a reserve currency and asset. My friend Vince Lanci will cover this last part, which is known as dedollarization.

We will start with a focus on the US government's fiscal condition.

The US Government has been "kicking the can" down the road with its finances because the secular bull market in Bonds has allowed it to do so. Interest rates had been in a secular downtrend for decades. The market wanted to buy US debt. However, that secular downtrend in interest rates and the secular bull market in Bonds is over.

In Figure 6.1 on the next page, we plot the yield on the 10-year Treasury Note and a total return calculation for the 10-year Treasury Note divided by the Consumer Price Index.

The yellow represents secular bear markets, as defined by the real total return in Bonds losing the 80-month moving average. A secular bear market began at the end of 1965, and one started in the middle of 2020. From 1982 to 2020, there were buyers of US Treasurys amidst secular downward pressure on bond yields. That is no longer the case, and it bodes negatively for the US financial condition as there will be upward pressure on borrowing costs.

Figure 6.1: Secular Bear Market in Bonds

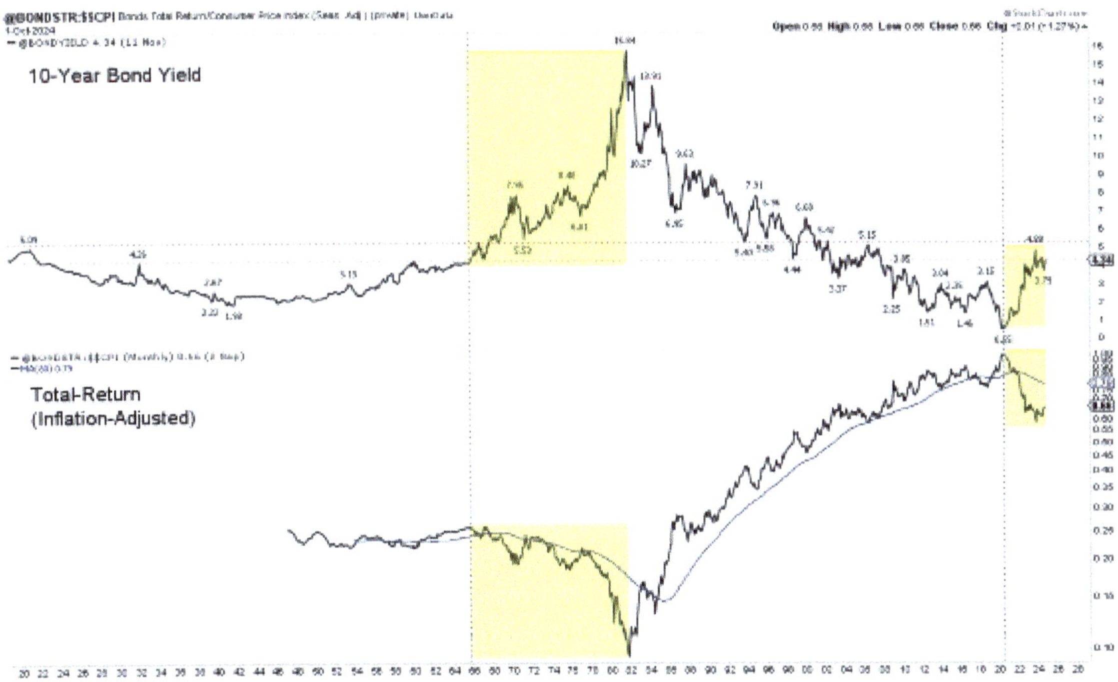

There is upward pressure on borrowing costs at a time when the US debt to GDP is threatening to hit 130%. In a deep study of the debt crisis, famed investor Ray Dalio found that in the last 120 years, after sovereign nations' debt to GDP reached 130%, 98% defaulted. Sovereigns can default by austerity (deep spending cuts), restructuring, or inflation (which was the result for most).

US debt to GDP hit 126% after COVID-19 but declined only slightly over the past few years. This is concerning because we are in a non-war and non-recession status with a large budget deficit, and interest payments on the debt are surging higher.

Figure 6.2 on the next page plots debt to GDP (right scale) and gross and net interest payments as a percentage of Federal Revenue. When debt to GDP hit 119% in 1946, interest payments were at much lower levels. Conversely, when interest payments were very high in the late 1980s and early 1990s, debt to GDP was only 45% to 60%. When interest payments were very high at the start of the Great Depression, debt to GDP was only 40%.

Figure 6.2: Debt to GDP & Interest Payments

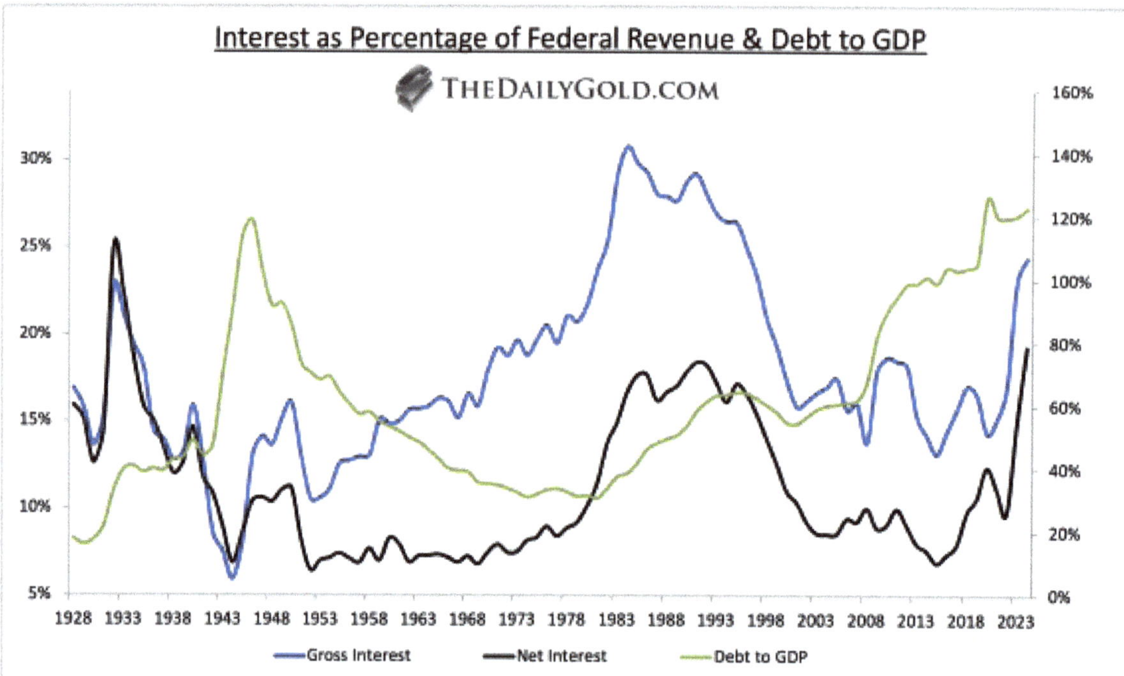

In other words, the problem today is that debt to GDP and interest payments are high, and the bond market is in a new secular bear market. The last time the bond market began a secular bear market was in 1965, when both net interest payments and debt to GDP were extremely low.

Figure 6.3 on the next page plots the US budget deficit and net interest expense. Since 2015, the net interest expense and the budget deficit have risen in tandem. The US must balance its budget to get debt to GDP down. However, this is becoming increasingly impossible as the net interest expense accelerates and comprises a bigger chunk of the overall budget. From 1990 to 2017, the net interest expense ranged from $200 billion to $250 billion. Since then, it has accelerated and reached nearly $1 trillion in 2024.

Figure 6.3: US Budget Deficit & Net Interest Expense

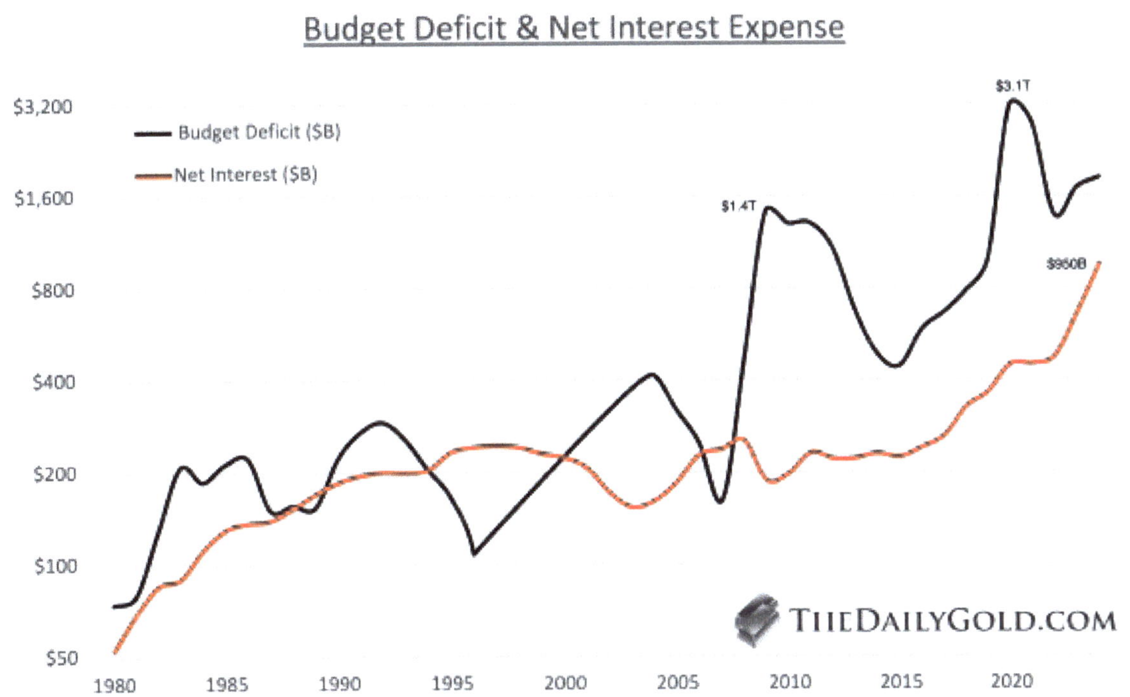

For debt to GDP ratios to decline, nominal growth (real growth plus inflation) must grow faster than debt. In other words, the economy needs to outgrow its debt. In doing so, the debt burden subsides. Hence, policymakers prefer 6% nominal growth with 3% inflation over 3% nominal growth with zero inflation. The real growth rate is the same, but stronger nominal growth (as the result of inflation) helps reduce the debt burden because the economy grows larger in proportion to the amount of debt.

The US will inevitably implement Yield Curve Control to cap bond yields and control the debt to GDP ratio and interest burden. Yield Curve Control occurs when the central bank purchases bonds to target an interest rate at a certain level. Quantitative Easing is more focused on the number of purchases by the central bank and tends to concentrate on shorter-duration (term) bonds. Yield Curve Control focuses on longer-term interest rates, also known as bond yields.

There have been two instances of Yield Curve Control in history. The first was in the US from 1942 to 1951, and the second is the ongoing program in Japan that began in 2016.

To manage the war effort and the ensuing debt, the Federal Reserve, at the behest of the US Government, kept short and long-term interest rates low for many years. They bought bonds to keep the 90-day T-bill rate below 0.5% and the Fed Funds Rate at 1% until the end of 1947. They also bought bonds to keep the 10-year Treasury yield below 2.5% through 1950.

Figure 6.4 on the next page shows the trends in inflation and interest rates from 1930 to 1961.

Figure 6.4: Yield Curve Control 1930-1961

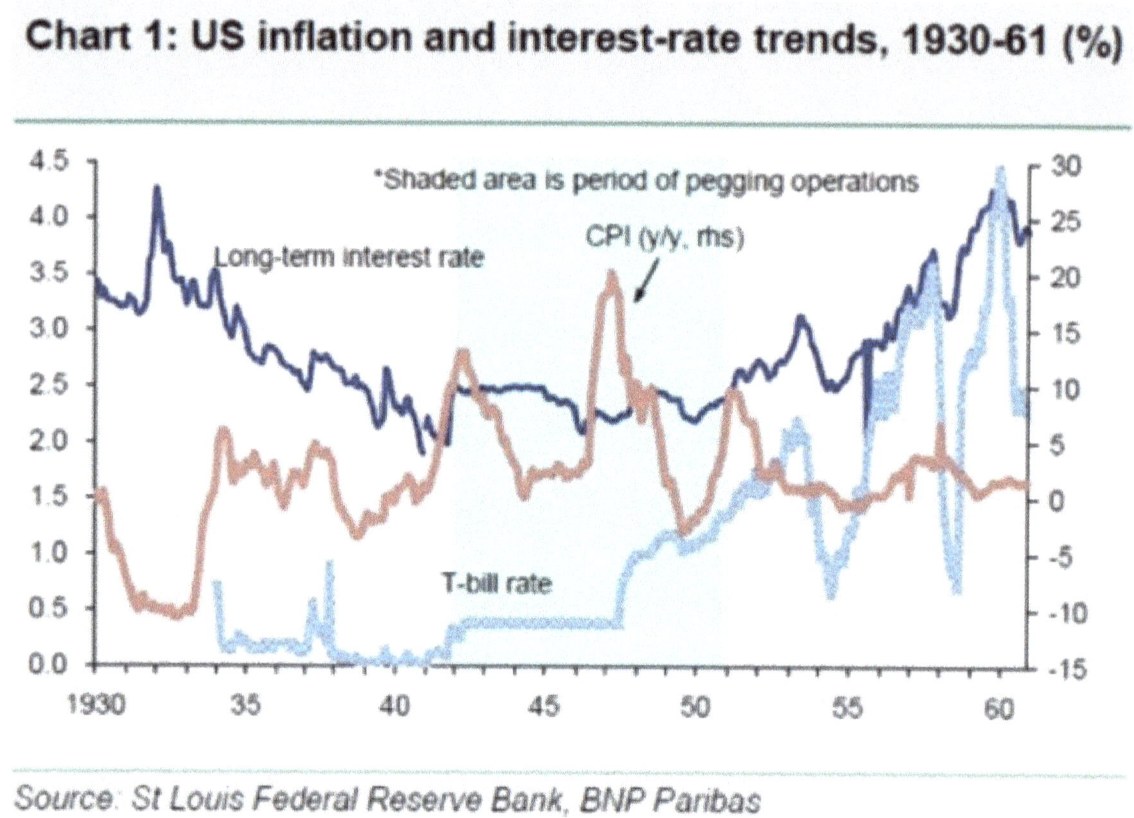

Though inflation raged, US debt to GDP was brought under control, and the debt burden was reduced. Debt to GDP peaked at 119% in 1946 and declined sharply over the next five years. It was due to inflation, not strong real growth. Real GDP growth, which was flat from 1943 to 1949, was only 6% from 1945 through 1951. Nominal GDP growth, which is essential in devaluing the debt burden, was 52% over the same period.

However, inflation spiraled higher in a volatile fashion in the 1940s. From the end of 1941 through 1950, the consumer price index (CPI) rose 85% or 7% per year compounded annually (CAGR). From the end of 1944 through 1950, the CPI rose 65% or 8.7% CAGR.

Japan implemented Yield Curve Control in September 2016 after the yield on the 10-year JGB (Japanese Government Bond) went negative. The Bank of Japan has sought to continue ongoing Quantitative Easing and Yield Curve Control until inflation reaches 2%. It reached 2% in 2022 and has remained elevated. As a result, the Bank of Japan has indicated it will phase out Yield Curve Control.

Japan is a different case than the United States. Although its debt to GDP has spiraled to over 200%, the Bank of Japan, which owns 53% of it, owns the debt internally. The country also has a strong culture of saving. Some analysts believe the United States can follow this path without major inflation or currency devaluation. That is highly unlikely, as Japan is a special case.

As we pen this chapter in mid-May 2024, we note that since the Bank of Japan implemented Yield Curve Control in September 2016, Gold has been up 85% in dollar terms but 180% in Japanese Yen terms. The Japanese Yen has declined 35% since then and currently sits at a 34-year low.

In summary, the United States' current fiscal and debt position is worse than in the 1940s and the early 1990s. debt to GDP has never been this high with the interest on the debt this high. And now, US Bonds are in a new secular bear market, which entails declining demand for bonds over time. The United States must turn to Yield Curve Control to alleviate the debt burden. The cost of the policy is accelerating inflation and severe bear markets in US Bonds and the US Dollar into the 2030s.

In addition to Yield Curve Control, the Federal Reserve will likely have to pursue debt monetization. When a central bank "monetizes the debt," it directly purchases large amounts of government debt to fund government spending. It is considered an extreme form of Yield Curve Control.

Given the recent breakout in Gold from a 13-year cup-and-handle pattern, the secular bear market in Bonds, and commodity price indices breaking to new all-time highs in 2022, it should not be a surprise that a new era of inflation has begun. This next section covers some of the larger macroeconomic drivers that will push inflation higher and keep it high deep into the 2030s.

These drivers include but are not limited to, global onshoring and regionalization, gains in labor relative to capital, fiscal stimulus over monetary stimulus, commodity underinvestment, and the prevalence of high debt and deficits. Rising global populism is the underlying root cause of these drivers. COVID-19 was not the root cause but an accelerant.

The first driver is the recovery of and growing popularity of labor. In 2022, Gallup reported that 71% of Americans approved of Labor Unions, the highest number since 1965. This number has steadily climbed since 2014. Republican approval of Labor Unions has increased from 26% in 2011 to 47%, a 20-year high.

In 2023, there were high-profile strikes from the United Auto Workers, Hollywood writers' and actors' guilds, and UPS workers. The power of labor is increasing.

Labor demographics also support higher inflation over the long run. Bloomberg Intelligence notes that labor force participation has declined for years. Aging baby boomers, declining fertility rates, and stricter immigration restrictions are contributing to labor shortages. Labor force participation has also declined in China, Brazil, and India.

The supply of labor is shrinking while labor is becoming more politically popular. This is a recipe for higher wages and lower margins. Figure 6.5 on the next page plots Labor and Capital's share of GDP. Corporate Profit Margins (capital) may have peaked in the wake of Covid while Labor has made a series of higher lows in recent years. This chart is from Q2 2023.

Figure 6.5: Labor & Capital Share of GDP

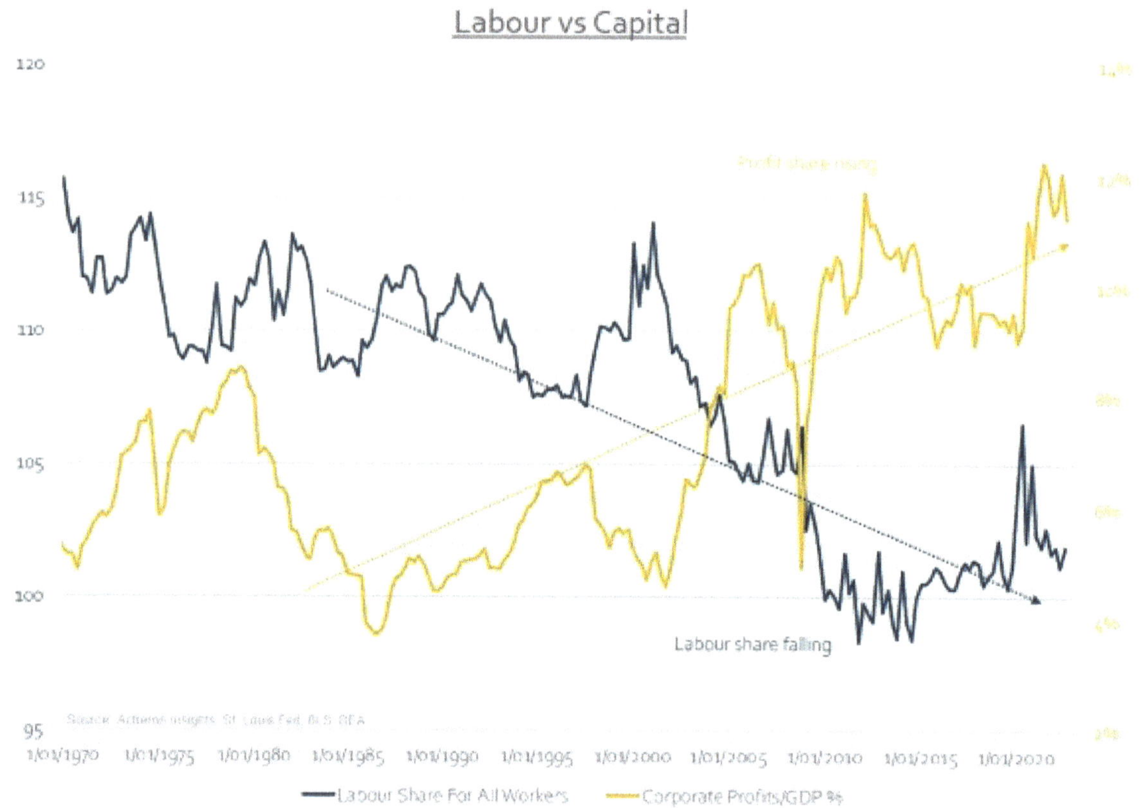

The growing popularity of and gains in the labor movement align with economic reshoring or the reshoring of supply chains. COVID-19 and escalating international tensions have accelerated this process.

Figure 6.6 on the next page displays the largest firms' mentions of reshoring in conference calls. Mentions grew steadily into the mid-2010s and truly exploded with the onset of COVID-19 in the spring of 2020.

Figure 6.6: Reshoring Mentions by Largest US Companies

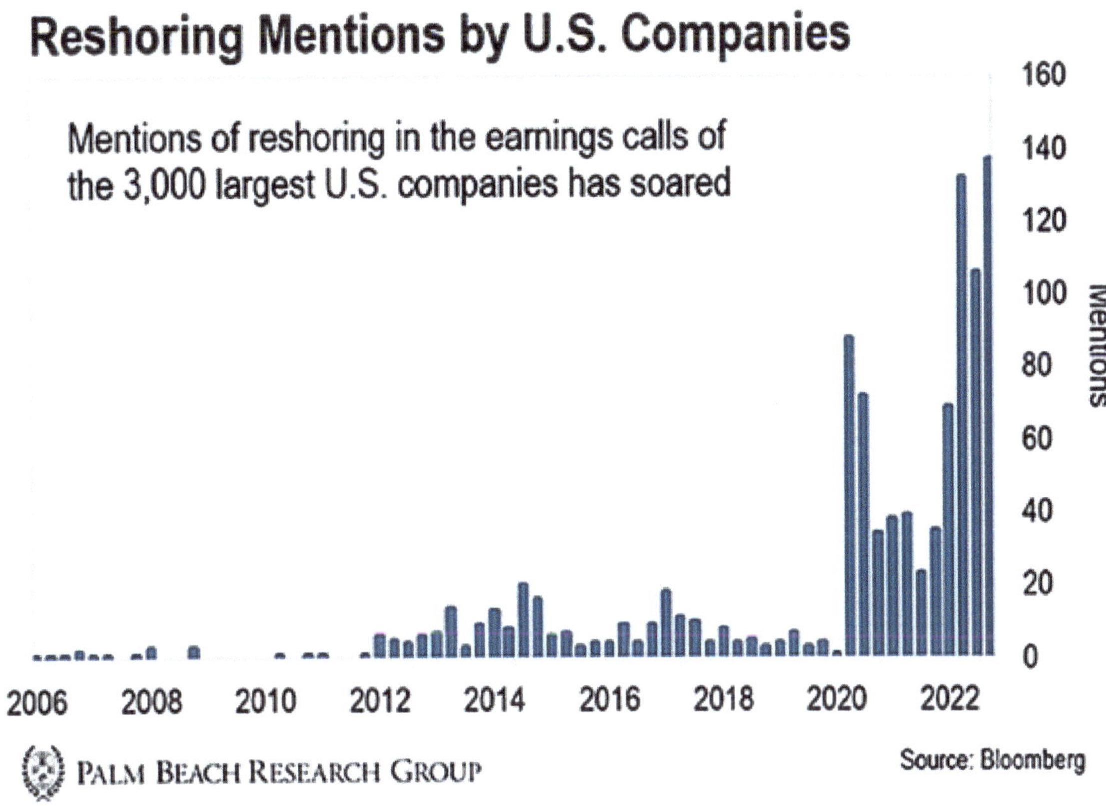

The federal government has paved the way for reshoring supply chains by providing $1.6 trillion in federal spending, which includes the Investments and Infrastructure Act, CHIPS and Science Act, Inflation Reduction Act, and United States Innovation and Competition Act. All were signed into law by the end of 2022.

The Investments and Infrastructure Act, which totals $1.2 trillion and is also known as the bipartisan Infrastructure Act, will fund the modernization and upgrade of the nation's transportation infrastructure. This will facilitate and support the move of several new-generation industrial facilities onshore.

The CHIPS and Science Act authorized $280 billion in new funding to boost domestic research, development, and manufacturing of semiconductors in the United States. This includes funding for investments in artificial intelligence, nanotechnology, and quantum computing. After the Act's passage in August 2022, announcements of investments from the private sector totaled over $200 billion.

The Inflation Reduction Act, which totals $250 billion, invests in domestic energy production, specifically clean energy. This entails funding new facilities and factories to spur the production of solar panels, lithium-ion batteries, and electric vehicles.

The United States Innovation and Competition Act authorizes $110 billion for technology research over a 5-year period. This includes investments in education and training programs in artificial intelligence, semiconductors, quantum computing, and biotechnology. In addition, over $10 billion was authorized to create ten regional technology hubs and a supply chain crisis-response program.

The Federal support for the reshoring of supply chains and domestic manufacturing renaissance highlights a new era of fiscal stimulus as the economic driver instead of monetary stimulus. This is a complete reversal from 15 years ago.

Recall the Global Financial Crisis, zero percent interest rates, quantitative Easing, and the anti-government spending politics that elevated the Tea Party Republicans to office in 2010. The nominal budget deficit contracted after 2010 and remained low until 2017.

The effects of those extreme monetary measures, along with minimal fiscal stimulus, helped elevate populism in the United States and elsewhere. Quantitative Easing, zero-percent interest rates, and bailouts inflated asset prices and Wall Street but not Main Street. Most economic gains were accrued by the top 1% and the top 0.1%, driving rising inequality and populism.

Fiscal stimulus is advantageous for policymakers because it is a direct response to political pressure and targets the real economy rather than Wall Street. The drawback is that it is more inflationary. It is money directly hitting the economy.

In addition, as discussed in the first part of this lesson, the increase in debt and record peacetime deficits caused by fiscal stimulus have set the US on a path toward Yield Curve Control.

Morgan Stanley notes in a report that the need for financial repression (another phrase for negative real interest rates) may be larger today than in the 1940s. They note that unprecedented debt burdens in most major economies are colliding with deficits that are becoming structural. They estimate that with GDP growth of 1.7% per year and a 5% budget deficit, real interest rates on government debt would need to be -3.3% to keep debt to GDP stable. That equates to an inflation rate of almost 8% on today's 10-year Treasury yield of 4.40%.

The last driver of secular inflation is the low capital investment in the production of commodities and energy, which will lead to higher commodity prices over the years and decades ahead.

From a bird's-eye view and macroeconomic standpoint, long-term trends in commodity prices adhere to the basic supply-and-demand relationship. Rising commodity prices incentivize growing capital investment, which leads to future supply and falling prices. Low prices disincentivize capital investment, which leads to shrinking supplies. This sets the stage for a rebound in commodity prices.

Figure 6.7 on the next page plots the capex of commodity sectors (blue) and technology sectors (black) in proportion to total capex in the S&P 500.

Capex in the commodity sectors tends to make a major turn a year after the major turn in prices. Commodity prices peaked at the end of 1980 and 2011. In each case, commodity capex peaked two years later. Commodity prices bottomed in 2001, a year before commodity capex bottomed. Finally, commodity prices bottomed with the onset of COVID-19 in March 2020, and as we will see in Figure 6.8, commodity capex rebounded.

Figure 6.7: Capex: New economy vs. Old economy

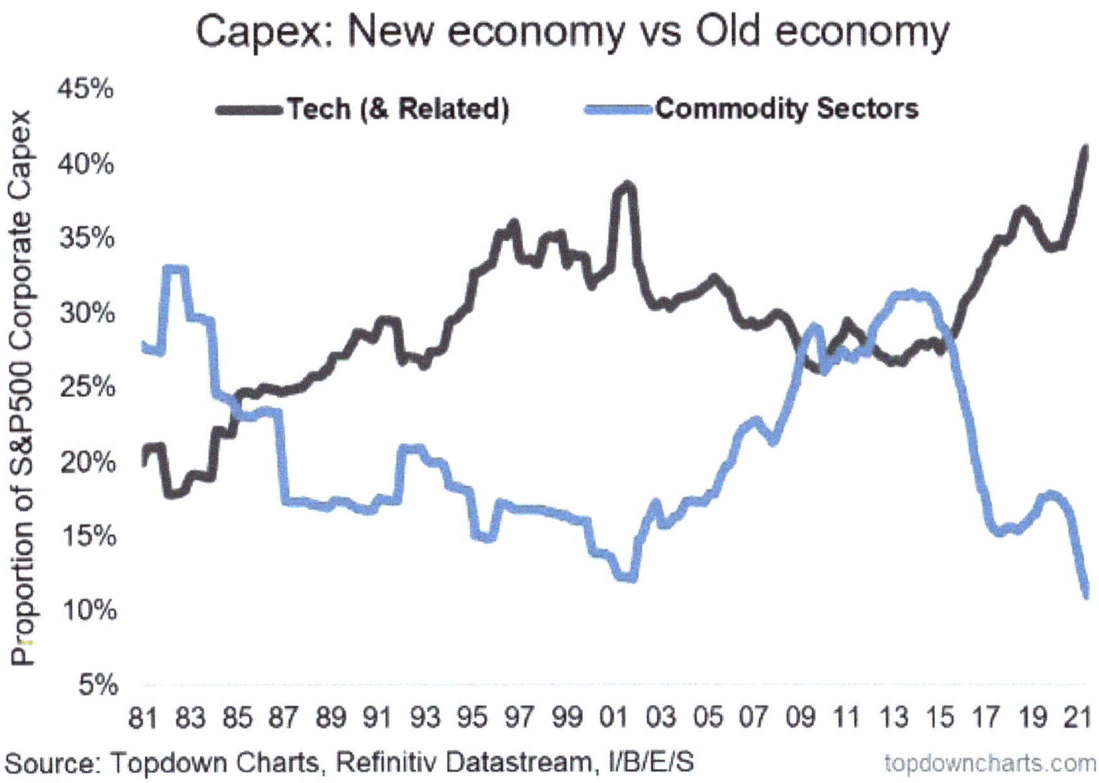

Figure 6.8 below is an updated version of Figure 6.7. It divides capex among the commodity sectors and measures the capex-to-assets ratio between them.

Figure 6.8: Capital Investment in Commodities

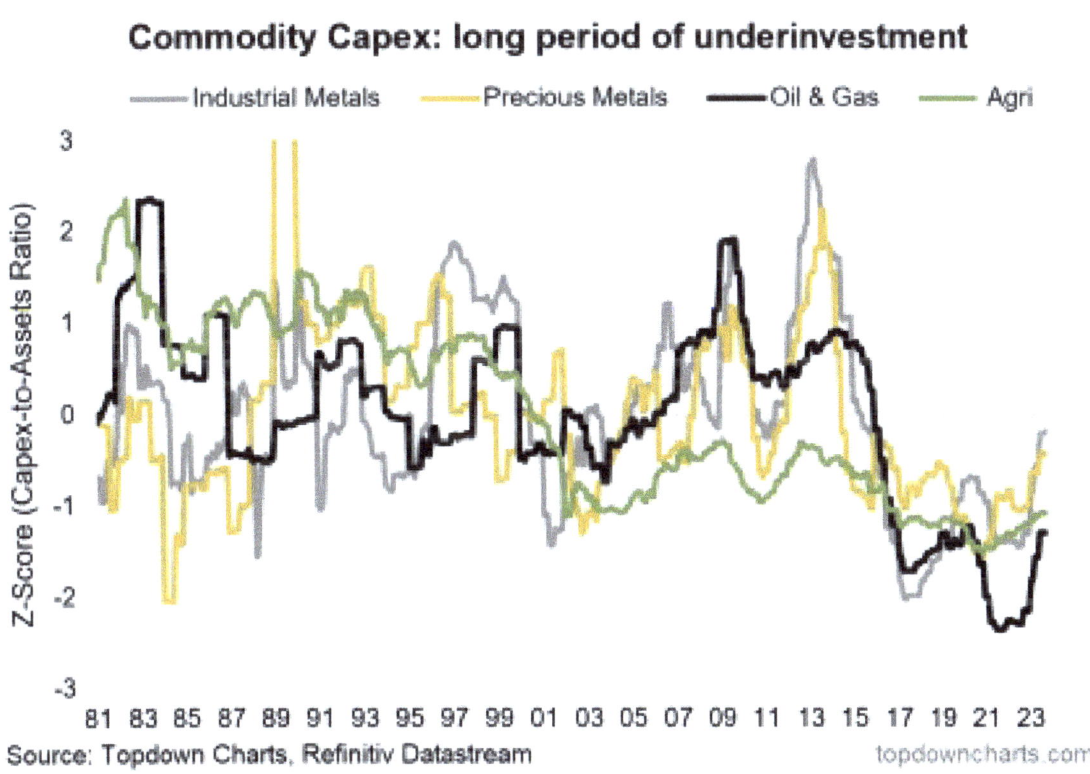

Commodity prices exploded after Covid, and capital investment started to increase naturally. However, note the decline in Oil & Gas investment since 2009 and its 40-year low after 2021. Agriculture capex was at a 40-year low in 2021. Higher prices always lead to higher supply, but this is only the start.

Chapter Summary

Multiple and specific fundamental drivers will power a new secular bull market in Gold, Silver, and commodity prices over the next 10 to 15 years. Chief among them, concerning Gold and Silver, is the US Government's debt and poor fiscal condition, necessitating extremely inflationary policies such as debt monetization. Due to a new secular bear market in Bonds, which is only the second one in the past 100 years, there is no more road to kick the can down.

There are also secular inflationary drivers in the economy. The rise of populism globally and COVID-19 has accelerated onshoring and regionalization, gains in labor relative to capital, and the preference for fiscal stimulus over monetary stimulus, which impacts the economy directly instead of the financial sector.

Finally, only a few years ago, capital investment in future production of industrial metals, oil and gas, and other commodities hit significant multi-decade lows. Previous levels of this capital investment marked secular lows in commodity prices and the birth of a new secular bull market.

Chapter 6: Part 2

Dedollarization

Vince Lanci of GoldFix

"We are witnessing the birth of Bretton Woods III—a new world (monetary) order centered around commodity-based currencies in the East that will likely weaken the Eurodollar system and contribute to inflationary forces in the West. As a result, Gold stands to benefit from this shift as a neutral reserve asset."

– Zoltan Pozsar (March 2022)

See Figure 6B.1 on the next page

Figure 6B.1: China's Gradual Move Away from US Dollar

Introduction: The Shift Away from the Dollar

Dedollarization is no longer a fringe theory. It's a real shift in global finance, driven by a range of factors from geopolitical tensions to sudden monetary policy changes. For decades, the US dollar ruled as the world's main reserve currency. Now, a growing number of countries are looking for alternatives. Sanctions, the "weaponization" of the dollar, and concerns over the Federal Reserve's policy swings have all pushed central banks and governments to diversify.

In this changing environment, Gold stands out. It's neutral, widely trusted, and isn't tied to any one nation's policies. Many see it as a hedge against political risks and inflation. As new financial arrangements emerge—like bilateral trade deals, regional payment systems, and talk of Gold-backed currencies—Gold's role expands. Below, we'll explore the causes of dedollarization, the factors pushing

Gold to center stage, and how nations are paving the way for a future less bound to the dollar.

Causes of Dedollarization

1. The Weaponization of the Dollar

US sanctions illustrate how the dollar can be used as a geopolitical tool. Freezing foreign reserves or denying access to dollar-based transactions puts countries like Iran, Russia, and Venezuela in a tough spot. After Russia's reserves were partially frozen following the Ukraine invasion, many nations realized the dollar isn't a neutral reserve asset. This move showed that heavy dependence on the dollar can be risky.

To reduce vulnerability, countries started diversifying their reserves. Gold, immune to sanctions and not controlled by any single government, became a top choice. Russia's big purchases of Gold showed how a country can insulate itself from dollar threats. Other nations took note. The fear that reserves could be locked at will has prompted them to hold more assets outside the dollar.

Figure 6B.2: Value of US Treasury Securities Held By Russians

2. Monetary Policy Volatility

The Federal Reserve's rapid policy shifts have also caused concern. In crises, the Fed injects liquidity through massive quantitative easing, which can weaken the dollar's value. When inflation rises, the Fed reverses course with sharp rate hikes, which can disrupt global markets. This unpredictable cycle leaves countries exposed if they rely too heavily on dollar reserves.

Holding Gold can offset this volatility. Gold doesn't hinge on the Fed's next decision. It's seen as a stable store of value, so central banks in emerging markets have increased their Gold reserves. This strategy helps them hedge against exchange rate swings and inflation spikes that can undermine the dollar. By diversifying with Gold, they're aiming for greater stability in a fast-changing monetary landscape.

3. Emerging Multipolarity

The rise of economies like China, India, and Russia has made global power more multipolar. The BRICS bloc (Brazil, Russia, India, China, and South Africa) is pushing for ways to bypass the dollar in trade and finance. China's deals with Brazil to use the yuan and India's push for rupee-based transactions are signs that these nations want to reduce dollar dependence.

In this environment, Gold's neutrality gains importance. It's a universal asset that doesn't favor any single economy. The idea of a BRICS currency backed by Gold or other real assets also shows how these nations might reshape global finance. By pooling resources, they hope to create an alternative financial structure that doesn't rely on US monetary policy or Western banking systems. If they succeed, the dollar's status as a universal yardstick could erode.

4. Commodity Trade and Settlement Shifts

Commodities—oil, metals, and agricultural goods—have long been priced in dollars. This "petrodollar" system cemented the dollar's global status. Now, countries like China are advocating for alternative pricing and settlement in their own currencies. Deals like the China-Brazil arrangement, which uses the yuan and real, are small steps in this direction.

As more trades move away from the dollar, the need for large dollar reserves declines. This is where Gold can step in. Gold's global acceptance makes it an attractive bridge when trust in paper currencies fades. Its liquidity and independence from political control allow countries to settle trades without relying on the dollar. Barter systems or partial payments in Gold can also bypass currency risk. Over time, these shifts break the dollar's monopoly on commodity pricing.

Figure 6B.3: Share of Commodity Trade & Settlement

Date	Renminbi		U.S. Dollar		Other
March 2010	0.3%	84%	84.3%		15.4%
March 2011	4.8%		81.3%		13.9%
March 2012	11.5%		77.1%		11.5%
March 2013	18.1%		72.7%		9.2%
March 2014	26.6%		64.8%		8.6%
March 2015	29.0%		61.9%		9.0%
March 2016	23.6%	43%	66.7%		9.7%
March 2017	17.6%		72.5%		9.9%
March 2018	23.2%		67.4%		9.4%
March 2019	26.2%		65.1%		8.7%
March 2020	39.3%		54.4%		6.3%
March 2021	41.7%	11%	52.6%		5.6%
March 2022	42.1%		53.3%		4.7%
March 2023	48.4%	1.7%	46.7%	Dedollarization Manifesting	4.9%
March 2024	52.9%	10.1%	42.8%		4.3%

Source: Bloomberg (2024)

Gold Benefits

1. Gold's Role as a Neutral Asset

Gold is viewed worldwide as a stable store of value. It doesn't depend on the creditworthiness of a single government and isn't subject to direct political pressure. If a country faces sanctions or central banks worry about the impact of another nation's monetary policy, Gold offers protection. That's a key reason countries with uncertain relations to the US are keen on expanding their Gold reserves.

Gold's intrinsic worth sets it apart from fiat currencies, which can be devalued through inflation or policy decisions. Its price can move, but Gold maintains appeal as a hedge. This impartial character makes it a logical choice in a world where alliances shift and confidence in fiat currencies can waver. When a nation parks part of its reserves in Gold, it gains a buffer against both political and financial shocks.

2. Gold in the BRICS Strategy

The BRICS nations are leading the way in reevaluating Gold. China discreetly increases its Gold reserves, while Russia openly does so. Both want to shield themselves from Western sanctions and reduce reliance on dollar-denominated assets. India, with its cultural affinity for Gold, also sees bullion as a strategic resource. This collective interest among large emerging economies boosts Gold's global stature.

A potential Gold-backed BRICS currency would be a game-changer. Linking their joint currency to a hard asset would address trust issues and unify member economies. It might offer a serious challenge to the dollar, especially if global traders see this currency as more stable than a floating fiat currency vulnerable to unilateral US actions. While it's still an idea under discussion, the mere possibility captures the world's attention. It highlights Gold's central role in the dedollarization narrative.

Figure 6B.4: China & Russia Gold Reserves

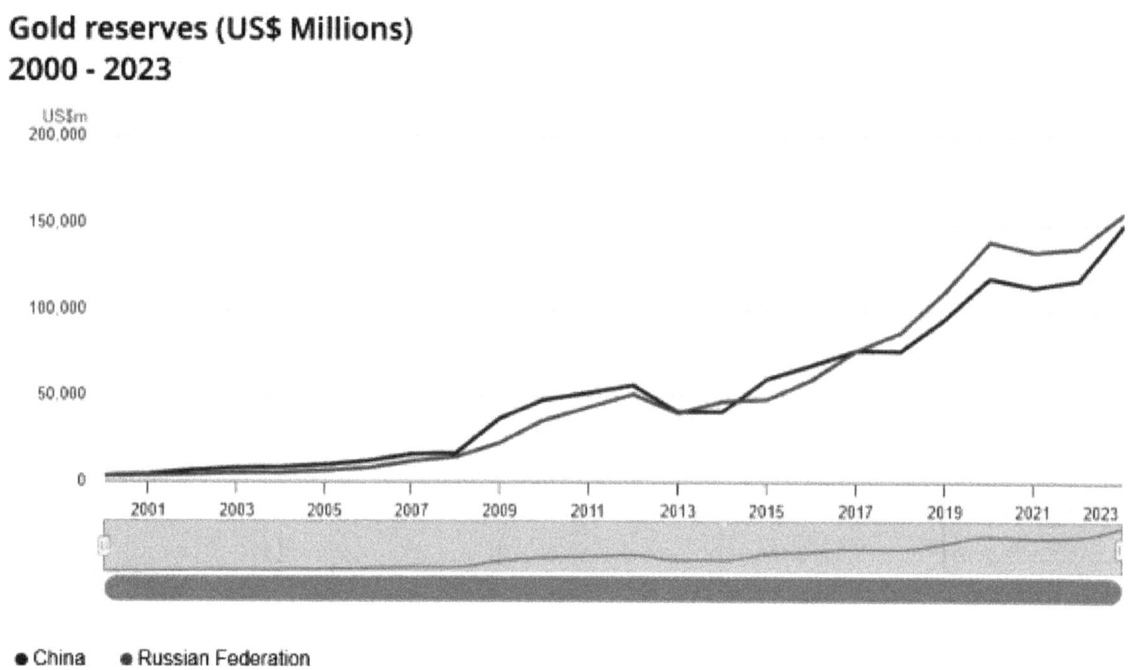

3. Facilitating Trade Settlement

Gold can serve as a neutral link in trade deals, especially when countries don't fully trust each other's currencies. It's an old concept dating back to mercantilist times, but it's getting a modern update. For example, countries can use Gold as collateral or as a direct settlement tool for cross-border trade. This bypasses exchange rates tied to the dollar.

China is testing such ideas in how it structures global payments, sometimes involving Gold-based arrangements. Digital platforms could soon make it easier to settle trades with tokenized Gold. That way, an exporter sending goods abroad can be paid in a Gold-backed digital asset, redeemable for physical bullion. This approach removes the risk of currency manipulation and aligns with the BRICS drive for independence from Western financial systems. Gold's universal recognition is key to its appeal in such setups.

Figure 6B.5: International Trade Settlement Using Tokenized Gold

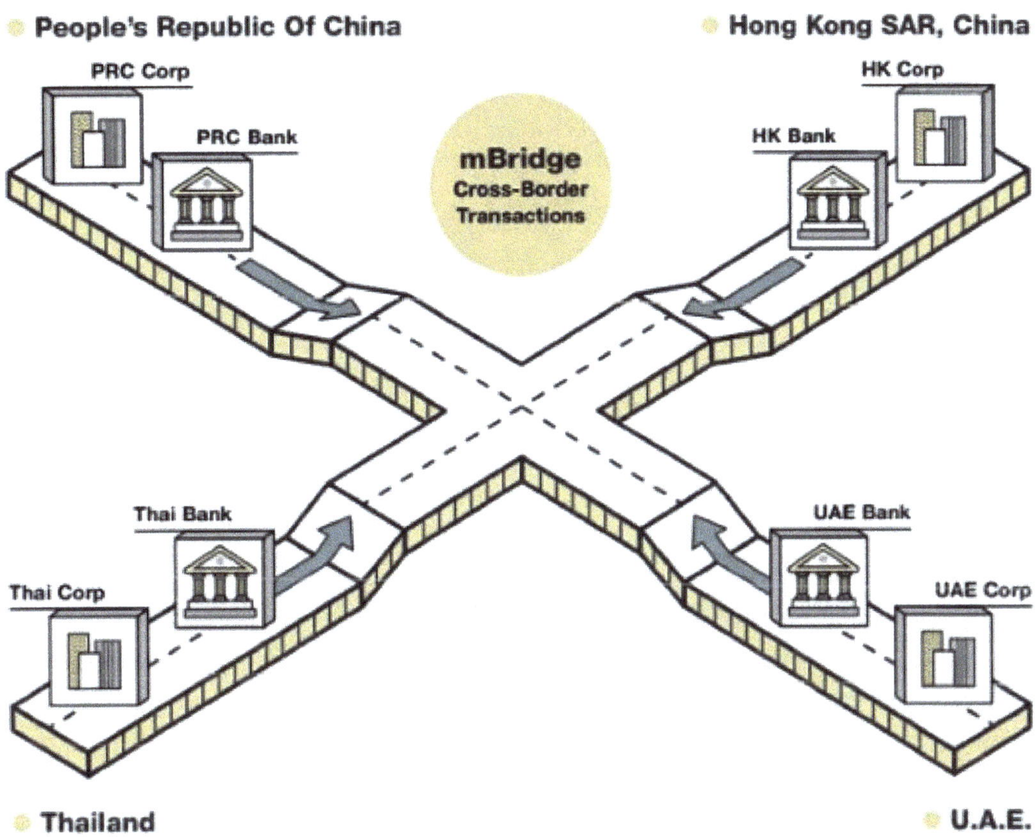

4. A Hedge Against Inflation and Currency Depreciation

Inflation undermines fiat currencies by eroding their purchasing power. Gold stands out as a store of value that often holds firm when prices rise. This makes it especially attractive for central banks in regions vulnerable to currency swings. If your domestic currency devalues, your Gold reserves typically become more valuable, protecting the bank's overall balance.

During past crises, Gold's safe-haven status has shone through. As countries pivot away from the dollar, Gold can help them navigate inflation or other financial pressures. Its longstanding track record offers comfort: When currencies falter, Gold tends to remain a reliable fallback. This stability is a huge draw for nations wary of tying their fortunes to the decisions of foreign central banks.

The Mechanisms of Dedollarization

1. Building New Payment Chains

Alternative payment systems are a cornerstone of dedollarization. The

BRICS nations, especially China, are pushing platforms like the Cross-Border Interbank Payment System (CIPS). CIPS reduces reliance on SWIFT, which is dollar-focused. Meanwhile, blockchain-based projects like mBridge aim to enable settlement in central bank digital currencies (CBDCs). These innovations allow countries to trade without going through US dollar channels.

Gold could tie into these systems if central banks decide to back their digital tokens with physical Gold. That would give added stability and offer a direct alternative to dollar-settled transactions. By sidestepping legacy networks, these new chains promote financial sovereignty. They also highlight how technology can accelerate the global pivot away from dollar-based structures.

2. Regional Trade Agreements

Regional and bilateral trade deals, denominated in local currencies, are expanding. China and Brazil have made headlines by shifting a slice of their trade to the yuan and real. This reduces the need for both sides to hold dollars. Over time, a web of such deals can chip away at the dollar's share of world trade.

Gold can play a supporting role. Countries can complement these local currency arrangements with Gold reserves. If trust in a partner's currency isn't complete, using Gold as a settlement option provides added security. This approach blends modern trade policies with a centuries-old asset. Nations forge closer ties and worry less about external sanctions or currency volatility. They can also tap into Gold-based instruments to smooth out imbalances in their bilateral deals.

3. Gold-Backed Financial Instruments

Beyond physical bullion, Gold-backed bonds or digital tokens are on the rise. Countries peg these instruments to actual Gold reserves, offering investors security. If a government defaults, holders still have a claim on the Gold. This structure can make the debt more appealing, possibly lowering borrowing costs.

Some central banks also consider partial Gold pegs for their currencies. By tying a portion of a currency's value to Gold, they signal a commitment to stability. The idea is that while the currency can float, a Gold buffer prevents extreme depreciation. Such steps align with a broader move to reduce exposure to dollar fluctuations. If enough nations adopt Gold-based financial tools, the collective effect can weaken the dollar's global grip.

4. Central Bank Accumulation

Central banks worldwide are boosting their Gold holdings. China, India, and Russia are the most prominent examples, but the trend isn't limited to them. As more banks add Gold, it diversifies their portfolios and reduces risk tied to dollar assets. It also shows a growing recognition that a more multipolar financial system is taking shape.

Large Gold holdings offer both economic and diplomatic advantages. If a crisis hits, countries can use Gold as collateral, easing access to credit. Domestically, Gold reserves back a currency's credibility, which can help maintain public trust. Internationally, Gold piles signal strength and independence, showing that a nation isn't at the mercy of external currencies or policies.

The Future of Gold in a Dedollarized World

1. Gold as a Reserve Asset

Gold's appeal as a reserve asset will likely grow. Central banks in emerging economies see it as a shield against currency volatility, and even some developed countries might boost their Gold percentage. This trend could push Gold prices higher, feeding back into further demand. While the dollar will still play a role, it may no longer dominate. Gold, by contrast, holds its neutral stance and global acceptance.

2. Gold-Backed Trade Settlement

Gold could also become the basis for trade settlement in a mercantilist-like approach. Countries that don't trust each other's currencies can settle imbalances in Gold. Modern systems can tokenize Gold, making these transactions efficient. Instead of shipping physical bars, digital tokens representing ownership can move instantly. This creates a trusted, real-time medium of exchange that doesn't rely on a single national currency.

3. Integration with Digital Currencies

CBDCs are on the rise in Asia, and Gold will be integrated into their frameworks. A Gold-backed CBDC offers the stability of an old-world asset combined with the speed of modern payment technology. This approach can draw in investors and trading partners who worry about the arbitrary expansion of fiat money. If a BRICS digital currency emerges with partial Gold backing, it could reshape global finance. Its success would rest on user trust, but the idea itself signals a major evolution in how nations handle their money.

4. A Stabilizing Force in Global Finance

As the dollar's dominance declines, currency markets could see more volatility and shifting alliances. Gold's role as a stabilizer becomes more valuable. It has survived countless economic crises, maintaining its core function as a hedge. In a multipolar environment, Gold helps keep financial flows anchored, preventing extreme swings. This steadiness attracts both policymakers and investors, who see Gold as a pillar in a time of transition. Its proven track record bolsters confidence when trust in fiat systems wavers.

Chapter Summary

Dedollarization marks a pivotal moment in global finance. Nations are rethinking their reliance on the dollar, prompted by sanctions, policy swings, and the allure of multipolar strategies. Gold emerges as a key ally in this shift. Its neutrality, track record, and resilience against political pressures make it uniquely suited to anchor new systems.

Still, the dollar's network effects won't vanish overnight. The move toward a more diverse monetary landscape will be gradual. Countries must invest in new payment platforms, negotiate trade agreements in local currencies, and possibly launch Gold-backed instruments. These processes carry costs and demand wide cooperation. Yet the trajectory seems set. A growing number of players, big and small, no longer want to be beholden to US financial policies.

In this evolving framework, Gold stands out as more than just a safe haven. It's a resource for trade settlement, a backstop for currencies, and a hedge against global uncertainties. It also symbolizes a broader shift toward financial autonomy. As the global order continues to adapt, Gold is poised to remain a central fixture, shaping trade, reserves, and monetary strategies in a world seeking an alternative to dollar supremacy.

Author: Vince Lanci
Professor of MBA Finance, University of Connecticut MBA
Publisher, GoldFix Newsletter

Chapter 7

Current Valuations of Gold & Gold Stocks

This chapter examines the current valuations for Gold and gold mining companies.

Gold is money and cannot be valued conventionally like a stock. We can only value it by comparing it to the other asset classes (Stocks and government bonds) and financial data series, such as the monetary base. We can compare Gold to anything with a historical dataset.

We can assess where these relationships stand today quantitatively in comparison to previous Gold market peaks like 2011 and 1980 and to previous Gold market bottoms like 1929, 1970, and 2000. Gold, being at nominal all-time highs, may appear expensive today, but in real terms, that is far from the truth.

Valuation data for gold mining companies is slightly elusive, but we can provide a rough history of conventional valuations, such as price to cash flow and price to net asset value, and how they compare to today's valuations.

To begin with, let us compare Gold to the stock market in the form of the S&P 500. Figure 7.1 on the next page plots Gold against the S&P 500 and Gold.

The ratio is only slightly higher than it was around the lows at the end of 1970. The only other period in which the ratio was lower than today was during the stock market bubble of the late 1990s and its aftermath in the early 2000s. Hence, from a historical perspective, Gold is quite inexpensive compared to Stocks.

Moreover, figure 7.1 shows that Gold has yet to begin a secular bull market. When it does, it will outperform the S&P 500 as it did in the 1930s, 1970s, and 2000s.

Figure 7.1: Gold vs. S&P 500

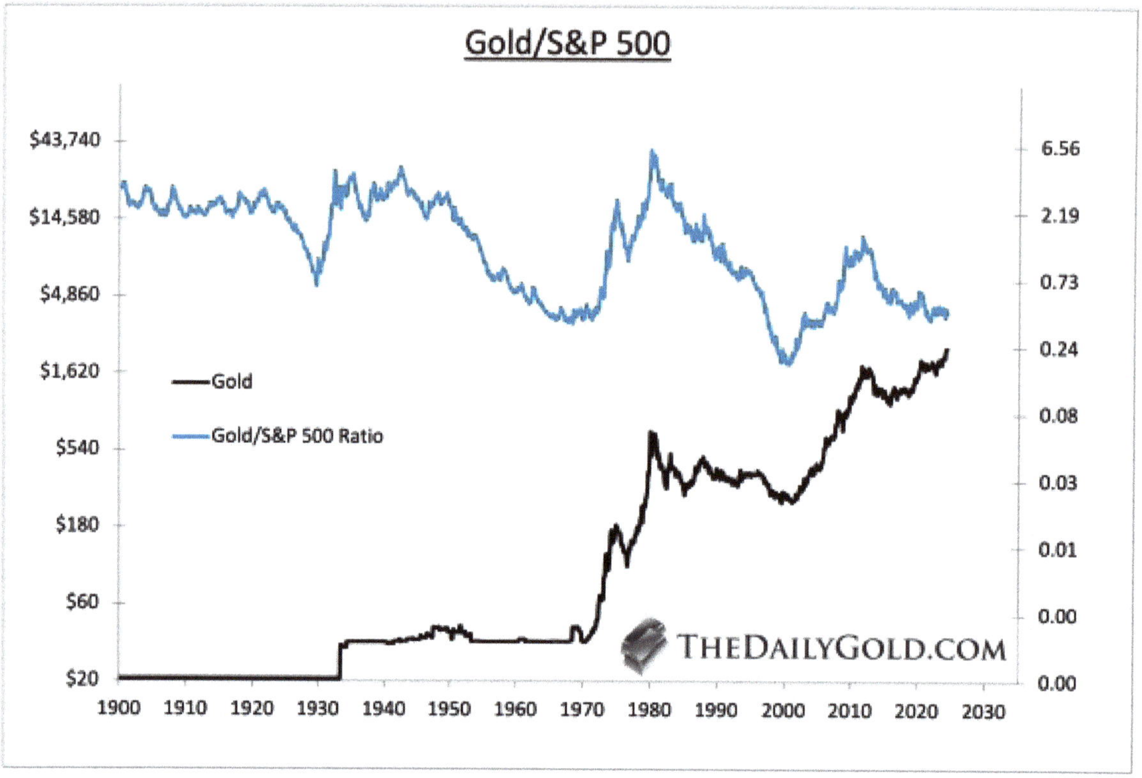

Figure 7.2 on the next page plots the Gold price against the Gold price levels that would back a portion of the US Monetary Base. The calculation accounts for the Gold price, the Monetary Base, and the value of US Gold Reserves (based on the Gold price). The amount of US Gold Reserves has not changed since 1977.

The Gold price exceeded 100% backing multiple times during the Great Depression and again during Gold's parabolic move and secular peak in 1980. Aside from the mid-1960s to early 1970s, the Gold price backed at least 40% of the monetary base until around 1990. The 1913 Federal Reserve Act mandated that there would be 40% backing under the Gold Standard.

Here are the important figures as of May 2024. A Gold price of $22000/oz would back 100% of the monetary base, and a price of $8800/oz would back 40% of the monetary base. In February 2008, amid the Global Financial Crisis, the Gold price backed 29.7% of the monetary base, the highest backing since 1991. That backing today would require a Gold price of $6500/oz.

Figure 7.2: Gold Price to Back Monetary Base

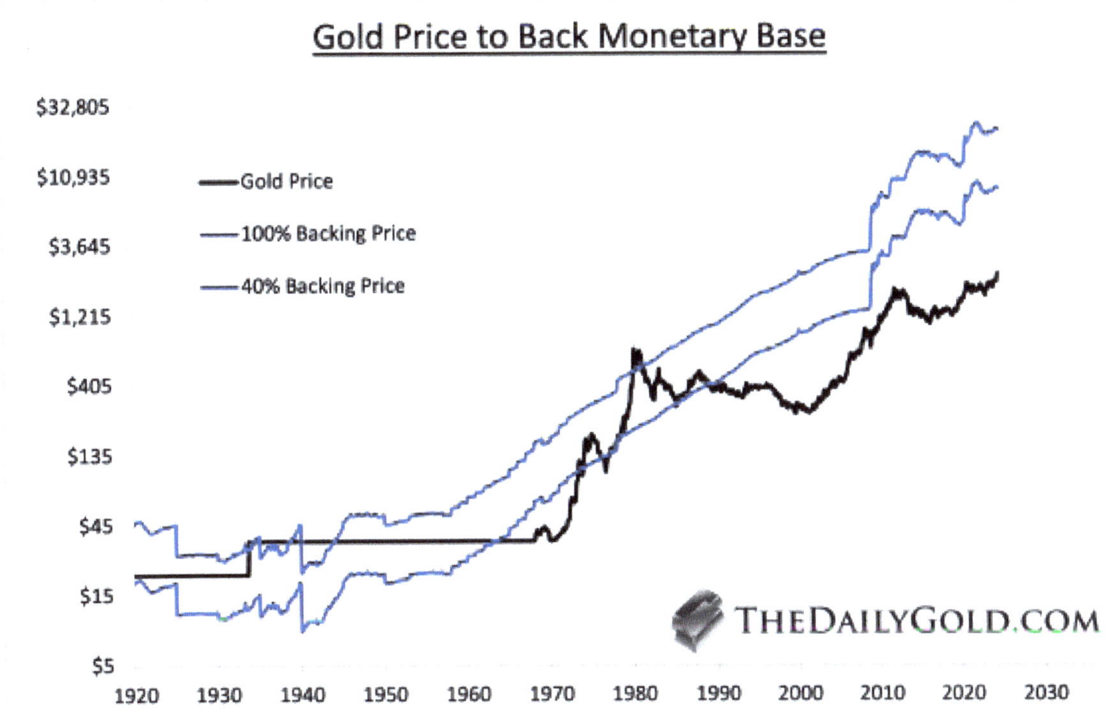

Figure 7.3 on the next page plots the percentage backing of the US Monetary Base. As of April 2024, the Gold price backs 10.4% of the US Monetary Base. The percentage backing during the secular bull market of the 2000s increased from 10.9% to 29.7%. That pales in comparison to what transpired in the 1930s and 1970s.

The percentage backing of the Monetary Base surged past 100% in the 1930s, 1940s, and 1980. Again, 100% backing today would require a Gold price of $22000/oz. The 1980 peak of 139% backing equates to a Gold price of nearly $31000/oz.

Figure 7.3: Gold Backing of Monetary Base (%)

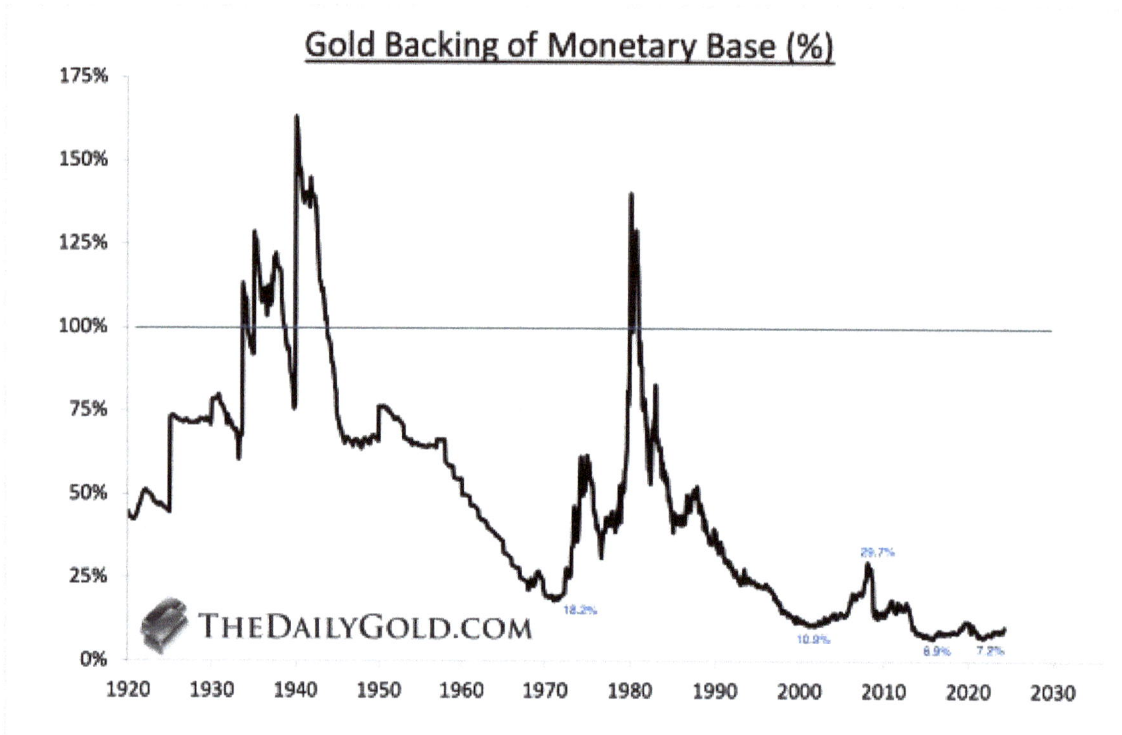

We can debate how high the Gold price could or should go, but there is a single unmistakable conclusion: Gold remains quite cheap historically. It is currently at one of the lowest levels ever relative to the stock market, but it is even cheaper than that, considering the percentage backing of the monetary base.

The conclusion remains the same when we assess the assets in Gold against all capital market assets. Figure 7.4 on the next page plots the assets in all ETFs as a percentage of all ETF Assets. A high reading would signal that Gold is more popular as an investment, whereas a low reading would signal that Gold is unpopular.

The share of Gold ETFs is barely above 1%, close to a 20-year low. The first Gold ETF was introduced in November 2004. Although the price of Gold has recovered and even doubled since the end of 2015, Gold remains as unpopular today as it was then. Moreover, note how low the share is relative to the peak of 8% around the end of 2011.

Figure 7.4: Gold ETF Assets as Percentage of All ETF Assets

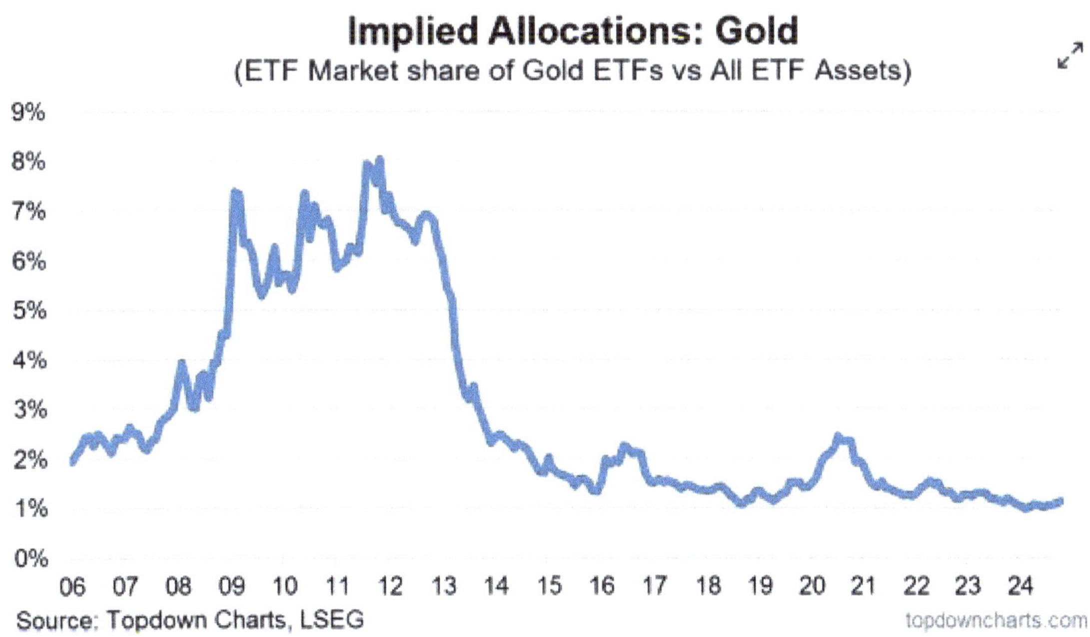

Gold's percentage of global financial assets is not as extreme but below past historical peaks. At the end of 2023, the CPM group estimated Gold at 0.63% of Global Financial Assets. This is less than one-quarter of the 1980 peak and roughly one-eighth of the level of 1960.

The figure grew from 0.15% to 0.72% during the last secular bull market and has not decreased much in the past decade. The reason is likely the growth in emerging markets and the rest of the world's affinity for Gold. Moreover, as we showed in Chapter 1, the price of Gold is much higher outside the United States. See Figure 7.5 on the next page.

Figure 7.5: Gold as a Percentage of Global Financial Assets

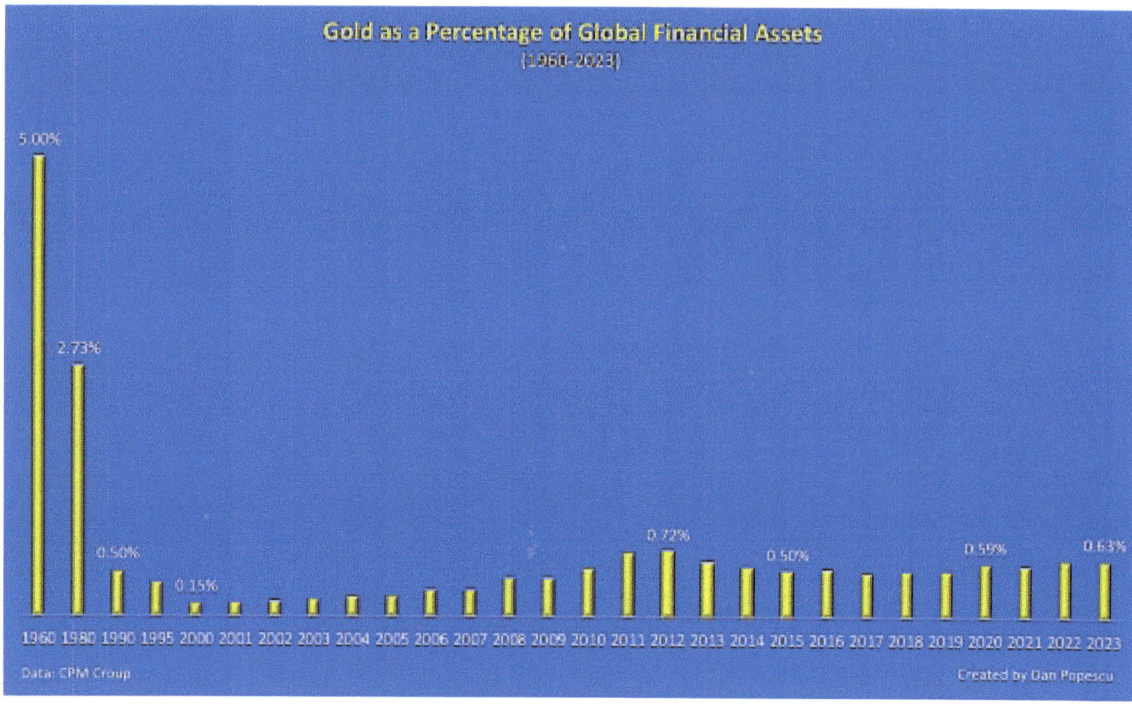

Gold mining companies' valuations are historically cheap for two reasons. First, they have been in a secular bear market since 2011. Valuations were higher during the previous secular bull market.

The second reason is the advent of exchange-traded funds (ETFs) for Gold and Silver, which made it much easier to buy and invest in Gold directly. These ETFs financialized Gold.

Before the introduction of the first Gold ETF, GLD, in 2004, gold mining companies traded at higher valuations because they were the easiest way to invest in Gold. With the advent of Gold and Silver ETFs, investors no longer had to choose between gold miners, futures contracts, or bullion. That removed a lot of buying of gold miners, starting in the mid-2000s.

Figure 7.6 on the next page plots gold miners' price to net asset value over the past 40 years. The data is from Scotiabank. Since 2011, the valuation has remained below 1.5x and 1.3x for the vast majority. In a secular bull market, we expect the valuation to climb above 2.0x.

Figure 7.6: Gold Stocks Price to NAV

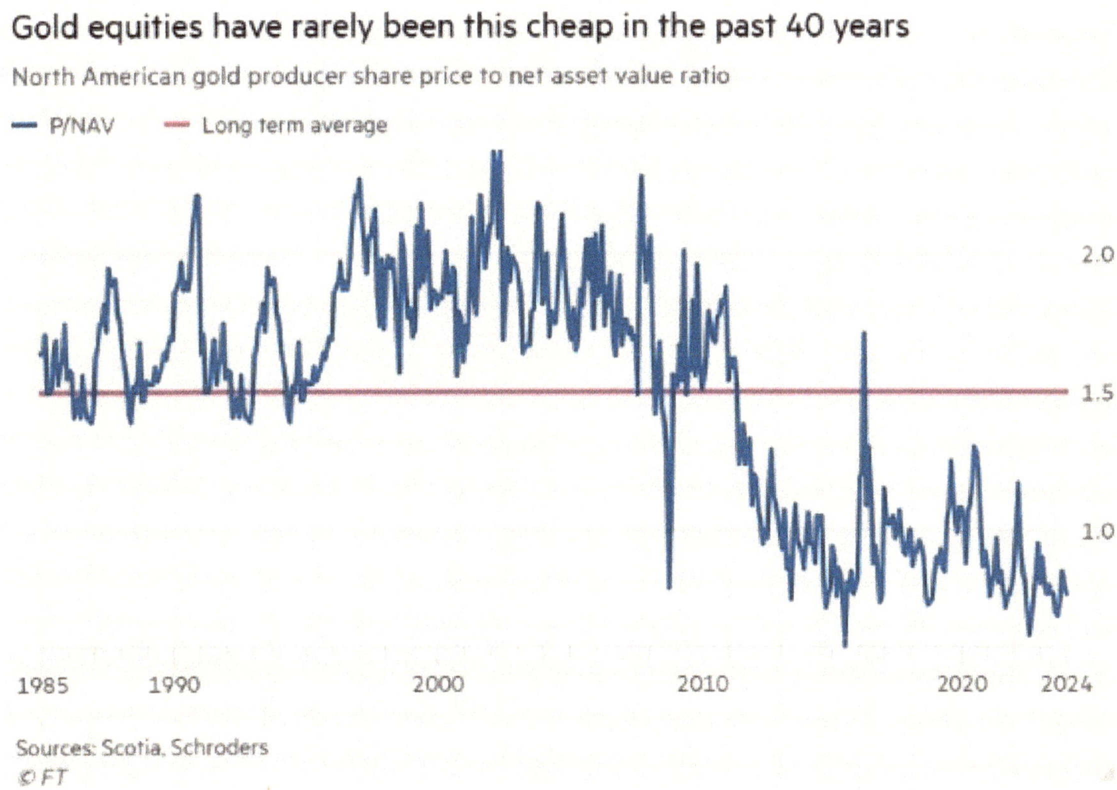

Figure 7.7 on the next page, courtesy of Bank of America Global Research and Bloomberg, plots the price to net asset value (NAV) valuation for several decades. It divides precious metals companies into four groups.

Senior producers, the largest miners, are valued at around 1.50x NAV. Between 1993 and 2008, their valuation touched 3.00x NAV at a handful of points.

The mid-tier producers are the cheapest in relative terms. They were valued at 2.0x to 3.0x NAV in the 2000s, 2.0x NAV at the 2016 peak, and close to 2.0x in 2019. Now, they are valued below 1.0x NAV.

Figure 7.7: Precious Metals Companies Price to NAV

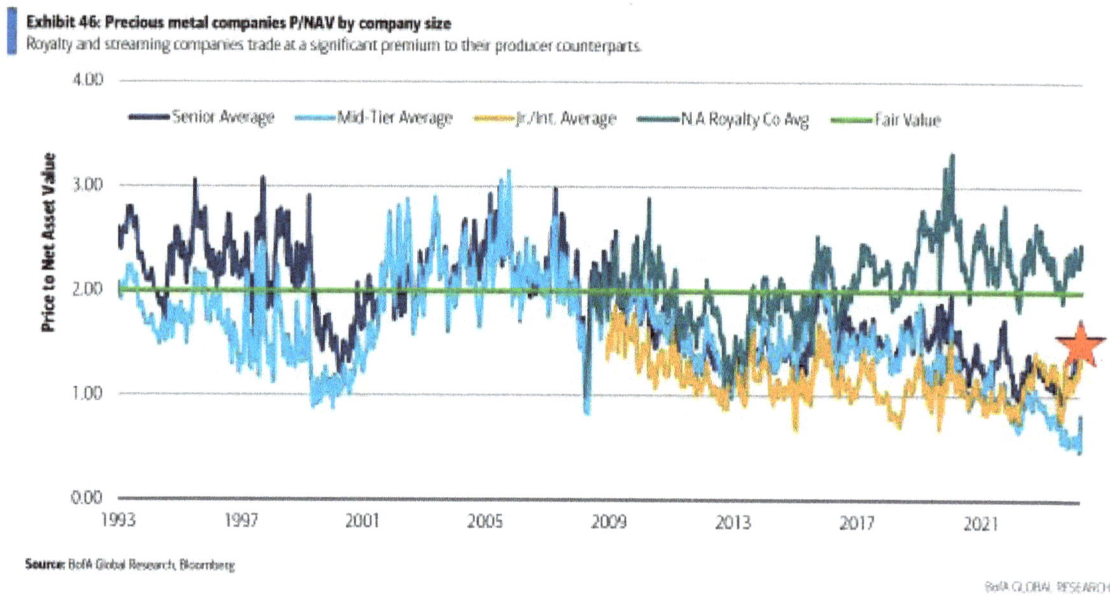

Figure 7.8 below, also courtesy of Bank of America Global Research and Bloomberg, plots the Enterprise Value to EBITDA (EV/EBITDA) valuation. It is similar to the price-to-cash flow valuation. The image divides the companies into four groups and includes an average.

The period is 2010 to autumn 2023 when mining companies have been in a secular bear market. The valuation for the average producer has ranged from 5x to 10x. It was nearly 10x at the end of 2010 and the summer of 2020. It currently is between 7x and 8x. According to data from Bank of America and Bloomberg, the valuation hit 14x multiple times from 2008 to 2010. The juniors, are currently valued above 8x. They have been valued at 12x to 13x a handful of times.

Figure 7.8: Enterprise Value to EBITDA Valuation

Figure 7.9: Gold Stocks Price to Cash Flow

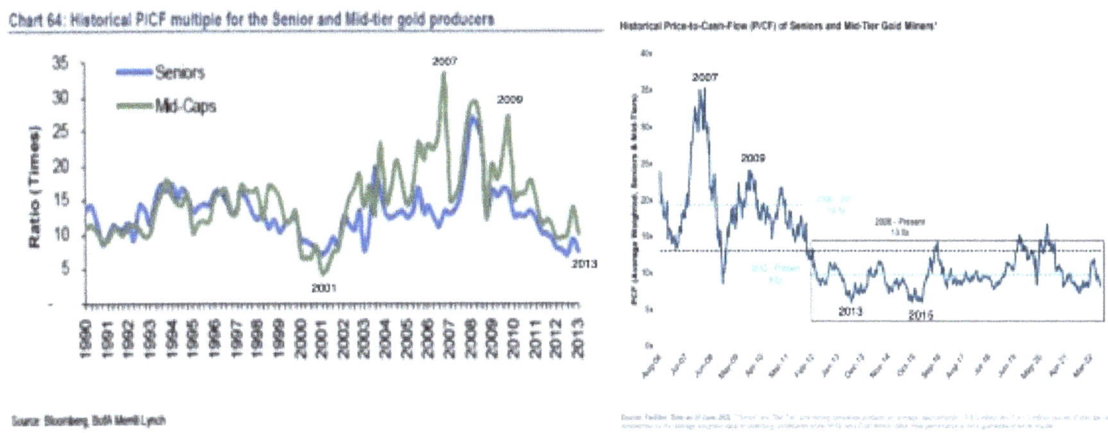

Figure 7.9 above is two images squeezed together. Both images plot the price-to-cash flow multiple for senior and mid-tier gold miners. The first image shows the valuation for each group from 1990 to 2013. The second image plots both groups' valuations from 2006 to June 2022. The data is from different sources, so the charts are not aligned perfectly.

The price-to-cash flow valuation peaked in the middle of the previous secular bull market (2000-2011), which was around the introduction and adoption by investors of the first Gold ETF. The peaks ranged from 25x in senior miners to as high as 35x cash flow for mid-tier miners. According to data from CIBC World Markets, the price-to-cash flow multiple for gold stocks reached 22x in early 1975 and 1980, which were near peaks during the secular bull market of 1970 to 1980.

The valuation of 6x cash flow at the 2001, 2013, and 2015 lows was near the lowest in recorded history. In recent years, it has fallen to 7x and 8x cash flow. At the gold stock low of October 2022, it fell to its lowest level since 2013 and 2015.

Since 2012, the valuation has ranged from 6x to 16x but mostly between 6x and 11x. At the 2016, 2019, and 2020 peaks, it reached 15x to 16x.

Although the investment banks and Bloomberg have not recently provided a price-to-cash flow estimate for gold stocks, I found a workaround. Adam Hamilton, publisher of Zeal Intelligence, a great newsletter covering gold stocks, recently posted a table that included the quarterly cash flow of the Top 25 companies in the GDX ETF.

After totaling the combined cash flow and market capitalization of the Top 25 companies in the third quarter of 2024 and annualizing it, I calculated a price-to-cash flow multiple of 6.5x. Had GDX not recently declined by 15%, then the price-to-cash flow multiple would have been 7.7x cash flow.

By combining the various historical information, we can say that senior gold stocks have historically traded from as low as 6x cash flow to as high as 25x cash flow.

With the price-to-cash flow valuation historically low, it should be no surprise that gold stocks are very cheap relative to both the price of Gold and the stock market. Figure 7.10 below plots the Barron's Gold Mining Index against Gold and the Barron's Gold Mining Index against the stock market. Note that 2015 marked a potential all-time low in gold-stock valuations in terms of cash flow and net asset value. Furthermore, 2015 marked an all-time low in the value of gold stocks relative to the price of Gold and the stock market.

Relative to Gold and the stock market, Gold stocks have rebounded since 2015. However, they remain near all-time low levels against both, particularly against the stock market.

Figure 7.10: Gold Stocks vs. Gold, Gold Stocks vs. S&P 500

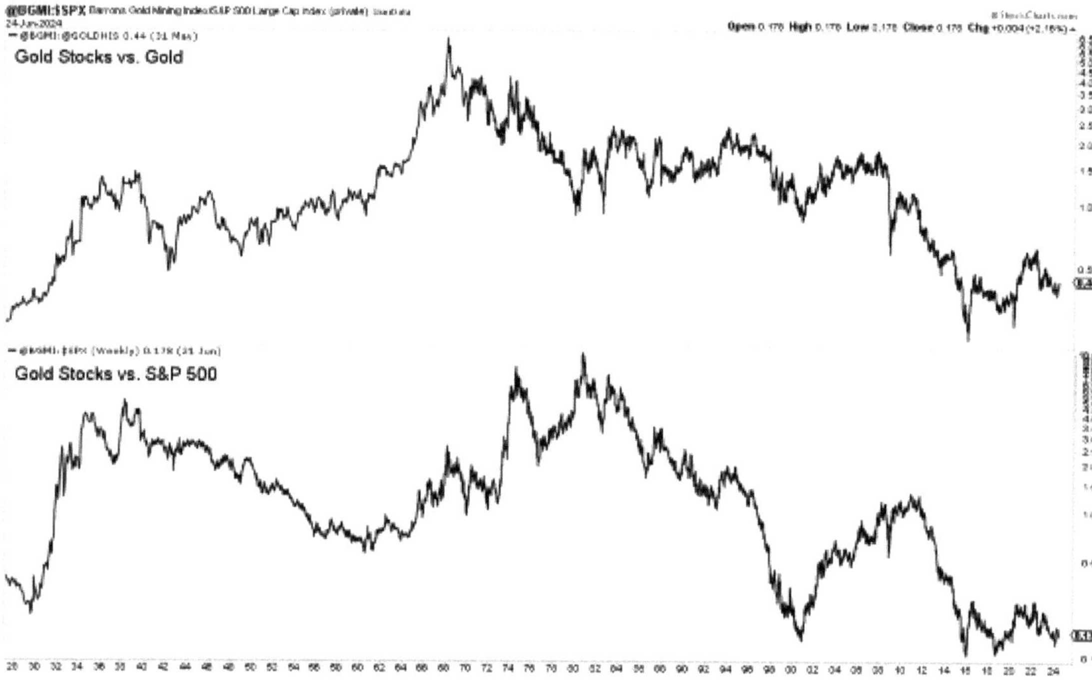

Finally, Figure 7.11 on the next page plots the share of ETF assets in gold stocks against the share of all ETF assets in equities. The current share is at a 17-year low, only months after a spectacular breakout move in Gold. No other chart is more bullish for gold stocks. This chart shows that gold stocks are extremely under-owned and have significant room to move once more capital moves into precious metals.

Figure 7.11: Gold Miners' ETF Assets As a Percentage of All Equity ETF Assets

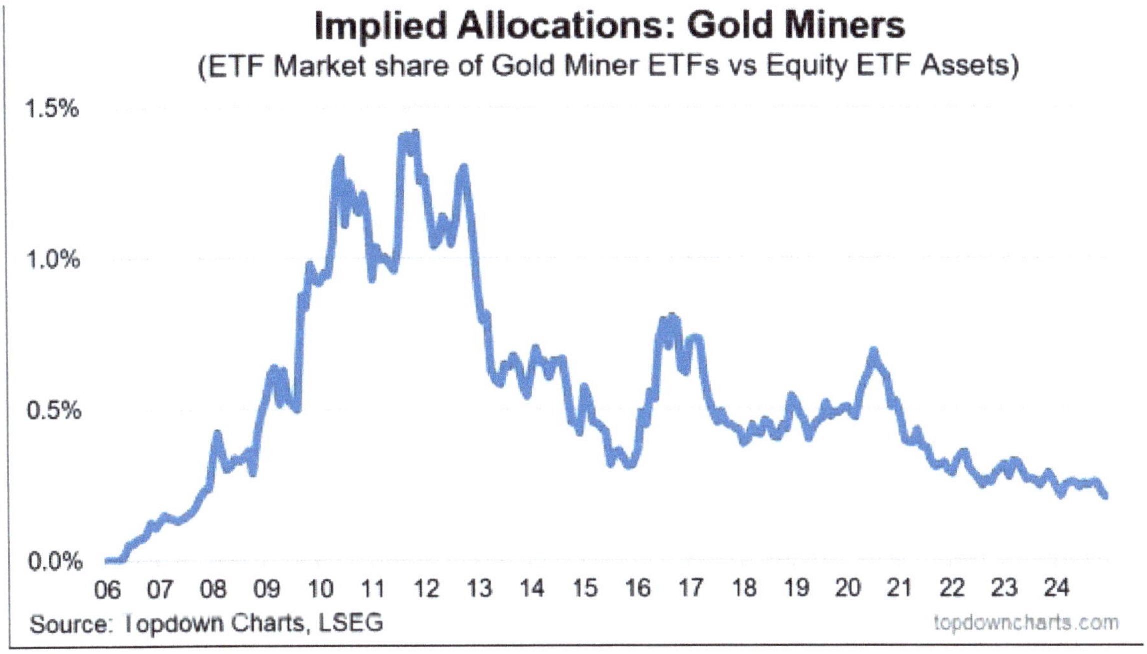

Chapter Summary

Although the price of Gold has moved well beyond its 2011 highs and is trading around all-time highs, it remains extremely cheap relative to the stock market and monetary base. In addition, it is cheap considering its value relative to US and global financial assets. Furthermore, Gold ETFs account for a little more than 1% of all ETF assets compared to 8% at the end of 2011. This information reflects that Gold has barely started to emerge from the secular bear market from 2011 until late 2023.

The gold mining sector traded at all-time low valuations in 2015 before Gold bottomed at $1040/oz. Although the Gold price has more than doubled in the last eight years, valuations for gold mining companies remain historically low and in bear market territory. Valuations have increased slightly since late 2022, when they were slightly above the 2015 lows. Moreover, the ETF assets in all gold stock funds relative to all equity ETF assets are at a 17-year low. This is shockingly bullish as it sets the stage for a secular bull market.

Chapter 8

All About Gold Mining Stocks

The gold mining sector has a boom-and-bust history, with spectacular long-term volatility over the past 100 years. This is the nature of resource markets due to volatility in commodity prices.

Although Gold and Silver are not valued based on supply and demand fundamentals, their drivers of investment demand and monetary factors are just as volatile and cyclical. The other reasons for their inconsistent and volatile long-term performance speak more about the mining business's long-term difficulties.

Mining firms consume their end product or asset, which is a finite resource. They need to grow to recover what they produce, which requires capital. This makes the mining business extremely capital-intensive. Firms rely on their ability to raise capital via equity or debt. Equity dilution hurts stock prices.

Finding new deposits and economic deposits is also becoming increasingly difficult for geological and political reasons. Average ore grades have declined consistently and significantly in recent decades. Throw in additional cost inflation, and new deposits are more expensive to find and build into mines.

Politics and geopolitics add another layer of risk. The best deposits are often found in jurisdictions with political and legal instability. Governments can change policies and laws quickly, circumventing recent investments.

Given the many risks, it is understandable why companies no longer outperform the price of Gold over extended periods. We will expound upon this in a moment.

First, let us delve more deeply into the history of gold mining stocks. In Figure 8.1 on the next page, we plot the Barron's Gold Mining Index and the price of Gold over the past century.

There have been spectacular bull markets in gold stocks, but there have been seven bear markets of 60% or more in the past 50 years! Four of those bears occurred during secular uptrends (1960-1980 and 2000-2011). Moreover, even during bullish cycles, the stocks can correct 20% multiple times per year, with corrections often reaching 30% or 40%.

The Barron's Gold Mining Index's performance relative to Gold has been horrible in recent decades. The price of Gold is well above its 1980 and 2011 peaks, but the gold stocks are not.

Figure 8.1: BGMI, Gold- 100 YEARS

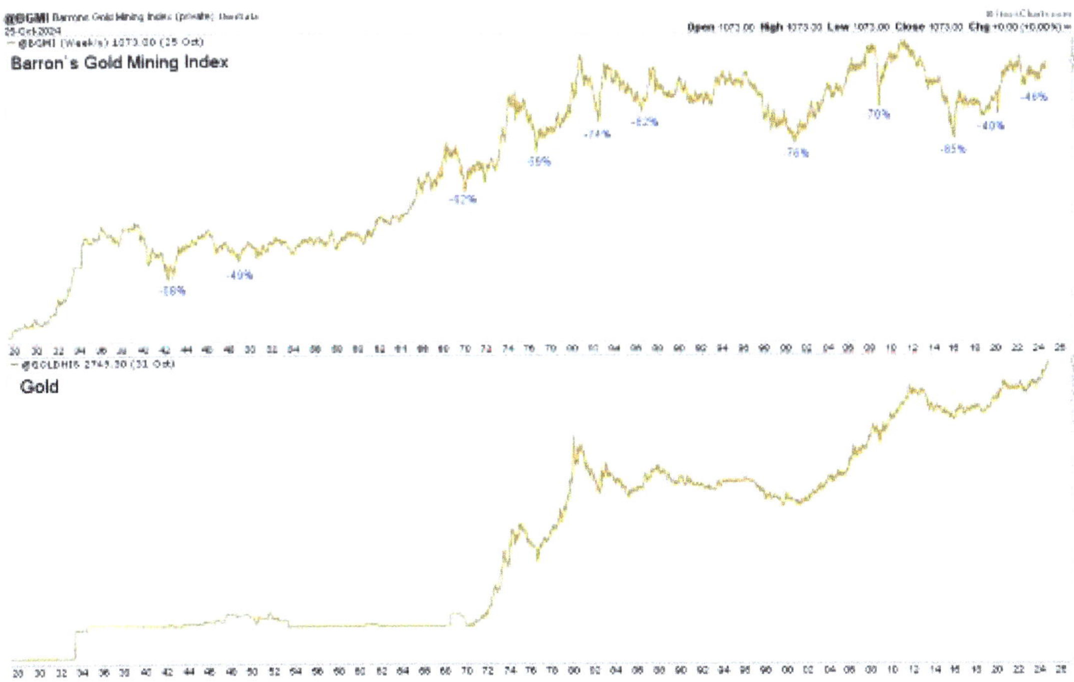

Figure 8.2 on the next page will help explain the discrepancy between the long-term performance of Gold and gold stocks and is one of the most important insights from this book. I discovered it a few years ago. In previous editions of this book, I highlighted the Gold-to-commodity prices ratio as a potential fundamental indicator for gold stocks. But its efficacy was lacking.

The best fundamental indicator for gold stocks is the inflation-adjusted Gold price. Gold mining companies do not follow the price of Gold; they follow their margins, which are the Gold price minus mining costs. The rate of inflation is a solid proxy for mining costs, so the inflation-adjusted Gold price serves as an excellent indicator of Gold mining margins.

Figure 8.2 plots the Inflation-Adjusted Gold Price and the Barron's Gold Mining Index. No indicator is perfect, but the two data series track quite closely. Each had significant peaks in 1980 and 2011. Barron's Gold Mining Index is lagging behind the Inflation-Adjusted Gold price, and that is due to the current, historically low valuations.

The Inflation-Adjusted Gold Price has a technical setup for an extremely significant breakout. Much like Silver, this looks to be a 45-year breakout. This is a major catalyst for the reintroduction of gold stocks into the mainstream.

Figure 8.2: Inflation-Adjusted Gold Price & Barron's Gold Mining Index

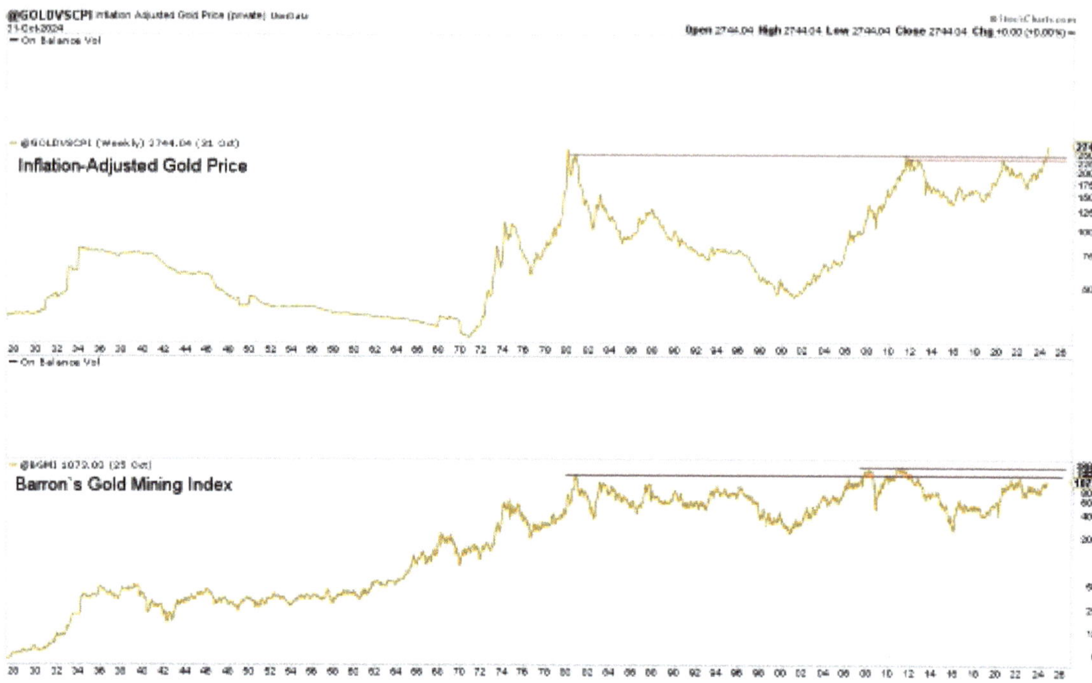

Gold against Oil (Gold to Oil ratio) or Gold against commodity prices can be a shorter-term indicator of gold miners' margins. Oil feeds inflation, and as much as 30% of the cost of open-pit mines is energy. If commodity prices and Oil outpace Gold, it's usually a negative signal for gold stocks.

The inflation-adjusted Gold price is the best indicator year over year. Tracking Gold against Oil and commodity prices is a better indicator month over month and quarter over quarter.

Aside from poor performance, there are key reasons why gold mining stocks disappeared from mainstream portfolios.

The first reason is the proliferation of mutual funds, exchange-traded funds (ETFs), and various investment products that helped create more competition for investment. The best bull markets in gold stocks occurred in the 1930s, 1960s, and 1970s. Sector-specific mutual funds, international stock mutual funds, and emerging markets mutual funds did not exist until after the 1970s. Today, there are a plethora of ETFs, including foreign currency ETFs and inflation-protected bond funds.

As an aside, gold stocks enjoyed a spectacular move in the 1960s (although the Gold price was fixed) because there was essentially no competition for an inflation-protection type of investment. Today, one can invest in Treasury Inflation-Protected Securities (TIPS), foreign currencies, emerging markets, and many other ETFs. Moreover, thanks to the many ETFs, one can easily buy Gold (and Silver). This was not the case before 2005.

Before the introduction of Gold and Silver ETFs in 2005 and 2006, the only way a portfolio manager or retail investor could buy Gold was through the futures market or a coin dealer. As a result, most investors could only gain exposure to

Gold through mining companies. Hence, they traded at much higher valuations. Figure 7.7 from the last chapter shows that the price-to-NAV valuation was much higher in the 1980s and 1990s than today.

Furthermore, gold stocks traded at much higher levels relative to Gold before the introduction of ETFs in the mid-2000s. Figure 8.3 below plots Barron's Gold Mining Index divided by Gold and the parent index of GDX divided by Gold.

As noted in the image, the recent poor performance of gold stocks against Gold is easily explained by two events. First, the first Gold ETF was introduced at the end of 2004. Second (and completely neglected) is the secular bear market in precious metals from the summer of 2011 until late 2023. The gold price was flat during that period, but the inflation-adjusted price was down 25%.

Figure 8.3: Gold Stocks vs. Gold

The introduction of Gold and Silver ETFs financialized Gold and Silver at the expense of mining companies. Portfolio managers and retail investors have largely abandoned these companies in favor of Gold ETFs. As a result of this and the secular bear market, gold mining stocks trade at historically low valuations and have been relegated to options on Gold.

Like options, gold mining stocks will underperform Gold over very long periods of time. However, during sharp rebounds or trending moves in Gold, gold stocks do outperform Gold. In other words, they outperform Gold during huge rebounds from a significant low or during and after breakout moves in Gold.

Figure 8.4 on the next page plots Gold and the gold stocks divided by Gold since 2000. It plots GDX divided by Gold and also GDXJ divided by Gold. GDXJ data is available from 2004 on the MarketVectors website. We attached data from our junior gold index from the end of 2002 to the end of 2003, which was an exceptional year for junior mining and exploration companies.

The vertical lines mark the breakouts in Gold, and the Ls mark important lows in Gold. The best performance in miners and juniors relative to Gold followed the L bottoms and breakouts in the Gold price. The worst performance follows peaks in the Gold price. See 2008, 2011, 2016, and 2020.

Figure 8.4: Gold Stocks vs. Gold

Chapter Summary

Gold mining is a boom-and-bust industry. Over the past century, it has experienced spectacular bull markets, but a 60% bear market followed each.

Gold mining stocks move based on the delta in their margins. The best fundamental indicator for gold stocks is the inflation-adjusted Gold price, which tracks industry margins fairly well.

The poor performance of gold mining stocks relative to Gold is due mostly to the secular bear market in precious metals (from 2011 through 2023) but also to the introduction of Gold and Silver ETFs in the mid-2000s. Before then, the easiest and only way in history to gain exposure to Gold was via mining companies.

Because of the Gold and Silver ETFs and many other investment products that dilute attention and capital, gold mining companies have been relegated to options based on the Gold price. They will outperform and leverage Gold after major Gold rebounds and during and after major breakouts in the Gold price. They will underperform Gold during long periods of time in which Gold is correcting or not trending higher consistently.

If Gold enjoys a secular bull market until the mid or late 2030s, we should expect the gold mining and junior gold companies (as a whole) to match or slightly outperform the Gold price from the start until the end. However, within that time, there will be multi-year and single-year periods in which the miners and juniors dramatically underperform Gold. There will likely be at least one 60% bear market along the way and another at the end of the secular bull market.

Chapter 9

All About Junior Gold Stocks

A junior resource company is involved in exploring, discovering, or developing a new mineral deposit that can become a producing mine. Juniors are speculative venture-style companies that, while extremely risky, serve as the mining industry's research and development arm. Juniors are trying to discover and define the next future mine, like a biotech company trying to develop the next blockbuster drug or a technology start-up trying to become the next Amazon or Facebook.

Junior resource stocks are listed mostly in Canada on the Toronto Stock and Toronto Venture Exchanges, London on the London Stock Exchange, and Australia on the Australian Stock Exchange.

The size of a junior company varies depending on your perspective as well as the current stage of the company. Investors and speculators in Canada and Australia view a "junior" as anything below $100 million in market capitalization and even below $50 Million in some cases. They tend to focus on the industry's smallest companies, primarily exploration-stage companies. These companies are exploring to discover a mineral deposit or drilling to grow an existing deposit to a larger size. Some of these companies can be classified as pre-resource or pre-discovery.

These companies carry the greatest risk but the greatest reward. Only one out of 1,000 exploration projects becomes a mine; some projects are never drilled. However, due to growing interest and their tiny size, these stocks can move from pennies and nickels to $1-$2 in a raging bull market. The ones that do make a major discovery that will become a significant mine, and I can think of only a handful in the last decade, can return 100-fold from their IPO price.

Investors and traders in the United States view juniors through the GDXJ exchange-traded fund. It is the most liquid and widely followed ETF for junior resource companies. GDXJ has been rebalanced in recent years, and its top holdings are mid-tier firms rather than juniors.

A long-time Canadian analyst, Bob Hoye, once called GDXJ the "senior juniors." The Top 20 holdings in GDXJ comprise roughly 60% of the fund and have market capitalizations of at least $2 billion. That does not sound "junior" to me. If one removed the top 20 companies, GDXJ would better fit its description. Yet, it would still be focused on the largest and most successful junior companies.

GDXJ is composed of juniors who became successful producers and juniors who are developing or building significant mines. There are no pre-resource or pre-discovery companies within the GDXJ. There are a few exploration companies, but only those that have already discovered or defined a meaningful deposit.

Let us discuss the stages of junior companies in greater detail.

Most juniors are exploration companies. These companies are searching for a new deposit (greenfield projects) or hoping to grow an existing deposit (brownfield projects) to reach critical mass. Some companies may have already defined a resource, while others are just getting started. When a company moves from publishing a resource estimate to an economic study (such as a preliminary economic assessment or pre-feasibility study), it can become a development company.

The development phase involves preparing for and actually building a mine. This stage involves infill drilling (filling in areas between known mineralization), permitting, and a definitive feasibility study. A company reaches the latter stages of development when it raises the funds to build the mine and begins building it. If the mine's construction is successful, the junior company becomes a junior producer.

Figure 9.1 below is one of the most important charts for understanding the evolution of a successful junior mining company. It was created by Pierre Lassonde, a former president of Newmont and the founder of Franco Nevada. The chart depicts the life cycle of a junior resource company, also known as the Lassonde Curve.

It shows the potential path of the stock price through exploration, development, and production. While every junior company won't necessarily follow the Lassonde Curve, it does help us understand where the risks and opportunities are.

Figure 9.1: Life Cycle of Junior Resource Company

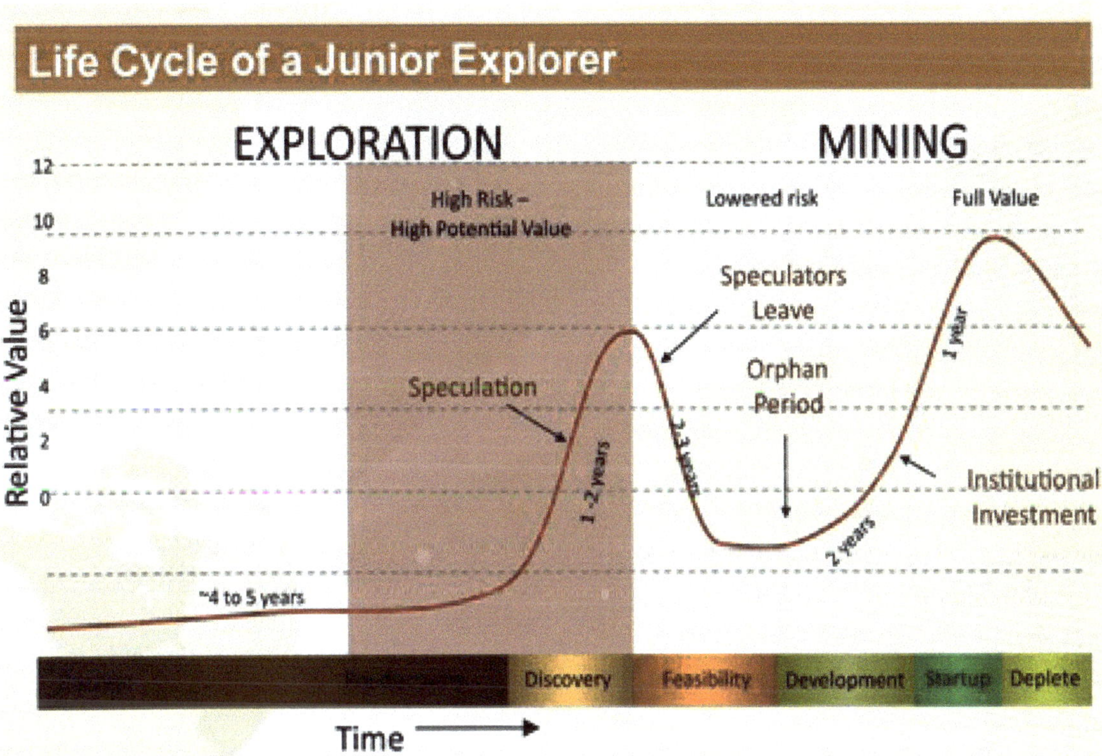

The major takeaway for investors and speculators is there are two buy points and one major sell point. The best times to buy are before or during a legitimate mineral discovery or during the final months of construction, leading to production. The major sell point is between those two stages when the company enters development and has to prove to the market and industry that the discovery can become a mine.

We want to buy exploration companies before they have maxed out their exploration potential and developers near the end of the development period, around the time construction begins. A successful exploration company will either be acquired by a larger company or successfully develop the asset independently and build a mine. A successful development company will raise the capital needed to build the mine and then build it successfully. Acquisitions occur most often at the development stage because the project has been de-risked.

Lobo Tiggre, the editor of the Independent Speculator, has deemed the buy point on the Lassonde Curve for developers the "Pre-Production Sweet Spot" (PPSS). Tiggre studied the outcomes of 124 first-time (company) mine builders dating back to the 1980s. The majority of cases are Gold and Silver mines, but the data includes some Copper and Uranium mines. He found an operational success rate of ~92% and 95.2% if a mine was built after a takeover.

In assessing stock performance, Tiggre compiled performance from a published construction decision (CD) or announcement that construction had begun to the announcement of first pour (FP) or reaching commercial production (CP). The average time from CD to FP was 569 days. Overall, 75.4% of cases delivered a positive return. The average gain from CD to FP was 97%, and the average gain from CD to CP was 111%. The average gain was 132.4% during bull markets, against a 20.2% gain during bear markets.

Why Focus on Producers and Developers

There are multiple reasons why I prefer to focus most of my research on developers and producers, and you should, too.

These companies offer the best value proposition. The market loves growth, and production growth offers leveraged upside in a bull market. As we have seen from the Lassonde Curve, the best point for owning developers or producers is near the end of a mine's construction when production is only months away. These companies receive a valuation bump or positive re-rating from construction to production.

Producers and developers have more predictable outcomes than earlier-stage exploration companies. It is much easier to project the value of producers and developers two to three years into the future at various metals prices. One can estimate the level of production, the Gold price, and costs to generate potential cash flow. Meanwhile, exploration companies are entirely dependent on the success of drill holes, which is much less predictable. They are also not necessarily leveraged to metals prices. Their leverage is based on their exploration success more so than metals prices.

Finally, you can invest in exploration by also investing in producers who commit to serious exploration. This is a lower-risk way of investing in exploration. These companies can fund exploration from their ongoing cash flow. However, exploration companies have to continuously issue shares to fund their exploration, which becomes extremely dilutive if they are not adding significant value with each raise.

Meanwhile, suppose a producer makes a discovery near or around an operating mine. In that case, it can add significant value to the company because the capital required to mine that discovery is usually extremely low. They often do not need to build a new mill or processing facility; the mining infrastructure already exists.

Generalist investors may recall Kirkland Lake Gold, which moved from below $2 in late 2015 to as high as $50 in 2019 and $57 in 2020 before being acquired by Agnico Eagle in 2021. Kirkland Lake Gold played a large role in multiple high-grade Gold discoveries at the operating Fosterville mine in Australia. The company acquired Newmarket Gold in late 2016, which discovered the ultra-high-grade Swan Zone. Crocodile Gold acquired Newmarket Gold in late 2015, which discovered the high-grade Eagle Zone at Fosterville.

By 2019, Kirkland Lake grew the Swan Zone to 2.34 million ounces of Gold at a grade of 49.6 grams per tonne (g/t), making it likely the world's highest-grade Gold deposit of that size. Production at Fosterville grew from 123,000 ounces of Gold in 2015 to a whopping 619,366 ounces in 2019. The mine, with a cash operating cost of only $119/oz in 2019, generated nearly $650 Million in operating cash flow, almost 20-fold greater than the cash flow it generated four years earlier.

Wesdome Gold is another example of a discovery that transformed a junior producer. In 2016, it discovered high-grade gold mineralization in the deep zone of an old mine (Kiena in Quebec, Canada). After the Gold price peak in 2016, the stock climbed from $1.70 in late 2017 to $14.85 in 2020. By the end of 2020, the Kiena Deep discovery had grown to 835,000 oz Au at a 17 g/t grade.

A gold discovery need not be 2 to 3 million ounces to be transformational for a producer or developer. In many cases, a small, high-grade discovery of half a million ounces or even less can materially raise the economics of a development project or add significant value to an operating mine.

Kirkland Lake Gold and Wesdome Gold are a few elite examples of what I deem "The Holy Grail" of junior mining. This is when a junior resource company boasts production growth potential with a significant value-adding mineral discovery from exploration.

Criteria for Producers & Developers

Broadly speaking, I am looking for junior producers and developers with the potential to appreciate by 5x to 10x in a cyclical bull market. That entails looking at companies with market caps below $200 million that have the potential to grow to $1 to $2 billion and for companies with market caps below $1 billion that have the potential to become $3 to $5 Billion. I usually avoid companies with market caps below $50 million and those that are essentially penny stocks.

The following criteria apply most to producers and developers but also relate to exploration companies.

Management

Many who speculate on or invest in junior gold companies say management is the most important criterion. The odds of success in this game are fleeting, and those who have had success in the past are more likely to have success in the future.

Management should have a track record of success when developing, building, and operating mines. Have they built mines? Have they worked in operations for a senior producer? Are they seeking to build the type of mine they built in the past?

In exploration companies, management teams with a track record of success have better odds of future success. They can attract strong backing, raise capital, and acquire the most prospective projects.

It is important to note that success in exploration can be quite elusive. Unknown geologists can make tremendous discoveries, while those that have in the past may not necessarily find success in the future. A track record is important, but do not overvalue it. The biggest names in the industry do not have a bulletproof track record. While they tend to come across the most prospective opportunities, success is never a guarantee. At the same time, many grifters run companies for the paycheck and do not do serious exploration.

Size

Size matters. Larger mines and larger projects attract more attention and investors and command a valuation premium. Those investors include fund managers, large institutions, and industry professionals. Larger mines and larger projects also have greater leverage to the upside of a bull market.

There are important thresholds. At a minimum, we should focus on companies or projects that contain or have the potential for 3M and the potential to produce at least 100K oz Au per year. For Silver, we focus on companies or projects that contain or have the potential for 80M-100M oz Ag-eq and the potential to produce at least 7-8M oz Ag-eq per year. And by Ag-eq, we are focusing on Silver and Gold and not base metals. Many Silver deposits contain other base metals like Zinc, Lead, and Copper.

The market cares about and values a producer growing production from 100K oz Au per year to 225K oz Au per year more than a producer growing production from 25K oz Au per year to 75K oz Au per year.

The +3M threshold is important for exploration because if these projects have high margins, they will attract big-money investors and interest from senior mining companies. One can make money on smaller discoveries and production growth from smaller projects, but there is more interest, money, and potential in the larger deposits.

Value

Speculators and investors should first value a company and its potential based on the current Gold or Silver price. Every project, mineral deposit, and operating mine will appear to be a great investment at a much higher Gold or Silver price. Focusing on value at only higher metal prices can lead you away from real value and real companies with good prospects. Besides, if a company is at a good value at the current Gold or Silver price or a slightly lower price, the odds are that it will be a big winner in a bull market.

Producers, developers, and exploration companies are valued differently. As already covered, the greatest valuation bump comes from moving from a late-stage developer to a producer. Hence, we prefer to focus on junior developers and junior producers.

One of my favorite areas for finding value is among underpriced developers likely to fund and successfully build a mine within the next few years. Perhaps the developer is trading below 0.20x its net present value. If it funds and successfully builds the mine, it can trade closer to 1.00x net present value a few years later. If the real price of gold moves higher, there is an additional upside.

The three drivers of price appreciation in junior producers are production growth, valuation, and margins. The ideal situation is to find a junior producer with production growth potential and the potential to trade at a higher valuation when that production growth is attained. A rise in the real Gold or Silver price will result in stronger margins. Those three things can lead to massive appreciation over a few years.

Insider & Institutional Ownership

Insider and institutional ownership are important for two reasons. First, it reduces the float (supply of stock actively traded), which, for juniors, will grow over time due to the need to raise capital by selling additional shares. A tighter float makes it easier for a stock to rise. Second, it adds credibility to the junior. Institutional ownership also includes ownership by a larger mining company. Ownership from the CEO and board of directors signals those at the highest level are aligned with shareholders and believe in the company's outcome.

Avoid These Fatal Flaws

Few mining properties are viable; even fewer (1 in 1000) become mines. This is because a fatal flaw or two prevents the project from ever being financed and built into a mine.

Some of these fatal flaws emanate from a single broad flaw, which, other than permitting difficulties, usually makes the project uneconomic. The reasons can relate to the deposit size, grade, or capital needed.

A common flaw is that the deposit's grade is not high enough. This is especially common with very, very large deposits. While the large endowment of Gold or Silver will excite some investors, the broader market ignores the size because it knows the low grade will prevent the deposit from ever becoming a mine.

Also, huge deposits typically require massive capital investment to become mines. No one will fund a billion-dollar construction if a project is marginal. Investors and financiers cannot assume the Gold or Silver price will rise and change the economics because that tends to be temporary and unsustainable over the mine's life. They want to fund projects that can work even if the real Gold or Silver price does not rise.

Some gold and silver deposits may have more than adequate grades but are too small. The market does not care much about small deposits. Moreover, because of cost inflation, building a small mine today is quite a bit more expensive than it was decades ago. A smaller project can only work if the potential margins are very high.

Some mines, especially underground mines, have technical or execution risks. There can be many reasons why a mine won't work. For example, a deposit's mineralization may be too narrow, making it difficult to mine. It may not have enough continuity. There may also be too much dilution from mining the ore to transporting it to the mill or processing facility.

Open-pit mines tend to have lower execution risk, but good metallurgy is essential, as these mines are lower grade and require strong ore recovery. Bad metallurgy can doom these types of projects, as it can entail rocks that are too hard, costly, and difficult to recover ore from.

Permitting risk, or jurisdictional risk, is a major fatal flaw, much greater than it was 20 years ago. In layman's terms, this means the project will never be built or will struggle to be built because it will never be allowed by local or national governments. For example, it is nearly impossible to permit a mine in California. This is also known as political risk.

Permitting and jurisdictional risk can also entail environmental risk and the risk of terrorism, which is a problem in parts of Africa.

It is important to note that jurisdictional risk is never a reason to focus solely on the best jurisdictions. You risk investing in many marginal projects and, perhaps, questionable companies. Many of the best discoveries and projects are located in places some investors deem undesirable and risky jurisdictions. The most successful speculators and investors in this space keep an open mind. Others only focus on North America and, therefore, miss out on some of the best opportunities.

Note that jurisdictional risk tends to be much greater before a project is developed and operating. Once it is permitted and operating, far more stakeholders are involved in the mine's success.

Why Focus on Juniors

Junior resource companies are a better option for investors or speculators seeking growth and capital appreciation, provided they spend significant time analyzing the viable companies in the space.

Juniors have far greater upside potential and leverage in a cyclical bull market, while senior miners do not necessarily possess a material advantage in protecting against the downside. Neither should be held throughout a bear market like blue-chip stocks.

Here is some data from the last secular bull market in precious metals. From 2004 to 2007, GDXJ gained 299%, while from 2004 to the peak in early 2008, GDX's parent index gained 187%. During the global financial crisis, GDX declined 71%, while GDXJ lost 81%. Then, from the 2008 low to the 2011 peak, GDXJ surged 578% while GDX gained 311%.

It's also possible for individual and retail investors to gain a significant information advantage in various junior companies. Many small juniors and even medium-sized juniors lack analyst coverage. Retail investors can become experts on these companies. In many cases, you can communicate with the company's CEO. You can become better informed on these companies than most market participants. That is not possible with the senior mining companies.

Furthermore, retail investors have a liquidity advantage. Big money cannot buy or sell these companies without having a huge impact on the market. It also has to be married to them.

Ultimately, the potential for significant and sometimes life-changing returns in juniors seduces us the most.

In Figure 9.2 on the next page, we plot the performance of a basket of 12 to 15 gold-focused juniors over different time frames. Interestingly, the two baskets appreciated around 13-fold over the first three years. The performance from 2008 to 2011 is more than double that of GDXJ during that period.

Figure 9.2: Junior Gold Stocks Bull Analog

In Figure 9.3 below, we plot the performance of a basket of junior silver stocks over several different periods. The last two cyclical bulls, which lasted multiple years (2008-2011 and 2005-2008), gained ninefold within three years.

Figure 9.3: Junior Silver Stocks Bull Analog

Unlike the secular bull market in precious metals from 2001 to 2011, the current one, which is just beginning, has the potential to evolve into a bubble and mania, which would entail much higher returns than in the 2001-2011 period.

In Chapter 5, we noted two major similarities between the new secular bull market and the bull market of the 1970s. Unlike in the 2000s and 1930s, Bonds are now in a secular bear market, as they were from 1965 to 1982. Also, like in the 1970s, Gold and Silver will have broken out to new all-time highs early in their new secular bull market. The preponderance of new all-time highs in Gold and Silver over the years ahead will lend itself to more speculation.

It is nearly impossible to find data on juniors' historical performance during the secular bull market of the 1970s. Still, the intrepid Jeff Clark of TheGoldAdvisor uncovered data on quite a few companies.

Figure 9.4 below shows the performance of 15 juniors in the final 15 to 24 months of the 1979-1980 mania. The average gain was 24-fold.

Figure: 9.4 Junior Gold Stock Performance 1978-1980

Returns of Juniors in 1979-1980 Mania

Company	Price on 12/29/1978	Price Peak	Date of Peak	Return
Carolin Mines	$3.10	$57.00	Oct. 80	1,738.7%
Mosquito Creek Gold	$0.70	$7.50	Oct. 80	971.4%
Northair Mines	$3.00	$10.00	Oct. 80	233.3%
Silver Standard	$0.58	$2.51	Mar. 80	332.8%
Lincoln Resources	$0.78	$20.00	Oct. 80	2,464.1%
Lornex	$15.00	$85.00	Oct. 80	466.7%
Imperial Metals	$0.36	$1.95	Mar. 80	441.7%
Anglo-Bomarc Mines	$1.80	$6.85	Oct. 80	280.6%
Avino Mines	0.33	5.5	Dec. 80	1,566.7%
Copper Lake	$0.08	$10.50	Sep. 80	13,025.0%
David Minerals	$1.15	$21.00	Oct. 80	1,726.1%
Eagle River Mines	$0.19	$6.80	Dec. 80	3,478.9%
Meston Lake Resources	$0.80	$10.50	Oct. 80	1,212.5%
Silverado Mines	$0.26	$10.63	Oct. 80	3,988.5%
Wharf Resources	$0.33	$9.50	Nov. 80	2,778.8%
AVERAGE				2,313.7%

in a

mania or a bubble. Several major mineral discoveries were made in the mid-1990s, which uncorked a frenzy in junior exploration companies during a cyclical bull market in resource companies from 1993 to 1996.

Figure 9.5 below, also courtesy of Jeff Clark, shows the performance of 15 exploration companies during a modest bull market for commodity prices.

Figure 9.5: Junior Gold Stock Performance 1993-1996

Returns of Juniors in Mid-1990s Bull Market				
Company	Pre-Bull Market Price	Price Peak	Date of High	Return
Cartaway	$0.10	$26.14	May 96	26,040.0%
Golden Star	$6.00	$27.50	Oct. 96	358.3%
Samex Mining	$1.00	$7.20	May 96	620.0%
Pacific Amber	$0.21	$9.40	Aug. 96	4,376.2%
Conquistador	$0.50	$9.87	Mar. 96	1,874.0%
Corriente	$1.00	$19.50	Mar. 97	1,850.0%
Valerie Gold	$1.50	$28.90	May 96	1,826.7%
Arequipa	$0.60	$34.75	May 96	5,691.7%
Bema Gold	$2.00	$12.75	Aug. 96	537.5%
Farallon	$0.80	$20.25	May 96	2,431.3%
Arizona Star	$0.50	$15.95	Aug. 96	3,090.0%
Cream Minerals	$0.30	$9.45	May 96	3,050.0%
Francisco Gold	$1.00	$34.50	Mar. 97	3,350.0%
Mansfield	$0.70	$10.50	Aug. 96	1,400.0%
Oliver Gold	$0.40	$6.80	Oct. 96	1,600.0%
AVERAGE				3,873.0%

Another mania in junior stocks occurred on the Spokane Stock Exchange in the 1960s. Silver rose from $0.90/oz in 1960, breaking above the 1920 high of $1.32/oz to $2.55/oz in 1968. Also, don't forget that the Barron's Gold Mining Index broke out from a 26-year base in 1964. Spokane, Washington, was the corporate headquarters for most of the region's gold, silver, lead, and zinc mines. According to HistoryLink, a free online encyclopedia of Washington State History, the average penny stock appreciated 160 times!

The post-World War II period saw not only restoration of its original name, but the admission to the trading floor of additional mining entrepreneurs, including Benjamin A. Harrison (d. 1993) and Harry F. Magnuson (1923-2009). These two were able to take advantage of the silver boom of the 1960s, during which the average penny stock appreciated 160 times. Participation in the Spokane Stock Exchange was vast, with more than 100,000 investors from all 50 states and many foreign countries. Barron's declared "Speculators in silver stocks have struck it rich in Spokane," and the Seattle Post Intelligencer called Spokane "the speculative darling of the industry" (Fahey, 121). Harrison's obituary describes him as "president of the Spokane Stock Exchange for 12 years ... and its most knowledgeable mining stock broker. ... The mining stocks Mr. Harrison traded brought immense wealth to northeastern Washington and northern Idaho" (The Seattle Times).

Chapter Summary

Junior resource companies are highly speculative venture-style companies that function as the research and development arm of the broader mining industry. They seek to explore for, discover, and, in some cases, build the mines of the future. There are thousands of these companies, and most are involved in exploring an asset to discover a future mine or grow an existing deposit. The vast majority of these companies are not viable and should be ignored.

Because exploration is very risky, we focus mostly (but not entirely) on the companies building a mine and/or growing production. One can also invest in exploration by investing in junior developers and junior producers who continue to fund exploration programs.

Many but not all junior companies will follow a Life Cycle, also known as the Lassonde Curve. It shows there are only two times to buy a junior company: before or during a major discovery and in the development phase when a company is building a mine and several months away from starting production.

There are key criteria to evaluate when researching individual junior companies. A management team with experience and a track record is almost essential. One should focus on projects and mines that have the potential to be large. The big money in this industry focuses exclusively on those assets. One should also evaluate a company's potential based on the current metals prices. Otherwise, you become too dependent on the rise in metals' prices.

Juniors are enticing because they will significantly outperform in cyclical and secular bull markets. They can offer significant leverage to rising metals prices. Senior mining companies are more stable but can experience catastrophic declines like juniors in a cyclical bear market. If they do their homework, retail investors can become experts on individual juniors, which lack analyst coverage and are not well understood by most investors.

Finally, the outlook for precious metals is extremely positive, raising the odds of the potential for a mania in junior resource stocks.

Chapter 10

Trading & Investing Rules for Gold Stocks

In this chapter, I will list and analyze some essential rules for trading and investing in individual junior companies and managing a diversified portfolio of junior companies. I developed these rules after trading and investing in the junior sector for 20 years. If I had followed these rules, I would have suffered fewer losses and secured higher profits.

Use a 20%-25% Mental Stop Loss

If a position drops 20% from its buy price, you should usually sell it. A 20% loss on a position of 5% of your portfolio limits your portfolio risk to 1%. Cutting losses is a vital piece of wisdom that has been passed down for decades from generation to generation.

In the junior mining sector, 20% losses can often become 50% losses, which can become 70%. Many of these companies do not have significant value to fall back on. You are not buying blue-chip stocks. Even companies with good assets can experience 70% losses.

There are only two times this rule will hurt you. First is if you buy something too early ahead of a major bottom. The second is if you have a bad entry point during a bull market and buy a stock at its interim peak. One way to prevent this rule from being triggered is to buy in tranches. You could buy a half position, and if the stock drops 25%, you could buy the other half. The stock would have to decline over 30% from the original buy price for you to be stopped out of your position.

Overall, this rule has a success rate of over 90%. It works because it keeps losses small and protects against small losses becoming more substantial, which happens frequently in this sector.

Trim a Position if it Becomes Too Large or Too Extended

Knowing when to sell is one of the most challenging aspects of trading and investing. There is no specific answer, but we have an answer concerning a diversified junior portfolio. If a stock becomes too large (as a percentage of your diversified portfolio), then you should sell one-third or half of the position. This is trimming. It allows you to lock in some profit and reduce risk while still partaking in the potential additional upside.

Many variables should be considered when judging how much of the position to trim and when to cut. Those variables include the company itself, its fundamental value, how much profit you have, and how much upside potential the company has.

For example, if a stock has 300% to 400% upside potential after a 150% gain, I would not sell half the position. In that case, I suggest selling one-third. However, if the stock has risen 200% and has a maximum of 50% to 75% additional upside, I would sell half.

This rule is especially important for early-stage exploration companies because they often make vertical moves, and most are not sustained. Some believe that for "drill plays" (a pre-discovery exploration company), one should sell half the position after it doubles.

Ultimately, one must distinguish between speculation (which will be rampant in junior companies during a bull market) and fundamental value. When speculation dominates market moves, traders and investors should be more aggressive about trimming their big winners.

Sell if Your Reason for Buying Changes or the Fundamentals Change

Many things can go wrong or off course, in mining and exploration. As a result, as a speculator or investor, you must remain aligned with your initial vision for your investment. When that vision is no longer valid, attainable, or changes, it is a sell signal. Do not justify holding onto your investment by creating a new reason.

For example, you invested in a developer because they would build a mine. If they are slow to execute that strategy or postpone construction to do more exploration, that is a reason to move on from the stock.

Another example concerns exploration companies. If you invested in one because of its exploration potential, but the company decides to focus on becoming a producer, that is a course change.

Other examples (sell signals) can include economic studies, resource estimates, or drill results that are underwhelming or below expectations.

One of my biggest losses in recent years was holding onto the stock of a company that reported a maiden resource. The grade came in much lower than expected, so I broke this rule by not selling and letting the stock exceed a 20% loss—I broke two rules!

When a company fails to meet your expectations, the story has changed, and it is time to sell and redirect that capital into better options.

Overweight & Underweight Certain Positions

A diversified portfolio of quality junior companies can outperform the sector but do not make the mistake of weighting each company equally.

The most significant and largest positions in your portfolio should be the companies you have the most confidence in and generally perform best.

The riskiest positions with the most potential should be underweighted. These include early exploration juniors, drill plays, and companies that have not proven much value yet. The smaller position size limits portfolio risk in absolute terms and liquidity terms.

Buy Value & Potential Based on Current not Future Metals Prices

The initial temptation is that because Gold and Silver are in a bull market, one should evaluate and find the companies with the most upside potential at a much higher metal price. However, this could immediately expose you to companies with flaws and, therefore, more downside risk. Moreover, if you want to bet specifically on higher metals prices, then do so without investing in a marginal company at the same time.

Investors and speculators should evaluate companies and their assets at current commodity prices to find underpriced and undervalued stocks. These companies will have significant upside and leverage to higher metals prices. Sometimes, that can include a marginal company or two with flaws. These companies may be so cheap and underpriced that they offer significant value at current metals prices despite a flaw or two.

Chapter 11

My Predictions

This chapter analyzes how the secular bull market in Gold and Silver will evolve and where and when it could end. The final targets are easier to measure than the timing and evolution, which are impacted by the end of the secular bull market in US stocks and Gold yet to break out against the 60/40 Portfolio.

Figure 11.1 below, an updated image from Chapter 7, plots the Gold price along with the price required to back the United States Monetary Base by 40% and 100%. The Federal Reserve Act of 1913 mandated a minimum backing of 40%. The calculation is derived from the current Gold price multiplied by US Gold Reserves and then measured against the Monetary Base.

Figure 11.1: Gold Price to Back Monetary Base

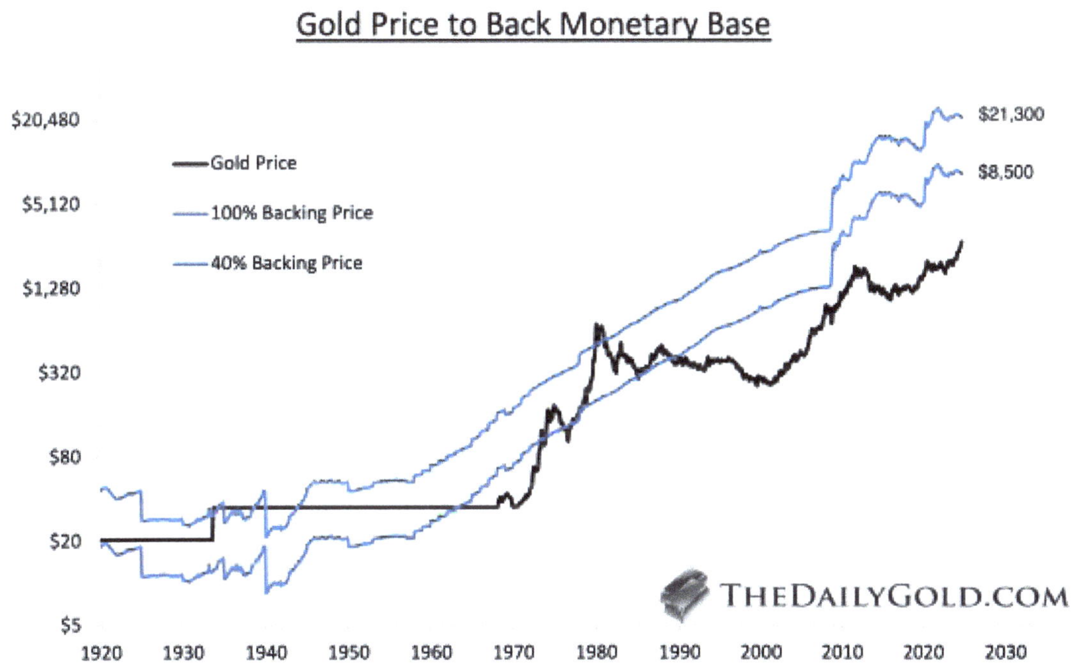

Around the time of secular peaks in Gold in 1980 and during the Great Depression (1940-1943 specifically), backing was over 100%. From the end of 1979 through 1980, backing exceeded 100% for 13 consecutive months and reached as high as 139%. From 1940 to 1943, backing reached as high as 163%.

Currently, 100% Gold backing of the monetary base requires a Gold price of roughly $21,300, while 40% Gold backing requires a Gold price of roughly $8500. The highest backing in recent decades was 29.7% in early 2008. That would equate to a Gold price of roughly $6300. Until 1990, Gold backing was at or above 40% throughout history, except for the late 1960s.

Circling back, we see that the Gold price at both historic secular peaks (1934, 1942, and 1980) achieved over 100% backing. Therefore, a reasonable target is the 100% backing price of $21,300. However, that price is based on today's snapshot. Consider how much higher the 100% backing price moved after the 2008 Global Financial Crisis and COVID-19 in 2020. Even one moderate recession could push that figure to $30,000.

Next is another look at Gold against the S&P 500 in Figure 11.2 below.

There have been three major peaks in the past 130 years. The Gold-to-S&P 500 ratio peaked at 6.2x in 1980 and 4.6x in 1934. Before that, it peaked at 5.4x in 1896. The peak in 2011 was at 1.5x.

Considering history, a target of 4x is reasonable. One could think that the ratio at 0.45x is historically low and will not be able to rise 9x from here. However, the ratio was at an all-time low in the late 1960s and rose 16-fold! Using daily closing prices, it rose 20x to nearly 7.5x!

The current S&P 500 of 6,000 multiplied by a ratio of 4x equates to a Gold price target of $24,000. An S&P 500 of 6500 multiplied by a ratio of 4.5x equates to a Gold price of nearly $30,000.

Figure 11.2: Gold & Gold vs. S&P 500

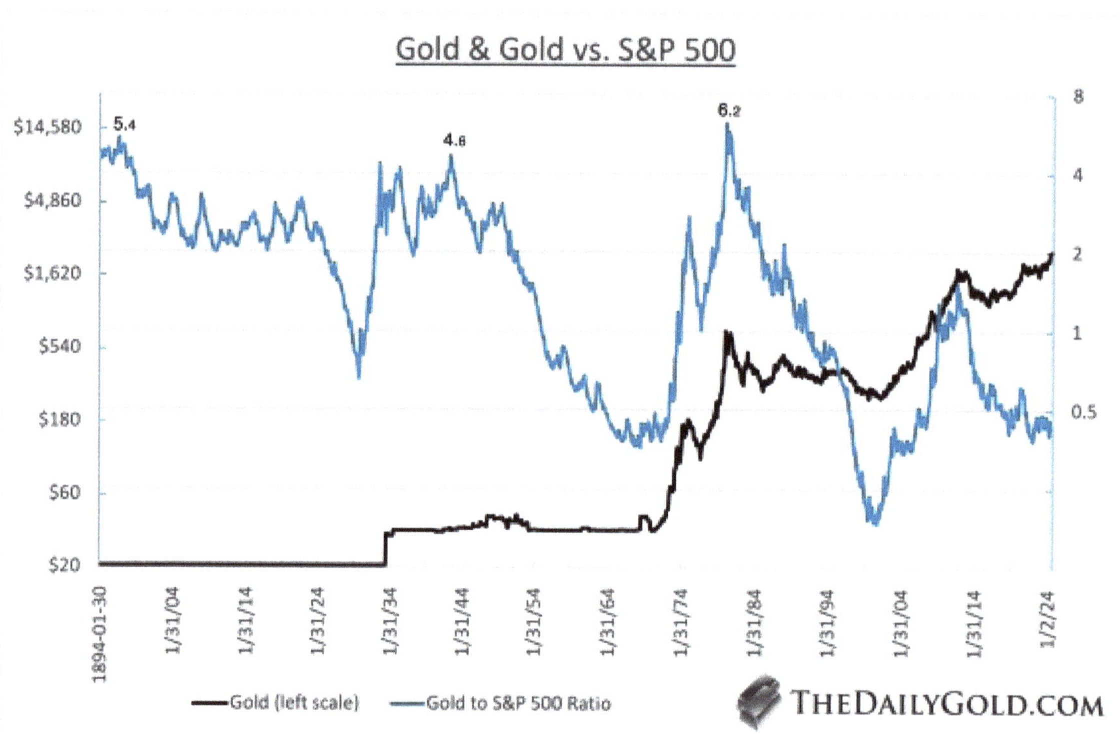

Let's consider Silver's upside potential in this secular bull market. After assessing Gold, we can evaluate Silver's upside potential using the Gold-to-Silver ratio, shown in Figure 11.3 below.

At the two most significant inflationary peaks of the 20th century (1920 and 1980), the ratio bottomed at 16x and 18x. It declined to as low as 14x in 1968 but was artificially low due to the Gold Standard. The low at Silver's 2011 peak was 32x. For most of the past 40 years, the ratio has ranged from 45x to 90x.

This sounds ridiculous, given that Silver is trading near $30, but Silver can reach $1000 in this secular bull market. We have shown the potential for Gold to reach $20,000 to $30,000. For Silver to reach $1000, a Gold-to-Silver ratio of 20x to 30x is required. A ratio of 20x and a Gold price of $25,000 equates to a Silver price of $1250.

Figure 11.3: Gold to Silver Ratio

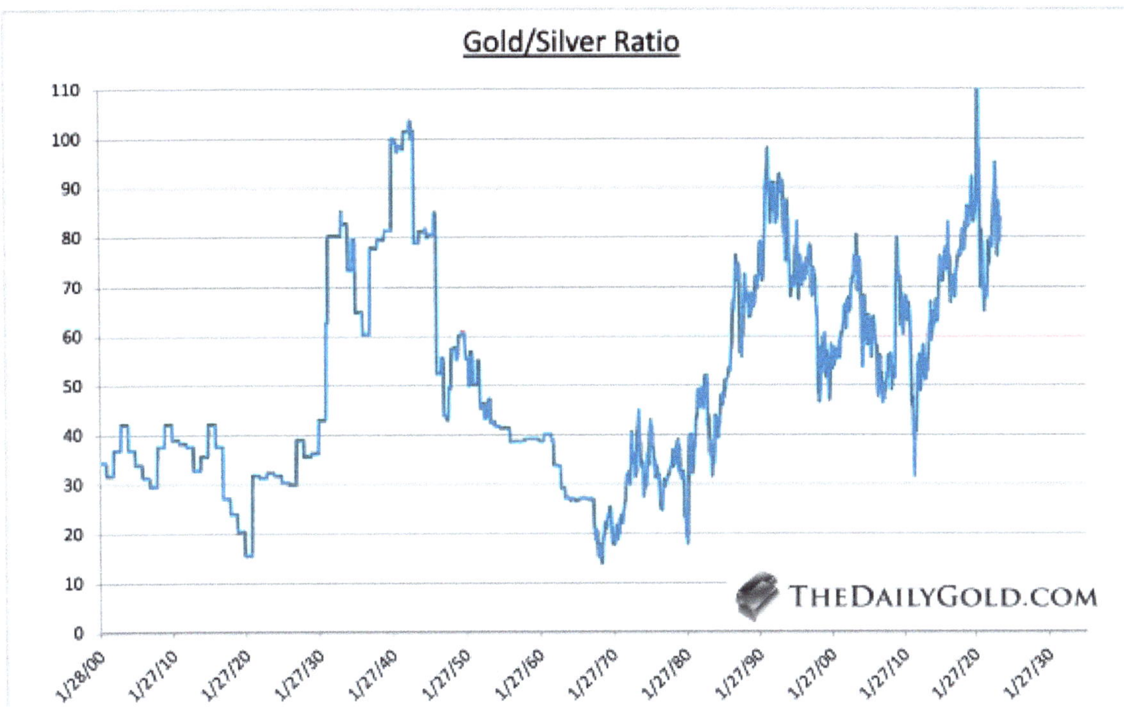

Moving on, let's take a look at the potential time frame for the secular peak.

First, we consider the time between past secular peaks in precious metals, peaks in the stock market, and bottoms in the Gold-to-60/40 Portfolio ratio. Note Figure 11.4 on the next page.

The last two secular bull markets in precious metals ended 11 years after the stock market's secular peaks. The S&P 500 has not reached a secular peak, but it's possible in 2025 or 2026. That would push the secular peak to the early second half of the 2030s.

Gold against the 60/40 Portfolio began moving toward important breakouts some nine and 10 years before the secular peak in precious metals. We are in 2025 and have yet to have that breakout signal.

Figure 11.4: S&P 500 Secular Peaks, Gold vs. 60/40 Portfolio, Gold

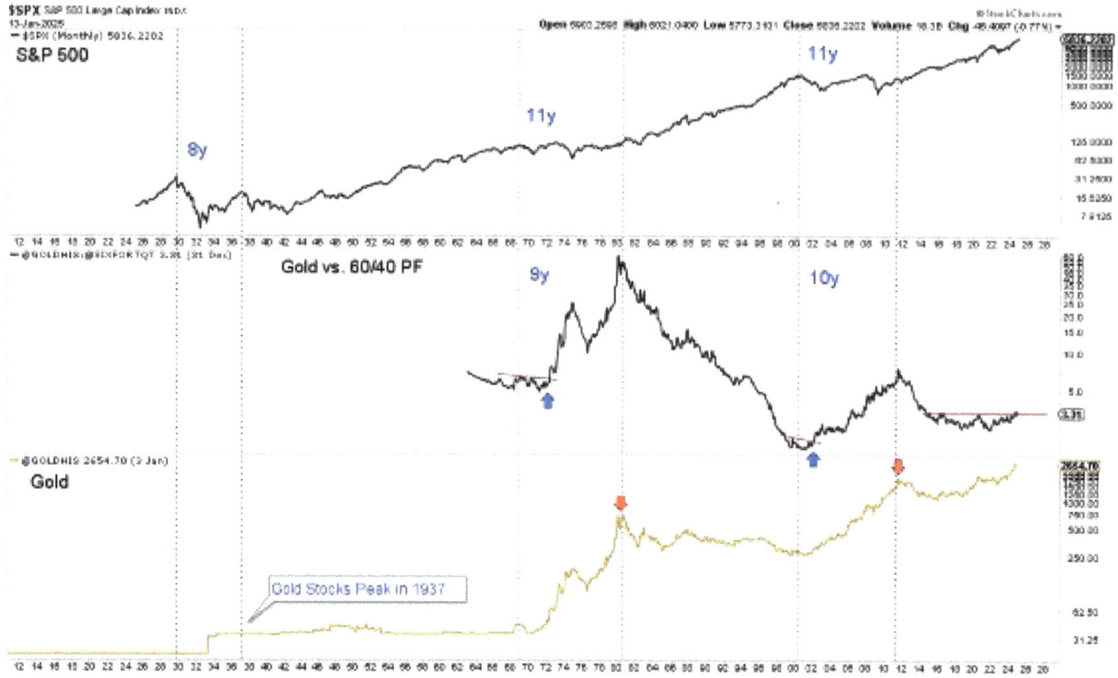

The status of the S&P 500 and Gold to 60/40 Portfolio Ratio suggest a potential secular peak in the mid-2030s, but there is a prominent cycle that argues for an even later peak.

I do not like most cycle analyses because cycles are subjective, but there is a strong track record in the following. There is a very long-term cycle of inflation and commodity price peaks because of the alternation between secular bull markets in US stocks and Commodities and the long-term cyclicality of commodity prices.

Figure 11.5 on the next page from Barry Bannister, Managing Director and Chief Equity Strategist at Stifel, shows the rolling 10-year annualized return in commodity prices. The peaks over the last century have been roughly 30 years apart, with major peaks every 55 to 60 years.

Figure 11.6 also on the next page, courtesy of Thunder Said Energy, shows an equal-weighted basket of commodity prices dating back over 200 years. Again, note the peaks are 30 years apart. I added the dates in Figure 11.6. As an aside, commodity prices exploding higher after 1971 was a breakout from over a 100-year-long base and the greatest breakout of all time.

Figure 11.5: 10-Year Rolling Return Compounded Annually

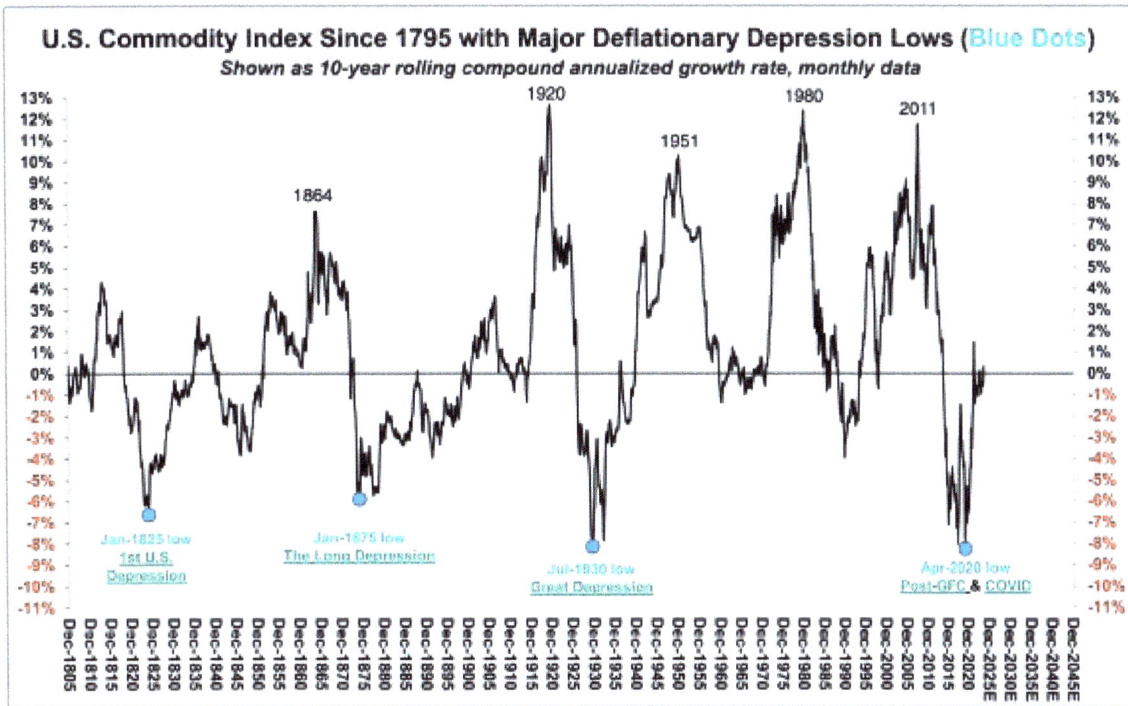

Figure 11.6: Equal-Weighted Commodity Prices

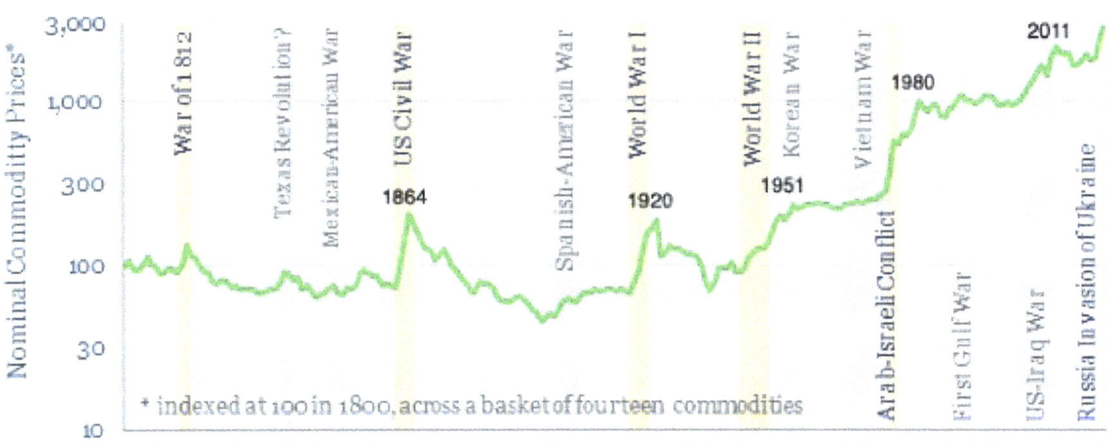

The prevalence of a 30-year cycle in commodity prices and inflation also necessitates a 60-year cycle, which carries more significance. Since the inflation of the Civil War, the 10-year Treasury Yield has made only two peaks: 1920 and 1981. (As an aside, the 10-year Treasury Yield surpassed its 1920 peak in the late 1960s, leading to the end of the secular bull market in US stocks). Also, the 1920 and 1980 peaks in commodity prices held for quite a bit longer than the peaks in 1951 and 2011. In short, history shows there could be an extremely significant inflationary peak at the end of the next decade (2030s).

Considering the above analysis, the secular bull market in precious metals could evolve in one of two ways. If the secular peak is to occur around the middle of the 2030s, then the template is a repeat of the previous two secular bull markets. That entails two major legs higher with a major downturn or crash in the middle. The other scenario is that the secular bull market will not peak until the end of the 2030s. That would entail three major legs higher and two cyclical downturns, similar to the secular bull market in gold stocks from 1960 to 1980.

There will be no hint about timing until we confirm that the secular bull market in the S&P 500 has ended and that Gold has clearly and convincingly broken out against the 60/40 Portfolio.

With respect to the next few years, whether Gold has broken out against the 60/40 Portfolio or not will inform us about the potential upside in both metals.

In Figure 11.7 below, we plot the four best cyclical advances in Gold on the scale of the current advance, which began in the fourth quarter of 2023. We mark the start of the advances, not necessarily from a price low but when Gold begins an impulsive and unimpeded advance.

Gold is closely tracking the average of the four best advances, which reaches $5000 by the end of summer 2026. For this chart to remain viable, Gold must break out convincingly against the 60/40 Portfolio at some point in 2025.

If that breakout proves the chart viable, given that Gold is in blue-sky territory and just broke out of a 13-year pattern, we should expect the advance to be stronger than average.

Figure 11.7: Gold Bull Analog

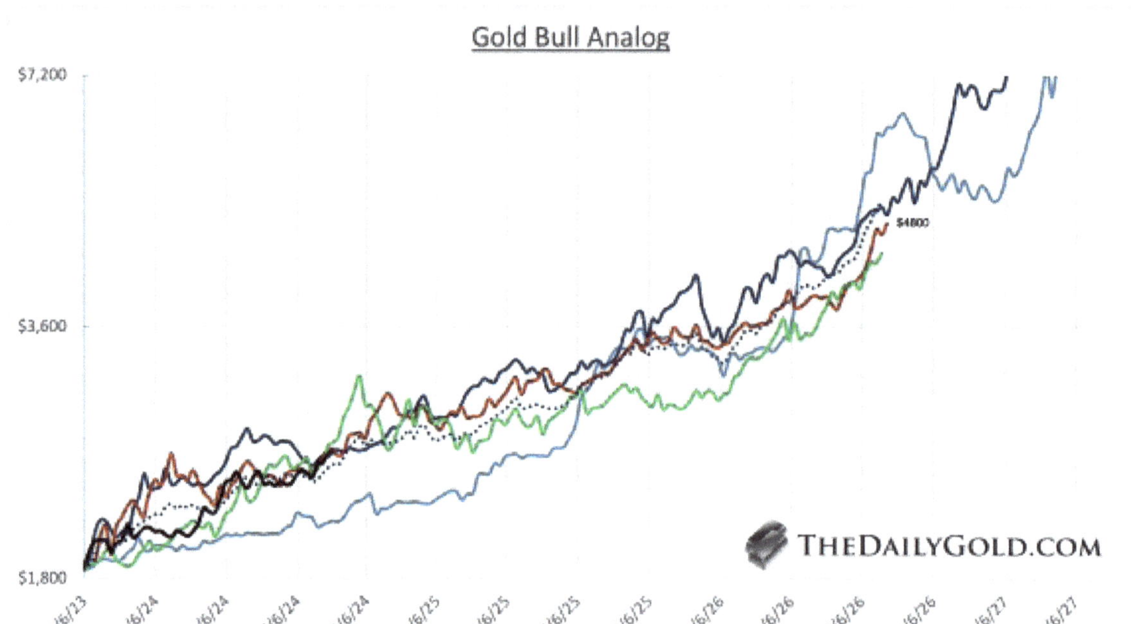

The two advances in the 1970s reached roughly $14,000 and $9000 in 2027. Those targets are excessive, as one was the final blowoff move, and the other began at an artificially low price.

Nevertheless, a target of $7000 to $8000 in 2027 to 2028 is not unreasonable. Keep in mind that the four best cyclical advances were followed by a 45% decline (1975-1976), two secular bear markets, and a 30% decline (2008). The more spectacular the move to the upside, the more likely a cyclical bear market will follow, entailing a 30% to 40% correction.

Figure 11.8 below plots Gold's performance following a sustained breakout to new all-time highs. There were four breakouts to new all-time highs, but we exclude the 2007 breakout, which was soon reversed during the Global Financial Crisis in 2008. We plot on the scale of the March 2024 breakout through $2100. The dotted lines show an average of the three breakout moves and an average of the two longest-lasting breakout moves.

For this chart to remain viable and for Gold to retain the momentum that emanates from a breakout to new all-time highs, Gold must break out against the 60/40 Portfolio in the first half of 2025. Gold has spent most of its breakout time below the averages.

Figure 11.8: Gold All-Time High Breakout Analog

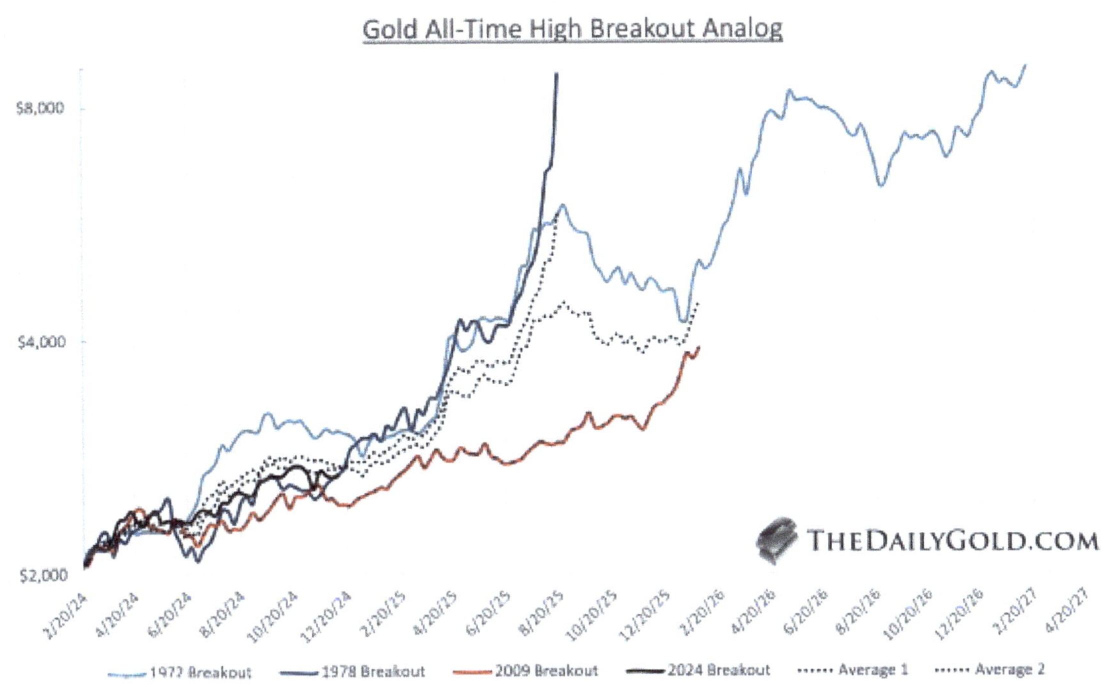

We can use the same analog charts to evaluate Silver. In Figure 11.9 on the next page, we plot the four best cyclical advances in Silver, which, in terms of the calendar, align very closely with the advances in Gold. We plot on the scale of the current advance, which began in February 2024. The dotted line is the average of the four advances.

Interestingly, the advances coalesce and hover around $50 for more than a few months. The average begins its move to $50 at the very end of 2025 and then breaks above $50 at the end of the first quarter of 2026.

Figure 11.9: Silver Bull Analog

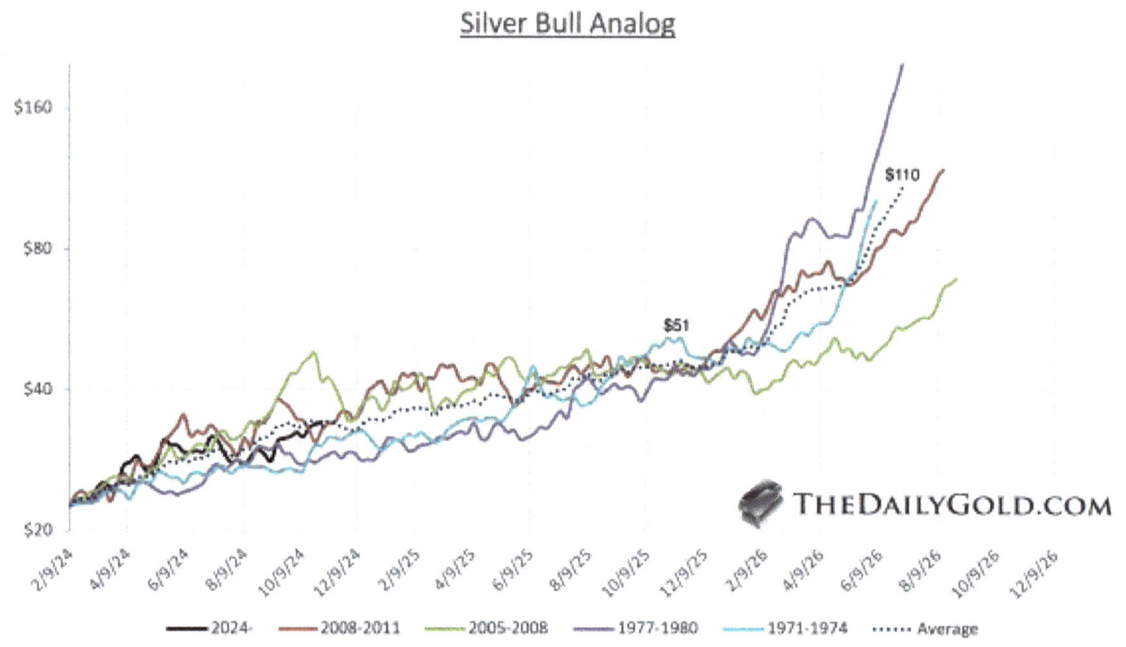

The analysis of the long-term technical outlook for Silver is simpler than Gold at this juncture, as Silver has yet to break past its massive base at $50. Upon a break past $50, Silver has a measured move of $96. In other words, a clean break above $50 should lead to $100.

We can evaluate a cyclical target for Silver using the Gold target and the Gold-to-Silver ratio. If the Gold target is $7000 to $8000 and the Gold-to-Silver ratio is 50 to 60, we have a target above $100, with a maximum of around $150. Note the Gold-to-Silver ratio chart in Figure 11.3.

Finally, it is important to note that precious metals will be negatively correlated to the stock market over a chunk (but not all) of the next 10 to 15 years. This occurs more so in inflationary periods but also around the time when the Gold to 60/40 Portfolio ratio confirms a secular trend change.

Figure 11.10 on the next page plots the various markets from 1969 to 1978. The blue line marks when the Gold to 60/40 Portfolio ratio began its secular breakout move (at the end of 1971). The two red lines mark the near 50% bear market in the S&P 500. Note that Gold, Silver, and the gold stocks made huge moves higher during that time.

The negative correlation between the stock market and precious metals continued into 1978. When the stock market and economy recovered in 1975, precious metals suffered and experienced a nasty cyclical bear market until the second half of 1976.

Figure 11.10: Precious Metals & Stock Market Negative Correlation 1973-1978

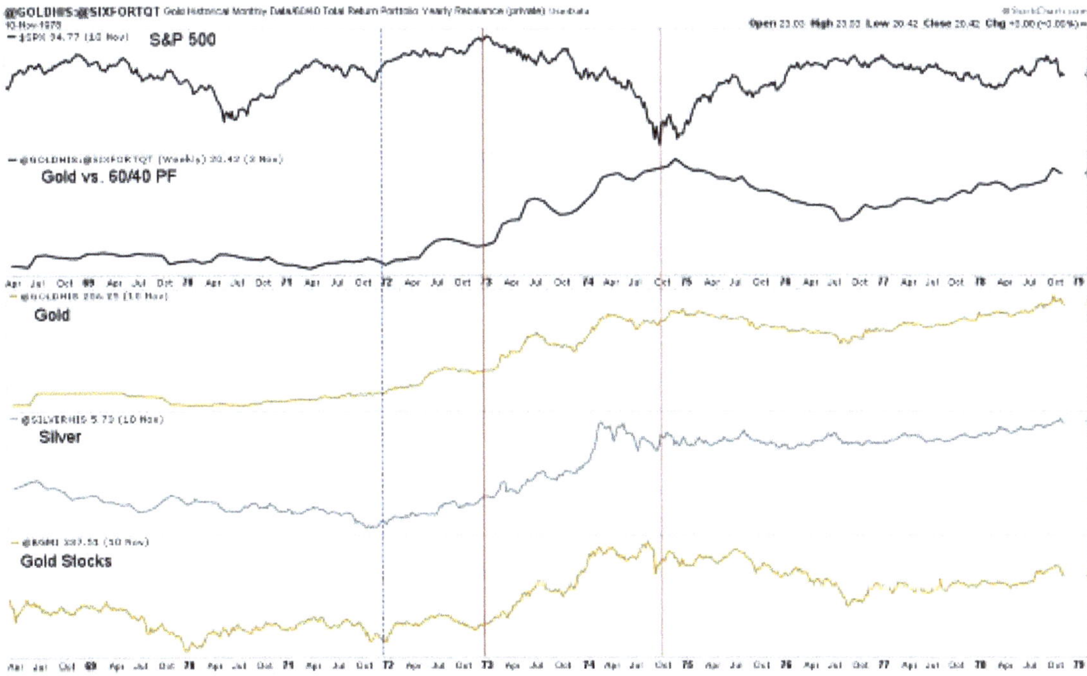

Precious metals were also negatively correlated with the stock market at the start of the previous secular bull market (2000-2011). Figure 11.11 on the next page plots the various markets from 1998 to 2003. The two red lines mark the extent of the bear market in the S&P 500 from March 2000 to October 2002. The blue line marks when Gold began its secular confirmation move against the 60/40 Portfolio (late 2001).

Gold stocks bottomed first, soon after the S&P 500's failed retest of the March high or double top at the end of summer 2000. Gold bottomed in the first quarter of 2001, and Silver bottomed at the end of 2001.

Figure 11.11: Precious Metals & Stock Market Negative Correlation 2000-2002

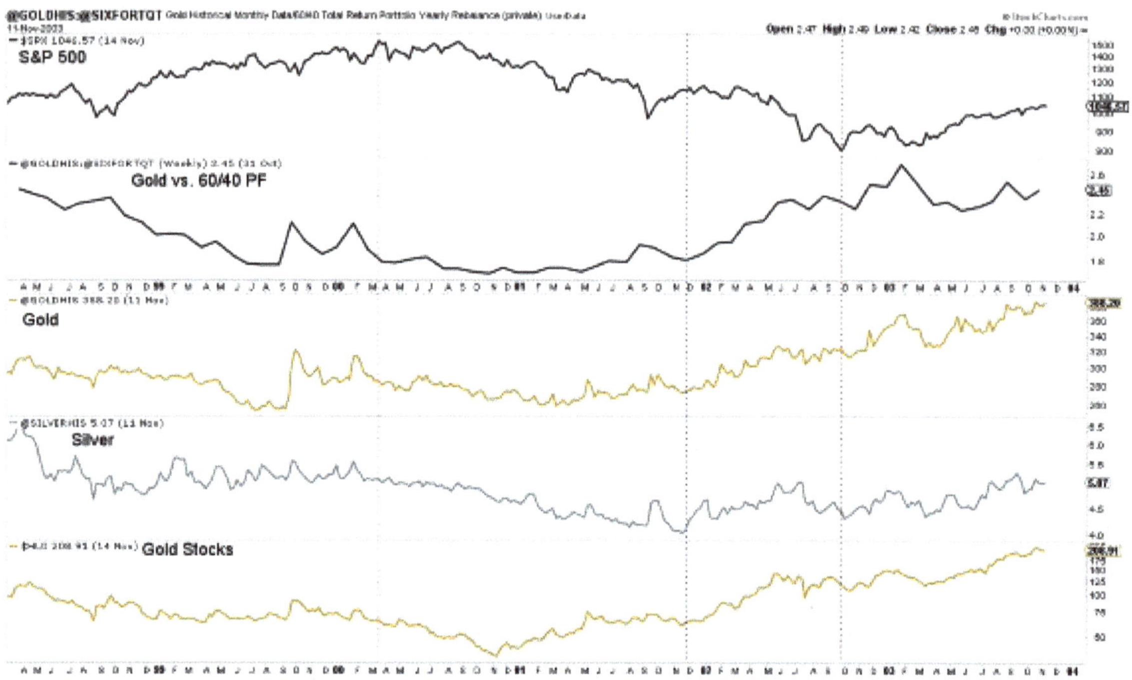

Recency bias is leading many to think precious metals cannot rise during a bear market in the S&P 500. After all, the two declined together through most of 2007-2008, the COVID-19 crash, and 2022. Therefore, they assume precious metals will fall during the next economic and market downturn.

However, history shows that when there is a secular turn in the Gold to 60/40 Portfolio ratio in favor of Gold, precious metals will trend higher in the face of a cyclical bull market. This happened during or around the start of the previous two secular bull markets in Gold.

This negative correlation occurs at the beginning of a secular trend change for two reasons. First, capital is over-invested in equities and conventional investments and under-invested in Gold and precious metals. There is little selling power in precious metals during the forthcoming downturn. Second, for there to be a secular shift in Gold's favor, there must be a clear period of negative correlation between precious metals and equities. Without that period, there is no secular shift. Hence, the negative correlation occurs at the beginning of the new secular bull market in precious metals.

Chapter Summary

A secular peak in Gold and Silver (and any market) has two parts: price and time. Regarding price, the first three charts in this chapter support targets of $20,000 for Gold and $1000 for Silver. Targets of $30,000 for Gold and even $1500 for Silver are not unreasonable. Remember that prices would spend little time in the upper half to the upper third of those targets.

Concerning timing, the secular peak could come from the mid-2030s to the decade's end. Considering the timing of the secular peak in the stock market and Gold breaking out against the 60/40 Portfolio, the peak could be closer to the middle of the next decade unless these events do not occur before 2027. Secular peaks in inflation and commodity prices have occurred roughly every 30 years, with historic inflationary and interest rate peaks occurring every 60 years. Both support a secular peak around 2040.

Precious metals are poised to benefit from the next economic and stock market downturn, which will occur when Gold breaks out against the 60/40 Portfolio, signaling a turn in the secular trend. For part of the next ten to fifteen years, there will be some negative correlation between precious metals and the stock market cyclically.

Bonus Chapter

In this bonus chapter, we share important charts that were not included in the other chapters but must be included because they provide additional valuable information.

In Bonus Figure 1 below, we plot various bull markets, including Gold from 1970 to 1980 and 2001 to 2011, on the scale of the current move in Gold, which began at the end of 2015. Gold would be closer to the pack if we had started the move in August 2018 rather than the end of 2015. But I digress.

Bonus Figure 1: Bull Markets & Bubbles Analog

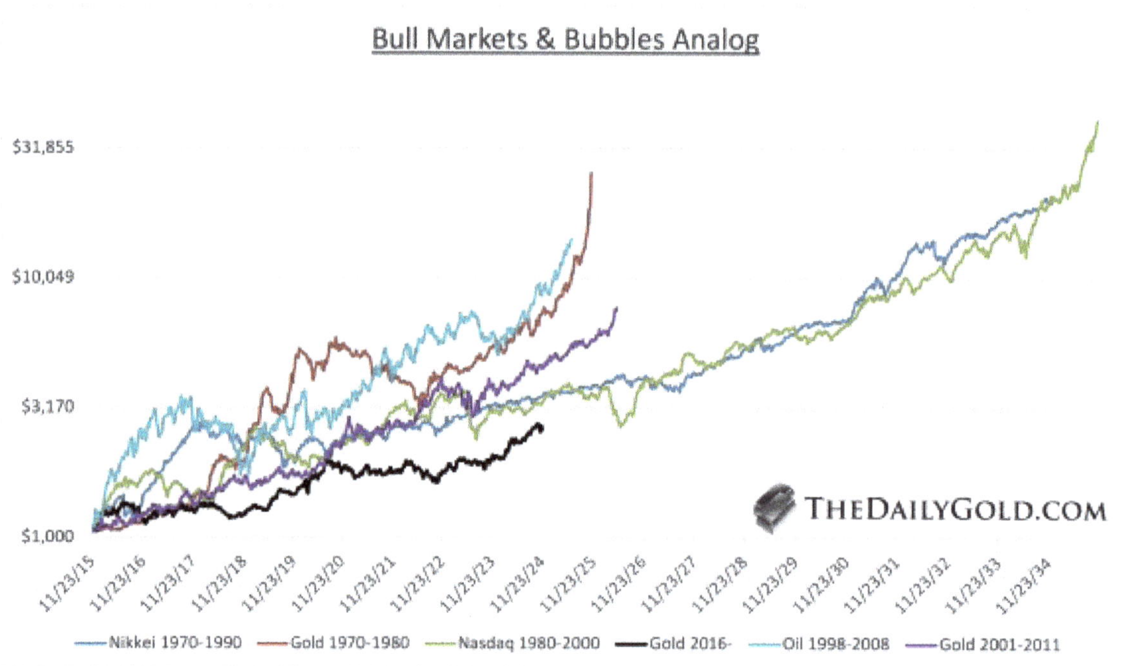

In Bonus Figure 2 on the next page, we compare the performance of gold stocks from 2016 onwards with that from 1960 to 1980. The data is from Barron's Gold Mining Index.

The current Barron's Gold Mining Index appears materially stronger than the various gold mining indices (HUI, GDX, etc). However, it is not too far off from the trajectory of the secular bull market of the 1960s and 1970s. That would entail an over 4x advance over the next roughly four and a half years, equating to a 5x move in GDX and potentially a 6x or 7x move in GDXJ.

Bonus Figure 2: Gold Stocks Secular Bull Analog

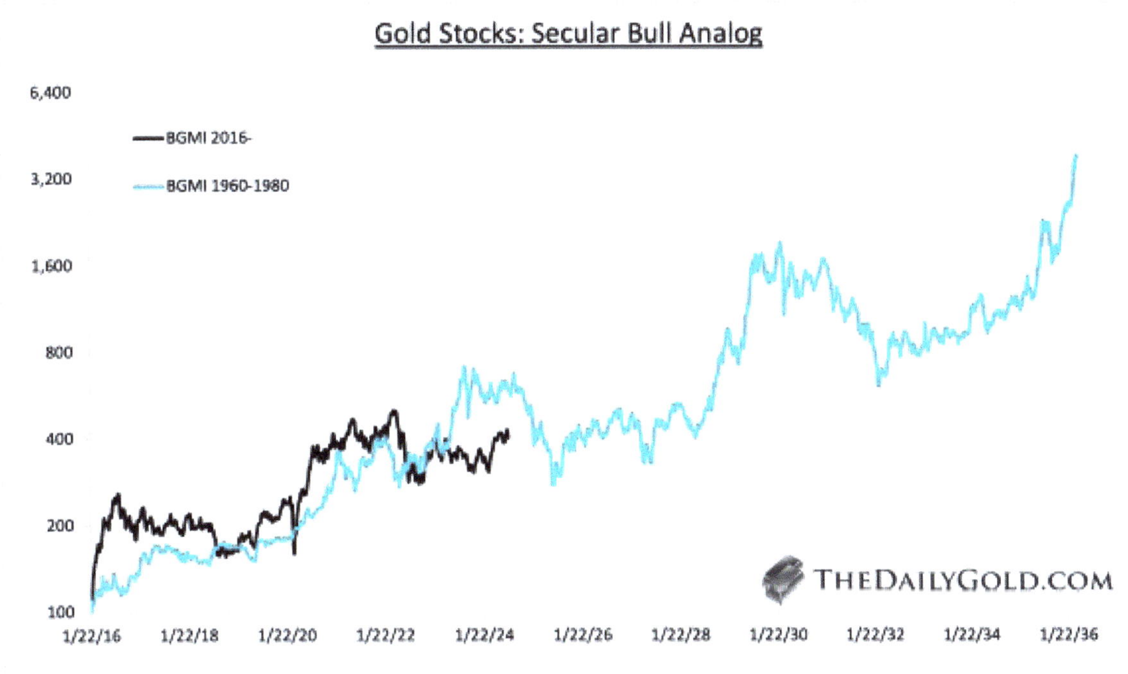

Bonus Figure 3 on the next page provides more evidence that the secular bull market in Bonds ended during COVID-19. There was a blowout in nominal and relative inflation assets. From the 2007-2008 peak, inflation assets increased by roughly 50% to 60%. During the same period, inflation assets tripled!

Bonus Figure 3: Fund Flows in Deflation Assets and Inflation Assets

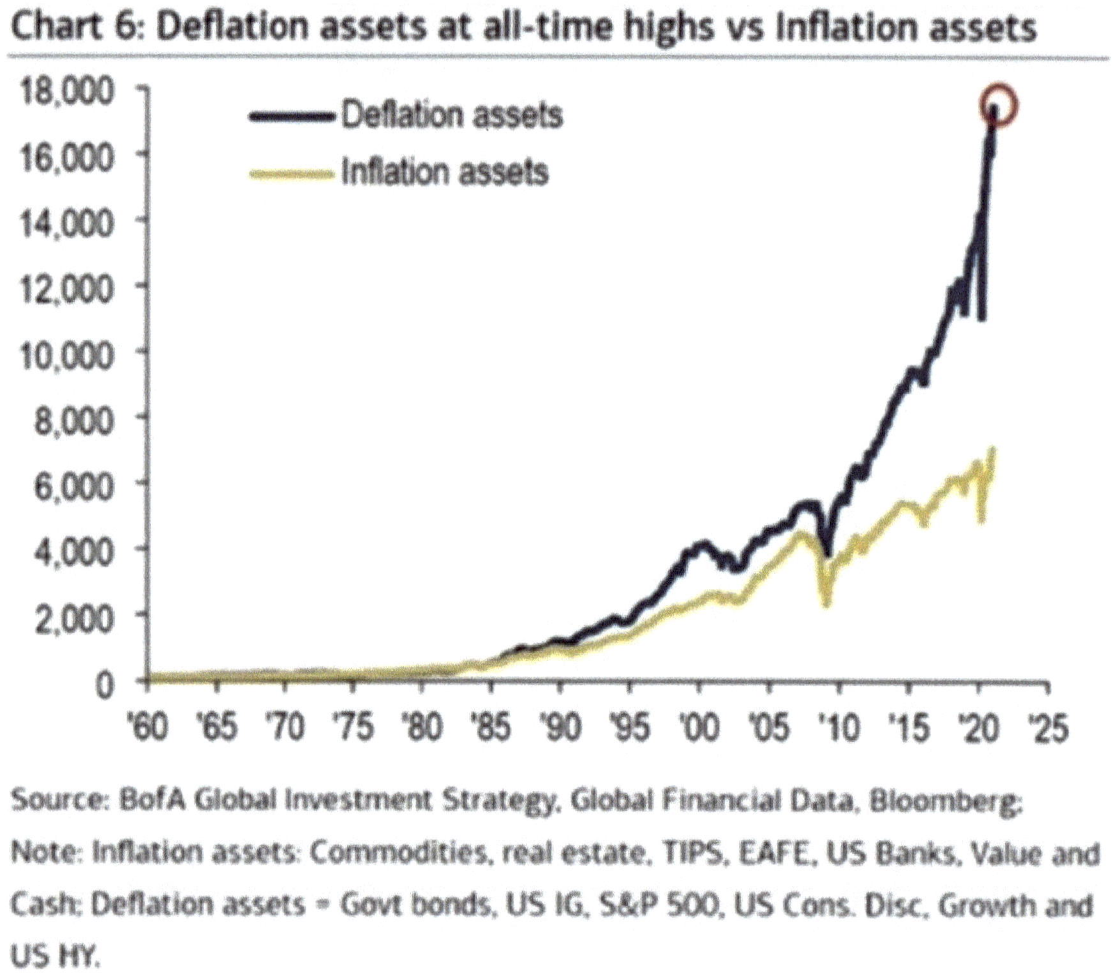

Bonus Figure 4 on the next page is one of my favorite charts. It plots the energy sector's weighting in the S&P 500 over the past 100 years! The weighting is not far off the all-time low during Covid. The major peaks align with the peaks in commodity prices (1951, 1980, 2011).

Our work focuses on Gold and Silver, but the secular trend in precious metals aligns with the energy sector. This sector also outperforms and can perform well during a secular bear market in US stocks.

Bonus Figure 4: Energy Weighting in S&P 500

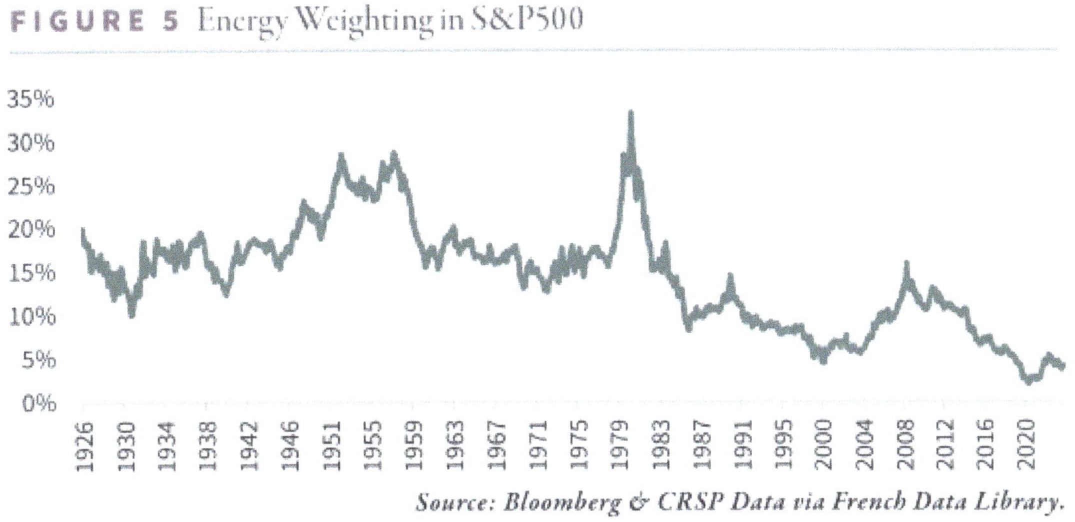

Bonus Figure 5 below, courtesy of RBC Capital Markets and FactSet, plots the Enterprise Value to EBITDA valuation for gold-focused producers and silver-focused producers. The data is from the past 11 years, which marks most, but not all, of the secular bear market in precious metals. Recall from Chapter 7 that gold stocks have been valued from mostly 5x to 10x.

Silver-focused companies and producers trade at a higher valuation due to the scarcity of pure Silver deposits or mostly Silver deposits. During the past 11 years, the valuation for silver-focused producers has ranged from 7x to 14x.

Bonus Figure 5: EV/EBITDA Valuation for Silver Producers vs. Gold Producers

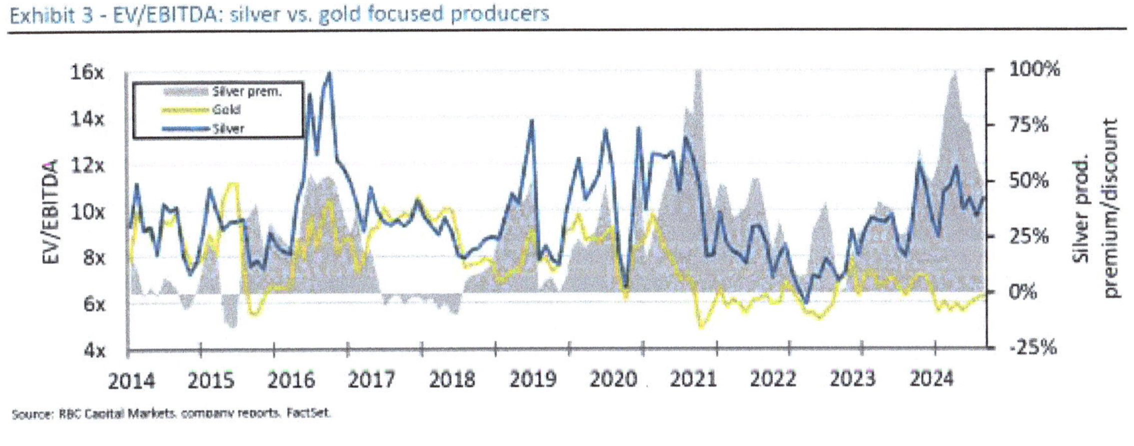

Bonus Figure 6 below shows the debt-to-income ratio for consumers, corporations, and the government during three recent time periods. I have a pet peeve about individuals forecasting a repeat of the crashes experienced in 1929 and 2008 when conditions are materially different.

The debt and leverage in the US financial system have essentially been transferred from individuals, households, and corporations to the government. Since the end of 2007, the debt-to-income ratio for the largest corporations has plummeted and also decreased for consumers. On the other hand, the debt-to-income ratio for the government has nearly tripled!

Bonus Figure 6: Debt-to-Income Ratio for Consumers, Corporations, Government

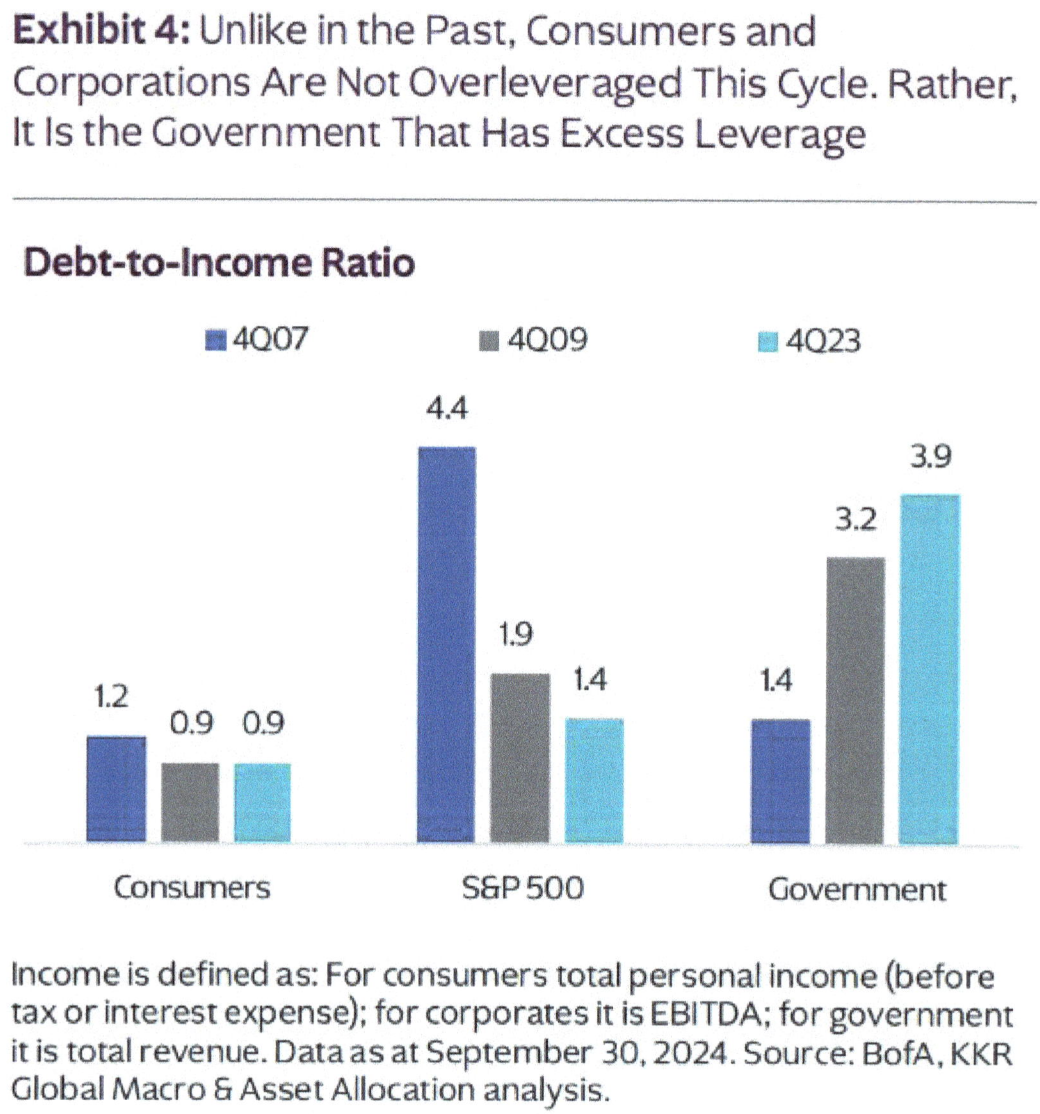

In Bonus Figure 7 on the next page, we plot Silver and Silver against the S&P 500 (chart inverted). The S&P 500 is trading at nearly 200x Silver. At the epic inflationary peaks of 1920 and 1980, the ratio was 6x and 3x (rounding up). The ratio was 16x and 28x at the other inflationary peaks of 1950 and 2011.

Bonus Figure 7: Silver vs. S&P 500

This is another excellent chart from Jurien Timmer at Fidelity. The chart is similar to the one in Chapter 2 but is on a different scale and has more annotations. It compares the current secular bull market in the S&P 500 to the ones in 1982-2000 and in 1949-1968. The chart argues we are ripe for a secular turning point in the next year or two.

Bonus Figure 8: Secular Bull Markets Analog

Bonus Figure 8 on the next page plots the forward PE ratio for the S&P 500 and its ensuing 10-year return. When the PE ratio has been this high, the forward 10-year total return has essentially been positive only once. It is only 1% per annum.

Bonus Figure 8: Secular Bull Markets Analog

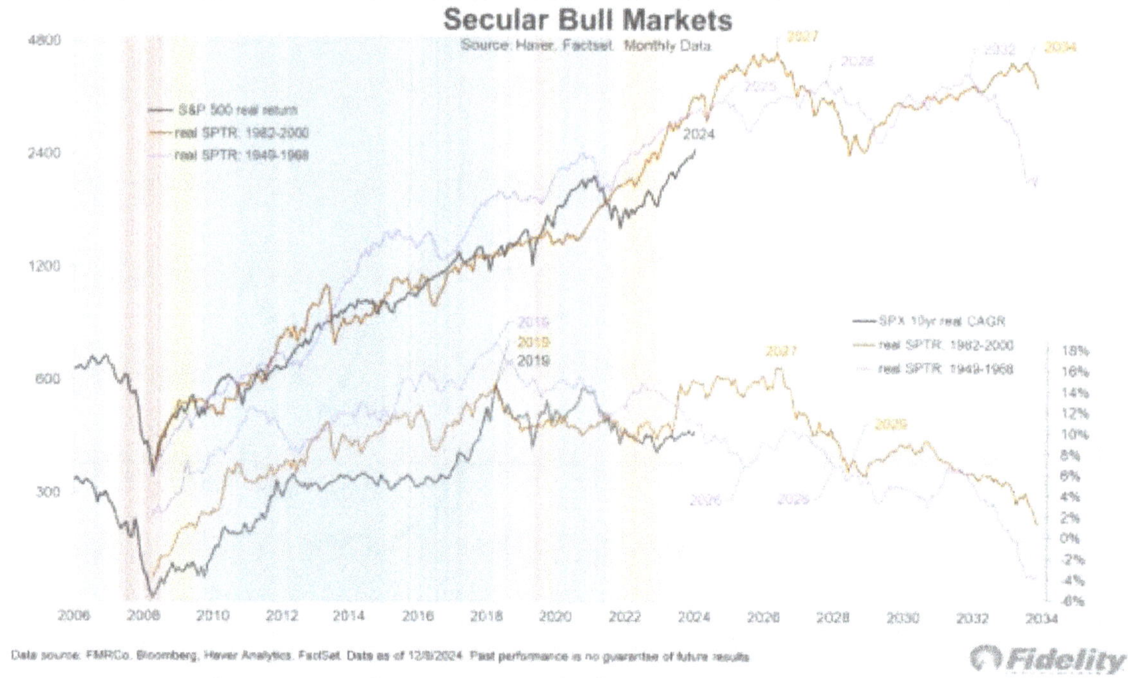

Bonus Figure 9 on the next page is from Francis Hunt, CMT, MBA, @themarketsniper. This chart plots the S&P 500 divided by the currency in circulation. It has reached a level commensurate with the previous two secular peaks and 1937. The extreme overvalued line serves as an excellent long-term sell signal, while the extreme undervalued line serves as an excellent long-term buy signal.

Bonus Figure 9: Price to Earnings Ratio & 10-Year Annualized Return

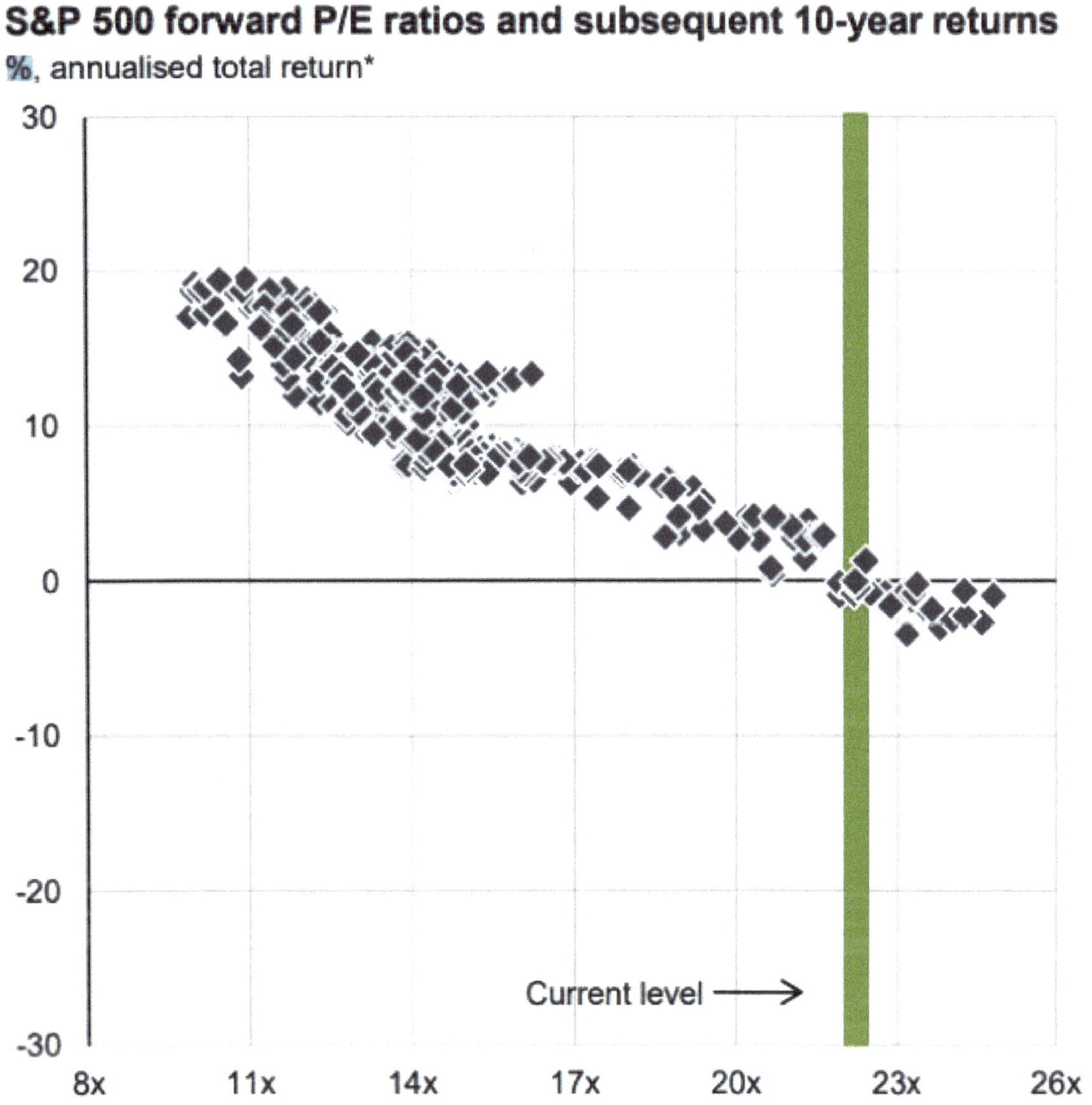

Bonus Figure 10 on the next page shows an inverted view of Gold against the 60/40 Portfolio. Gold is the denominator in this calculation. The blue lines represent the nominal lows in Gold, and the start of the portfolio's breakdown move against Gold.

Note the importance of the 40-month moving average in the context of the breakdown below the trendlines in 1972 and 2002. The ratio has already failed twice in the last 12 months when testing the 40-month moving average. At present, it is well below the moving average, which is also sloping downward. That is a negative sign, which is very positive for Gold.

Bonus Figure 10: S&P 500 vs. Currency in Circulation

Bonus Figure 11 on the next page from RBC Capital Markets and Bloomberg plots the price-to-cash flow and Enterprise value-to-EBITDA valuations for the S&P TSX Gold Index of gold stocks. In Chapter 7, I had to manually calculate and estimate a price-to-cash-flow valuation for gold stocks because no investment bank had published anything for a few years. This chart became available just as we went to publish.

The price-to-cash flow valuation is currently 8x, and the Enterprise value-to-EBITDA valuation is slightly above 6x. Recall that the price-to-cash-flow valuation has historically ranged from 6x to 25x. The valuation remains low but is off the record lows of 2013 and 2015 when it was below 6x. During the secular bear market, the enterprise value-to-EBITDA valuation ranged from 5x to 10x.

Bonus Figure 11: Gold & 60/40 Portfolio Against Gold

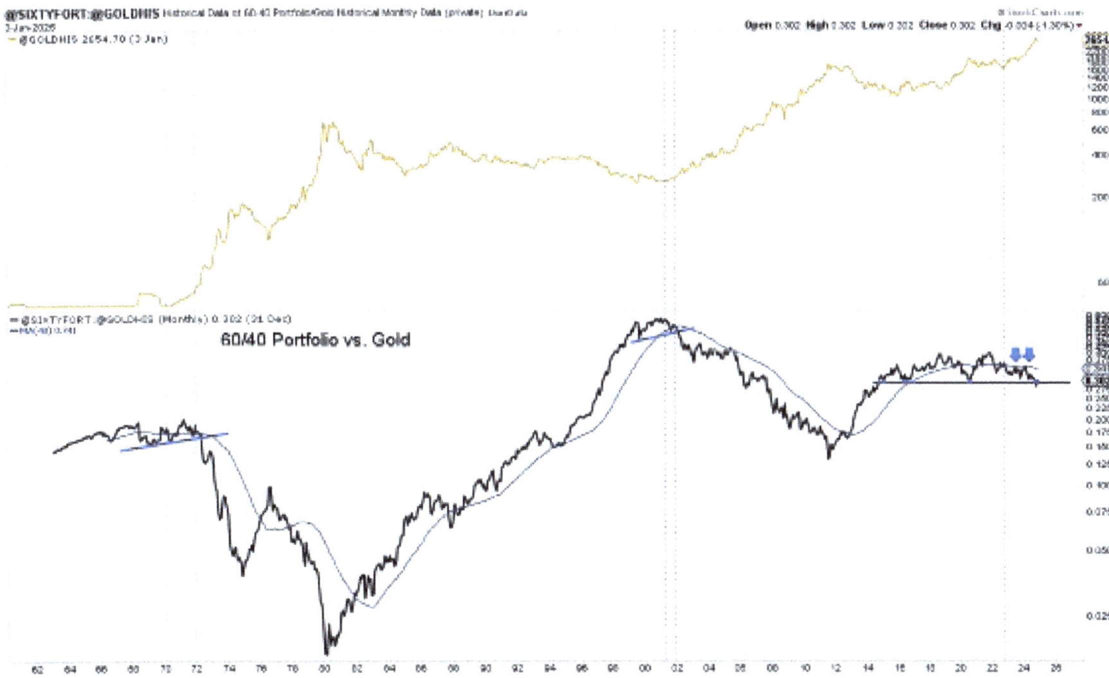

Bonus Figure 12: Gold Stocks Price to Cash Flow

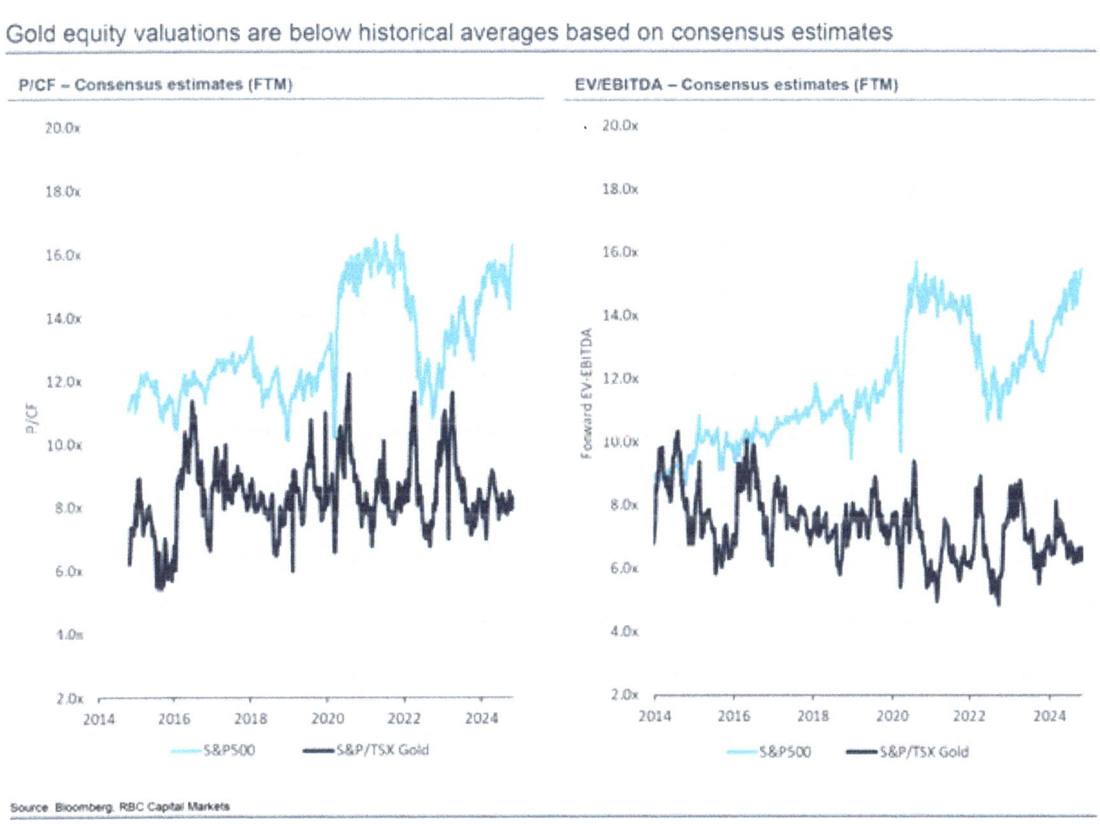

References

Chapter 1

Pimco: Understanding Gold Prices
https://www.pimco.com/us/en/resources/education/understanding-gold-prices

CPM Group: Gold Investment Demand
https://www.kitco.com/news/article/2024-10-09/global-uncertainty-enough-push-gold-and-silver-new-all-time-highs-2025-cpm

World Gold Council: Gold Demand Trends 2023
https://www.gold.org/goldhub/research/gold-demand-trends/gold-demand-trends-full-year-2023/central-banks

World Gold Council: Gold Demand Trends Q2 2024
https://www.gold.org/goldhub/research/gold-demand-trends/gold-demand-trends-q2-2024

The Hierarchy of Money & Case for $8000 Gold
https://www.gainesvillecoins.com/blog/hierarchy-of-money-case-for-8000-gold

MishTalk: Misconceptions about Gold
https://mishtalk.com/uncategorized/misconceptions-about-gold/

Chapter 2

Barron's Gold Mining Index & Other Data from Nick Laird/Gold Charts R US
https://www.sharelynx.com/

Stocks & Bonds Total Return Data from Professor Robert Schiller
http://www.econ.yale.edu/~shiller/data.htm

Business Insider/Goldman Sachs: The S&P 500's Golden Decade of Returns is Over
https://markets.businessinsider.com/news/stocks/stock-market-outlook-sp500-future-returns-decade-forecast-goldman-sachs-2024-10

Banc of America Future Returns Forecast
https://x.com/iceberg_fin/status/1851581598837223437

Chapter 4

The Silver Institute: Silver Supply & Demand from Metals Focus/GFMS
https://silverinstitute.org/silver-supply-demand/

Sprott: Silver's Critical Role in the Clean Energy Transition
https://sprott.com/insights/silver-s-critical-role-in-the-clean-energy-transition/?alttemplate=printblogarticle

LBMA: London Vault Data
https://www.lbma.org.uk/prices-and-data/london-vault-data

CME Group: Comex Vault Silver Totals
https://x.com/mikesay98/status/1820544217980252268

Carbon Credits: Soaring Demand Outstrips Supply, Pushing Prices to The Roof
https://carboncredits.com/silver-lining-soaring-demand-outstrips-supply-pushing-prices-higher-solar-energy/

Chapter 6

Bipartisan Policy Center: Net Interest on US Government Debt
https://bipartisanpolicy.org/explainer/net-interest-us-gov-debt/

Fiscal Data US Treasury: Interest Expense on Public Debt Outstanding
https://fiscaldata.treasury.gov/datasets/interest-expense-debt-outstanding/interest-expense-on-the-public-debt-outstanding

Committee for a Responsible Federal Budget: 2023 Interest Costs Reach $659 Billion
https://www.crfb.org/blogs/2023-interest-costs-reach-659-billion

Cato Institute: Federal Interest Costs 1790-2033
https://www.cato.org/blog/federal-interest-costs-1790-2033

Long-Term Trends: US Debt to GDP
https://www.longtermtrends.net/us-debt-to-gdp/

Historical Statistics of the United States 1789-1945 https://www2.census.gov/prod2/statcomp/documents/HistoricalStatisticsoftheUnitedStates1789-1945.pdf

Annual Report of the Secretary of the Treasury, 1947
https://fraser.stlouisfed.org/files/docs/publications/treasar/AR_TREASURY_1947.pdf?utm_source=direct_download

Federal Reserve Bank of St Louis: Federal Surplus or Deficit
https://fred.stlouisfed.org/series/FYFSD

US Inflation Calculator
https://www.usinflationcalculator.com/inflation/consumer-price-index-and-annual-percent-changes-from-1913-to-2008/

Gallup: US Approval of Labor Unions Highest Since 1965
https://news.gallup.com/poll/398303/approval-labor-unions-highest-point-1965.aspx

Wikipedia: Chips and Science Act
https://en.wikipedia.org/wiki/CHIPS_and_Science_Act

Wikipedia: Innovation and Competition Act
https://en.wikipedia.org/wiki/United_States_Innovation_and_Competition_Act

Wikipedia: Inflation Reduction Act
https://en.wikipedia.org/wiki/Inflation_Reduction_Act

Morgan Stanley: Stars Aligned for Higher Inflation
https://www.morganstanley.com/im/publication/insights/articles/article_staralignedforhigherinflation_us.pdf

Bloomberg Intelligence: Secular Inflation Regime Change Firmly Rooted in Three D's
https://www.bloomberg.com/professional/insights/markets/secular-inflation-regime-change-firmly-rooted-in-the-three-ds/

Advisor Perspectives: The Case for Secular Inflation
https://www.advisorperspectives.com/commentaries/2023/04/06/the-case-for-secular-inflation

Chapter 7

World Gold Council: Above Ground Stock
https://www.gold.org/goldhub/data/how-much-gold

Econ Fred: US Monetary Base Data
https://fred.stlouisfed.org/series/BOGMBASE

Gold Stocks Price to Cash Flow Chart 1975-1981
https://mikesmoneytalks.s3.us-west-2.amazonaws.com/wp-content/uploads/2011/09/01011244/DRUS09-21-11-1.gif

Adam Hamilton: Gold Miners Q3 2024 Fundamentals
https://www.zealllc.com/2024/gmq324fn.htm

Chapter 8

FundGuard: 100 Years of Mutual Funds
https://www.fundguard.com/100-years-of-mutual-funds/

World Gold Council: GLD ETF Launches November 18, 2004
https://50years.gold.org/moment/34/gold-etfs-enhance-access

iShares Silver Trust: Launches April 21, 2006
https://www.ishares.com/us/products/239855/ishares-silver-trust-fund

Chapter 9

Lobo Tiggre, Independent Speculator: Pre-Production Sweet Spot
https://independentspeculator.com/the-lowest-risk-strategy-for-the-highest-gains-ive-ever-seen

Kirkland Lake Gold 2019 Results
https://www.globenewswire.com/news-release/2020/02/20/1987567/0/en/Kirkland-Lake-Gold-Reports-Record-Operating-and-Financial-Results-in-2019-and-Q4-2019.html

Fosterville Gold Mine 2015 Production
https://www.streetinsider.com/Press+Releases/Newmarket+-Gold+Achieves+Record+Gold+Production+of+222%2C671+oz%2C+-Cash+Costs+of+%24704oz+and+AISC+of+%24987oz+In-Line+With+2015+Guidance%3B+Announces+2016+Guidance/11224974.html

Kirkland Lake Gold Swan Zone
https://www.canadianminingjournal.com/news/gold-kirkland-lake-hits-more-high-grade-at-fosterville/#:~:text=The%20mine's%20most%20recent%20estimate,grading%2049.6%20g%2Ft%20gold.

Wesdome Gold Mines Kiena Deep Resource
https://www.globenewswire.com/news-release/2020/12/15/2145774/0/en/Wesdome-Announces-Updated-Mineral-Resource-Estimate-for-Kie-

na-Mine-Complex-With-a-Significant-Increase-in-Indicated-Mineral-Resources-in-the-A-Zones.html

History Link: Spokane Stock Exchange
https://www.historylink.org/File/8883

Acknowledgments

This book would not be possible without the contributions of the following people.

Thank you to my friend David Skarica for inspiring me to write this book many years ago. Before you suggested it, I had never considered writing a book.

Thank you to Nick Laird, who runs the most comprehensive precious metals-focused charts website (goldchartsrus.com), for generously providing your historical Gold & Silver data.

Thank you to StockCharts.com for providing the best technical analysis software, specifically for the ability to upload data and create charts.

Thank you to Bob Moriarty of 321Gold.com for publicizing and promoting my work to your thousands of readers. Without your support, my audience would be much smaller.

Thank you to Yale Professor Robert Schiller, who graciously provides so much historical data on Stocks and Bonds on his website.

Thank you to Al Korelin for inviting me to my first property tours and publicizing my work.

Thank you to my good friend Andrew Percival for calculating the 60/40 Portfolio with proper rebalancing.

Thank you to my brother Aristotle for your promotional designs, including the cover, and for your wisdom and counsel.

Thank you to Vince Lanci for your wisdom, friendship, and big contribution to this book.

Thank you to my friend Ryan Parker who inspired my study of technical analysis and led me to precious metals in the early 2000s.

www.ingramcontent.com/pod-product-compliance
Lightning Source LLC
LaVergne TN
LVHW071343210926
848486LV00003B/216